# A Compelling Case
# for Universities

# A Compelling Case for Universities

Gaudeamus Igitur – So Let us Rejoice

**Quintin McKellar**

UNIVERSITY OF HERTFORDSHIRE PRESS

First published in Great Britain in 2025 by
University of Hertfordshire Press
College Lane
Hatfield
Hertfordshire
AL10 9AB

© Quintin McKellar 2025

The right of Quintin McKellar to be identified as the author of this work has been asserted by him in accordance with the Copyright, Designs and Patents Act 1988.

All rights reserved. No part of this book may be reproduced or utilised in any form or by any means, electronic or mechanical, including photocopying, recording or by any information storage and retrieval system, without permission in writing from the publisher.

British Library Cataloguing in Publication Data
A catalogue record for this book is available from the British Library

ISBN 978-1-912260-70-6

Printed in Great Britain by Henry Ling Ltd

# Contents

| | | |
|---|---|---|
| Introduction | | 1 |
| 1 | Evolution and Revolution: History | 5 |
| 2 | British Universities: Development and Growth | 19 |
| 3 | Access and Equity: Entry | 27 |
| 4 | Illuminating Minds: Education | 64 |
| 5 | Beyond the Curriculum: The Experience | 90 |
| 6 | Earnings and Happiness: The Benefits | 101 |
| 7 | The Triumph of Discovery: Research | 118 |
| 8 | Innovation and Entrepreneurship: Business Engagement | 149 |
| 9 | A World of Learning: Internationalisation | 168 |
| 10 | How to Pay For it All: Funding | 186 |
| 11 | Decree or Support: Governance | 205 |
| 12 | After and Beyond: Employability, Alumni and Community | 225 |
| 13 | Splendid Institutions: Evolving and Improving | 240 |
| Bibliography | | 255 |
| Index | | 281 |

# Introduction

This book unapologetically celebrates the achievement of the University. Only religion can boast international longevity and success on the scale of universities, and while religion is in general decline across the world, university education is still in its ascendancy. Politicians and the commentariat have criticised aspects of university education because they see it as a 'soft target' and they invariably do so to support their own self-interest or topical populism. Universities are more generally considered good things and the vast majority (96%) of mothers want their children to attend one.[1] They are the source of enlightenment, the pioneers of progress, the engines of the economy and the wellspring of joy and understanding.

The author is a practitioner of education and research, an academic of forty years immersion, who has led an animal disease research institute (Moredun, Edinburgh), a specialist, research-intensive higher education institution (the Royal Veterinary College, University of

---

1  D. Budge, 'Millennium Mothers want University Education for their Children', Centre for Longitudinal Studies, Institute of Education, 2010, <https://cls.ucl.ac.uk/millennium-mothers-want-university-education-for-their-children/>; K. Hansen, E. Jones, H. Joshi and D. Budge (eds), *Millennium Cohort Study, Fourth Survey: A User's Guide to Initial Findings* (London, 2010), <www.cls.ioe.ac.uk/MCSFfindings>.

London) and a large, post-92, multi-faculty university (the University of Hertfordshire). Having conferred degrees on more than 50,000 students and spoken to many of them, he cannot recall any who were disappointed by their experience of university, and while there are no doubt a vanishingly small number who have been dissatisfied, it is nevertheless likely that the learning and personal development which the experience bestowed on them will have contributed to a richer and more satisfying life.

Several of the chapters in the book have emerged from annual public lectures given at the University of Hertfordshire by the author, and from his contribution to a series of congresses and subsequent book chapters on higher education, published by Springer Nature Switzerland (2018–22).[2] The book embraces a global perspective but with a UK focus. After a brief history of the evolution of the modern university, the book broadly follows the student journey from admission to graduation and beyond. It takes excursions into research and innovation and considers funding and governance. The concluding chapter draws together some proposals for change but within the current model of higher education which it concludes is both highly effective and sufficiently adaptive.

As the book neared its completion, the government of the UK changed. After a 14-year period during which the Conservative Party governed, the Labour Party won by a substantial majority in the July 2024 election. Higher education did not feature extensively in the Labour Party manifesto, however they did commit to the creation of a funding system which would provide a secure future, they promised to replace short funding cycles for key research and development institutions in favour of ten-year budgets, and proposed to reform the apprenticeships levy. Following their election, the newly appointed Secretary of State for Education, Bridget Phillipson, gave a speech at

---

2   A. Badran, E. Baydoun and J.R. Hillman (eds), *Higher Education in the Arab World: Research and Development* (Cham, 2022), <https://doi.org/10.1007/978-3-030-80122-9>.

the Embassy Education Conference,[3] committing the new government to providing opportunity for everyone and thereby explicitly supporting the Robbins Principle (see Chapter 2) whereby university places should be available to all who are qualified for them by ability and attainment.[4] She also stated emphatically that 'international students are welcome in the UK. This new government values their contribution to our universities, to our communities, to our country' and importantly confirmed the 'opportunity *for international students to remain in the UK on a graduate visa for two years after their studies*'. The detail behind the new government's commitments is still lacking, but where their proposals are likely to change policies and practice, I have attempted to speculate, throughout the book, what that might mean for universities. Perhaps more important than the detail of policy changes is the commitment by the new Secretary of State to reset the relationship between government and education providers, putting 'education at the heart of change on the forefront of national life'.[5]

I am immensely grateful to three extraordinary colleagues, Julie Newlan, Mairi Watson and Andrea Nolan, who read and critiqued the text, steered me away from intemperance and greatly reduced my overindulgence in the exclamation mark. Julie and Mairi were my deputies at the University of Hertfordshire and Andrea the Vice-Chancellor of Napier University. I am also indebted to Jane Housham, my publisher from our University of Hertfordshire Press who, with some perseverance, adapted my scientific hard wiring to a humanities style and referencing.

---

3   Bridget Phillipson's speech at the Embassy Education Conference, 23 July 2024, <https://www.gov.uk/government/speeches/bridget-phillipsons-speech-at-the-embassy-education-conference>.
4   *Robbins Report*, Report of the Committee on Higher Education (London: HMSO, 1963).
5   Letter to the education workforce from Education Secretary Bridget Phillipson, <https://educationhub.blog.gov.uk/2024/07/08/letter-to-the-education-workforce-from-education-secretary-bridget-phillipson/>.

My deepest gratitude also goes to Kate Singer who typed the text, interpreted my hieroglyphics and was consummately patient with my rewrites and updates.

Although the pervasive mood of the book is positive, it does not shy away from the difficult issues which face universities and the students who attend them. On almost every aspect of university activity it derives satisfaction from great achievement.

Universities are undoubtedly splendid things 'so let us rejoice' in them – *Gaudeamus igitur*.[6]

---

6 'Gaudeamus igitur' is a celebratory Latin song, which has been, and in many universities still is, sung at graduation ceremonies. In the early days of the European university, when Latin was commonly spoken, it was a beer-drinking song.

# CHAPTER 1
# Evolution and Revolution: History

The foundations of the modern university lie in medieval communities, which gathered to learn and share knowledge across Europe. They remained the preserve of the privileged until relatively recent times. Growth in the second half of the last century and first quarter of this has been explosive and predictions suggest it will continue, with global numbers of students worldwide more than doubling from 216 million in 2016 to 472 million in 2035.[1] This growth has demanded new models of funding and the many new providers who have emerged have added diversity and complexity to the traditional idea of a university.

Knowledge has been harnessed, valued and disseminated since antiquity. In ancient Egypt, the Vizier, or administrative head, is thought to have taught secular and religious instruction at a 'higher' level to the Pharaohs and nobles. The Babylonians developed advanced mathematics and astronomy, and created scribal schools known as *edubas*, and the ancient Chinese (2000 BC) taught literature, rituals and archery. In all the ancient civilisations, higher-level education was confined to aristocrats and the priesthood.

---

[1] 'Study Projects Dramatic Growth for Global Higher Education through 2040', *ICEF Monito*, 3 October 2018, <monitor.icef.com/2018/10/study-projects-dramatic-growth-global-higher-education-2040>.

Much of 'western' modern higher education owes its evolution to the Greek philosophers. Whether the theorem ascribed to Pythagoras was indeed his by invention is open to debate, but there is no debating the pivotal role of ancient Greece in the way we teach and learn. Socrates (470 BC), arguably the founder of western philosophy, embraced dialogue in his teaching methodology, thereby encouraging contact between student and faculty – a principle of teaching excellence emphasised more than two millennia later.[2] It is instructive that Socrates was accused by politicians of the day of corrupting the minds of the youth – *plus ça change, plus c'est la même chose*. Fortunately, his trial and subsequent execution (by ingestion of hemlock) was more draconian than that meted out to today's educationalists who are merely pilloried by politicians and the press. Pythagoras and Socrates greatly influenced Plato, who evolved and developed political philosophy, and who established what may have been the first recognised institution of higher education in the western world. Plato's 'Academy' may have been named for the Grove of Academus in which it was established and which was in turn named after Academus, a hero of Greek mythology.[3] Whatever the source of the name, the 'Academy' has certainly stuck and is now used to refer to the physical entities which comprise institutions of higher education, the body of teachers and researchers which make up the faculty of the institution, and also to the members of learned societies. Aristotle was one of Plato's students and an extraordinary polymath who developed a systematic study of biology and the physical sciences, evolved logic, and expanded philosophy. Like Plato he established his own school of 'higher education', the Lyceum, and like Plato his observations that 'to experience is to

---

2  A.W. Chickering and Z.F. Gamson, 'Seven Principles for Good Practice in Undergraduate Education', *AAHE Bulletin*, 3 (1987), pp. 3–7, <https://eric.ed.gov/?id=ED282491>.
3  L. Schmitz, 'Academus', in W. Smith (ed.), *Dictionary of Greek and Roman Biography and Mythology*, vol. i (London, 1867), p. 5; E. Hamilton and H. Cairns, 'Introduction', in E. Hamilton and H. Cairns (eds), *The Collected Dialogues of Plato: Including the Letters*, Bollingen Series LXXI (Princeton, 1961).

learn'[4] are reflected in the active learning proposed by Chickering and Gamson, in their seminal work on principles for good practice. Aristotle's legacy had a major impact on Judeo–Islamic teaching and subsequently on western teaching throughout the Middle Ages and up to the present day. During the Roman and Byzantine eras education was generally provided by personal tutors to the rich rather than in organised academies, although from about AD 425, when Theodosius II founded the Pandidakterion (forerunner of the Imperial University of Constantinople, now Istanbul) there was an academy of sorts, teaching Greek, Latin, law, philosophy and rhetoric to those wishing to gain public office or enter the church.[5] The expansion of Islam led to the establishment of the University of al-Qarawiyyin (Al-Karaouine) in Fez, Morocco (AD 857–9) and although it was established as a mosque it can legitimately claim to have delivered 'higher education' since its opening and may have been the first to confer degrees. It is thought to have taught rhetoric and astronomy as well as the Quran and Fiqh or jurisprudence. Al-Qarawiyyin may therefore be the oldest existing and continually running university in the world, although this could be disputed by historians who consider the autonomy, community, and educational level essential defining characteristics of a university.[6] This golden age of Islam also galvanised the creation of great libraries in Baghdad, which housed texts from Greece, Persia and India, in what was then the intellectual centre of the world. In this period the University of Al-Azhar was established in Cairo (AD 975) and medical schools (*bimaristan*) were created to confer diplomas throughout the Islamic world.[7] In many European countries, in the second half of the

---

4 N. Evans, 'Diotima and Demeter as Mystagogues in Plato's Symposium', *Hypatia*, 21/2 (2006), pp. 1–27, <https://doi.org/10.1111/j.1527-2001.2006.tb01091.x>.
5 A. Markopoulos, 'Education', in E. Jeffreys, J.F. Haldon and R. Cormack (eds), *The Oxford Handbook of Byzantine Studies* (Oxford, 2008), pp. 785–95.
6 J. Verger, 'Patterns', in H. De Ridder-Symoens (ed.), *A History of the University in Europe, vol. I Universities in the Middle Ages* (Cambridge, 1991).
7 S.F. Alatas, 'From Jami'ah to University Multiculturalism and Christian–Muslim Dialogue', *Current Sociology*, 54/1 (2006), pp. 112–32, <https://doi.org/10.1177/0011392106058837>.

first millennium, higher education took place in monastic or cathedral schools, under instruction from monks and nuns.

## China

Chinese education was greatly influenced by Confucius, who lectured on ethics and morality at around 500 BC, and by 200 BC China had developed imperial colleges, teaching up to 30,000 students each year, primarily for the civil service. An organised system of education beyond the age of seventeen was developed during the Han empire (about 202 BC–AD 220), at which time the number of scribes educated for government service increased to about 120,000 per cohort, for whom there were three years of formal training, with rigorous written and oral tests. Although the principle purpose was probably to learn the communication skills required for governance and government, the Han scholars studied the classics and canon of Confucius and Chinese history. In the later and relatively short-lived Sui dynasty, around AD 580, Emperor Wen created the Jinshi, a prestigious degree, based on an examination system, which consolidated the idea of meritocracy in education. A true renaissance in culture and education began in the late tenth century under the Song dynasty (AD 960–1279). Utilising wood-block printing, encyclopaedias, compendia, dictionaries, Buddhist canon and Confucian classics were produced or reproduced, great libraries were established or re-established, and printed material became available and affordable to many. To reach the top civil-service jobs might take up to ten years of study, and the examinations, held every three years, were remarkably tough: in AD 1002 only 219 passed out of a cohort of 14,000 entrants. While much of the learning was undertaken by the individual, perhaps with a personal tutor, the Song rulers also consolidated university education with the university in Kaifeng (the capital at the time), hosting 4000 students in AD 1103. The educational backdrop to the Song era led to extraordinary scientific and cultural progress. From the invention of smelting to the magnetic compass, it was a period when China was, by a substantial margin, the most educated, progressive and innovative country in the world. (The information on Chinese higher education is taken from Wood and is expanded in his marvellous book *The Story of China*.)[8]

China now has one of the fastest growing and improving higher-education systems. It suffered from the purges of the cultural revolution (1967–76), when student numbers fell from 674,000 to just 48,000, but now boasts the largest number of students of any country (40 million[9]) in more than 3000 universities and colleges. It now also produces more research publications than any other country[10] and is a major destination for international students, particularly from elsewhere in Asia[11] and Africa.[12] China has a centrally directed programme to develop elite universities and is investing heavily in 140 universities in this programme. Entrance to university in China is dependent upon success in the National Higher Education Entrance Examinations (Gaokao), which varies somewhat between provinces but has a similar structure throughout the country. In 2021 approximately 10.8 million students sat the Gaokao.

## The western model

The University of Bologna is considered the oldest university in the 'western world'. Established in 1088 for the study and teaching of canon

---

8  M. Wood, *The Story of China* (London, 2020).
9  Z. Shuo, 'China's Higher Education System is World's Largest, officials say', *China Daily*, 3 December 2020, <https://www.chinadaily.com.cn/a/202012/03/WS5fc86ab2a31024ad0ba9999e.html>.
10  J. Tollefson, 'China Declared World's Largest Producer of Scientific Articles', *Nature*, 553/390 (2018), <https://doi.org/10.1038/d41586-018-00927-4>.
11  S. Kelsey, 'Explore the World's Top Universities', *US News & World Report*, 8 Oct 2013, <news.yahoo.com/explore-worlds-top-universities-142243604.html?>.
12  N. Moore and V. Breeze, 'China tops US and UK as Destination for Anglophone African Students', *The Conversation*, 27 June 2017, <https://theconversation.com/china-tops-us-and-uk-as-destination-for-anglophone-african-students-78967#:_:text=According%20to%20the%20UNESCO%20Institute>.

or religious law, it is likely that the broader study of Roman law at Bologna, derived from the legal systems developed in ancient Rome, led to its widespread embrace as the basis of legal systems throughout the western world and beyond. Bologna counts three Popes among its alumni and now boasts around 100,000 students in its twenty-three schools.

Bologna was closely followed in its establishment by the University of Oxford (from 1096) – also founded to produce men (and of course only men) able to run church and state. It has produced twenty Archbishops of Canterbury, twelve saints and, as of January 2024, thirty Prime Ministers of the UK![13] Later in England came the University of Cambridge (1209) and southern Europe (Salamanca, Spain, 1134; Padua, Italy, 1222; Naples, Italy, 1224) also opened early universities, roughly following the model which has survived to the present day. Most were established by royal decree from the reigning monarch or by papal bull (a type of charter named for the leaden seal used to confirm authenticity). Cambridge and Padua were formed respectively by academics from Oxford and Bologna, who broke away from their parent institution as a result of political or academic disagreements – university politics have always been bitterly fought. The early universities were communities of scholars ('university' translates roughly to an association or 'guild' of people),[14] speaking and teaching in the common language Latin, which permitted easy movement between institutions. For example, the fifteenth-century mathematician and polymath Nicolaus Copernicus, who formulated a model of the universe with the sun at its centre, was educated at the University of Krakow (1491–5) but also studied at Bologna (1496–1500), Padua (1501–3) and Ferrara (1503), before returning to Warmia in Poland as a cathedral chapter canon. Most early universities taught logic,

---
13 <https://www.ox.ac.uk/about/oxford-people/british-prime-ministers>.
14 C.T. Lewis and C. Short (eds), *A Latin Dictionary: Founded on Andrews' Edition of Freund's Latin Dictionary* (Oxford, 1963).

philosophy, law and medicine, with those in northern Europe focusing on theology and the arts, and those in Italy on medicine and law. By 1400 there were still fewer than thirty universities in Europe, however during the renaissance of the fifteenth and sixteenth centuries there was rapid growth in numbers – almost doubling in the fifteenth century alone.

This was a period of remarkable evolution of the arts, sciences and culture, no doubt greatly accelerated by the invention of the printing press by Johannes Gutenberg in Germany in 1440. Scotland could claim three universities by 1500 (St Andrews, 1413, Glasgow, 1451 and Aberdeen, 1495). Each was established by local bishops and confirmed by papal bull. The University of Edinburgh was established in 1583 by a royal charter granted by James VI and a second university (Marischal College) established in Aberdeen, at which time the city alone had the same number of universities as England. The modern version of Aberdeen University was created by the merger of the original university (Kings College) and Marischal College in 1860.

The early universities embraced a number of characteristics which may have contributed to their longevity and which have certainly contributed to the evolution of knowledge and its dissemination. Firstly, they mostly had a degree of autonomy. That is not to say that sovereigns and religious leaders did not try to influence them – just as today's politicians challenge the autonomy of contemporary higher education institutions. The extent of political interference has waxed and waned but is arguably no greater now than it was in the nineteenth century, when during a thirty-year period from 1854 there were ten reforming acts of Parliament in relation to Oxford and Cambridge universities alone.[15] Universities have always valued academic freedom – which has helped them to challenge dogma for more than a millennium. Secondly, they comprised communities of scholars

---

15  E. Byrne and C. Clarke, *The University Challenge: Changing Universities in a Changing World* (London, 2020).

– both to advance knowledge and understanding through debate and discourse and for their own self-governance – the senior governing bodies of Oxford and Cambridge still comprise about 5000 academics and officers of each university (the Congregation and Regent House respectively).

For the first 600 years change was incremental rather than radical. The range of subjects expanded, but the approach to teaching would have been familiar to Aristotle, and research, such as it was, was somewhat haphazard. Universities remained the preserve of the advantaged and produced men for church and state. During the early seventeenth century, the French philosopher René Descartes laid the foundations of rationalism, which helped catalyse a scientific revolution. In 1660 the establishment of the Royal Society in London introduced more structured empirical methods of research. One of its early fellows, Francis Bacon, believed in critical observation and 'sceptical methodology'.[16] It was however the great Prussian educationalist Wilhelm von Humboldt who helped establish what is now Humboldt University in Berlin in 1810, and who perhaps made the most radical change towards modernity in the sphere of higher education. He advocated and created a learning environment in which both teaching and research were embraced and in which they became integrated and mutually supportive. The Doctor of Philosophy (PhD) featured a dissertation focused on advanced research, and has become one of the staple currencies of academia since that time, being embraced throughout Europe and, following its adoption by Yale University in 1861, throughout North America. The success of Humboldt University in Berlin is reflected in its 57 Nobel laureates and notable faculty or alumni including Karl Marx, Albert Einstein and Friedrich Engels. In France, following the Revolution of 1789, a specialist group of *grandes écoles* developed in parallel with the public

---

16   E. Cassan, '"A New Logic": Bacon's *Novum Organum*', *Perspectives on Science*, 29/3 (2021), pp. 255–74, <https://doi.org/10.1162/posc_a_00368>.

universities. These institutions are fiercely competitive and selective, teach a limited range of subjects such as public policy, engineering and business administration and provide many of the graduates for the French civil service.[17]

In the Americas, universities were established under Spanish influence in what is now the Dominican Republic (University of Santo Domingo, 1538) and Mexico (University of Michoacán, 1539) before Harvard (1636), William and Mary (1693), Yale (1701) and Princeton (1746) were established – as in Europe, mostly by religious groups: Puritans (Harvard and Yale), Anglicans (William and Mary) and Presbyterians (Princeton). In 1862 the Morrill Act was passed in the US, which granted lands to established agricultural and engineering institutions. These land-grant colleges evolved into many eminent universities including the Massachusetts Institute of Technology (MIT) and Cornell University.

Entrance to and progress in higher education differs across the globe. In the US, which has the largest number of universities ranking highly in global league tables, students normally enter four-year bachelors' programmes which comprise an initial two years, undertaking core courses in subjects like literature, maths, history or languages. Students then select a 'major' for the remaining two years, in a subject of their choice. Many students move between universities in the US, either to more selective institutions or to those offering desired courses. Although there are private providers in the UK higher education system, the substantial majority of universities are still classified as public bodies or at least not-for-profit organisations. The US has a much broader range of university types – with public and private universities, liberal arts colleges, community colleges and for-profit colleges. In the US, state and federal funding for public universities has fallen from 60% in the 1970s to about 34% today.

---

17  O. Rollot, 'C'est quoi une Grande École?', *Le Monde*, 11 Feb 2011, <https://www.lemonde.fr/education/article/2011/02/11/c-est-quoi-une-grande-ecole_1477588_1473685.html>.

Perhaps by virtue of age, prestige and innovation, the University of California deserves mention. It comprises ten campuses and several research institutes and evolved from the original University of California founded in state legislature and embracing Morrill Land-Grant Acts, in Oakland in 1868, but soon (1873) to move to Berkeley. Several branch campuses were established over the 80-year period, until Clark Kerr was appointed president in 1958. He effectively created the University of California system, by which the branch campuses acquired their own chancellors and considerable autonomy. Kerr developed a federated system of substantially independent campuses, with their chancellors reporting to the president but retaining executive powers and engaging pluralistic decision making, but within a legally unitary university.[18] Further campuses have been added to the original 'branch' campuses of UC Berkeley, and the system now embraces University of California – Berkeley, Davis, Irvine, Los Angeles, Merced, Riverside, San Diego, San Francisco, Santa Barbara and Santa Cruz. The president now has a centralised office in Oaklands near the original university site, and the university maintains common standards and approves academic programmes across its constituent parts. It hosts around 294,000 students and has produced at least 71 Nobel prize winners.

## Emerging models of universities

Very large universities have emerged in India, Bangladesh and Turkey. The world's largest is Indira Gandhi National Open University, with headquarters in New Delhi, India, claiming an enrolment in excess of 4 million students, taught in person and at distance. Indeed, there are three other universities in India (Mumbai established in 1857, Savitribai in 1948 and Chaudhary in 1965) which can claim around half a million students each, and which teach predominantly

---

18  C. Kerr, *The Gold and the Blue: A Personal Memoir of the University of California 1949–1967*, vol. i (Berkeley, CA, 2001), p. 218.

in person. The National University of Bangladesh in Gazipur has about 2 million students, taught in person, and Anadolu University in Eskisehir, Turkey, a similar number taught in person and at distance. The growth of universities in the second half of the twentieth century, and since, has been spectacular, and the size of the 15–29-year-old populations in India and Bangladesh (more than 150 million and 50 million respectively) no doubt contribute to the mega-versities in these countries. At the other end of the scale, the relaxation on student number controls and easing of requirements to obtain degree awarding powers has led to a substantial growth in smaller providers in the UK. There are now 416 (2022) providers in the UK, up from 131 in 2002.[19] However, the vast majority of the new entrants teach relatively low numbers of students; many small specialist institutions in the UK have acquired degree-awarding powers, and comprise performing and visual arts, conservatoires and specialist medical (St George's, University of London), veterinary (the Royal Veterinary College, University of London) and agricultural institutions (the Royal Agricultural University and Harper Adams University for example). St George's merged with City University in 2024 to form City St George's, University of London. The last thirty years have also seen the emergence of large corporate higher education providers beyond the private universities which were established and flourished in some countries such as the US (Stanford, Yale, MIT for example). Perhaps the largest of the new corporates is Laureate Education Inc., which has about 875,000 students (2023), taught globally by both in person and distance provision.

The means of delivering teaching material evolved rather slowly over the first 800 years of the 'modern' university (see Chapter 4).

---

19   H. Carasso and A. Plume, 'To Measure is to Know: Two Decades of Change in UK Higher Education through the Lens of the Sector's own Statistics', in H. Carasso (ed.), *UK Higher Education – Policy, Practice and Debate during HEPI's First 20 Years*, Higher Education Policy Institute (HEPI) report 161 (Oxford, 2023).

Distance education enabled by the delivery of printed material was pioneered by the University of London from 1858, and through television by the Open University since 1969. It is, however, with the advent of the computer, and internet and video communication, that technology has contributed to a revolution in methods of delivery and access, not only to information, but also to those who might colour it with explanation and engage in learning dialogue. Online delivery need not of course be 'distant', indeed the majority of participants engaged in online education in the US are doing so from a provider located within their own state (see Chapter 9).[20] The emergence of the Massive Open Online Courses (MOOCs) at the end of the first decade in the twenty-first century (by Stanford and MIT amongst others), where courses were initially provided free online, was seen as a potential education disrupter of massive proportion. Indeed, some very successful private online delivery companies can trace their roots to the MOOC revolution – Udacity and Coursera (from Stanford in 2012) and edx from MIT, also in 2012. Nevertheless, the MOOC has not resulted in the demise of the campus university, and at least in its original form had two major drawbacks. Many students starting MOOCs failed to complete the course, and nor did these courses offer a monetised way of rewarding the investment in their creation. This is not to say that distance or online education has not been successful, nor that it is unlikely to grow as a useful addition to the conventional university. Online education is now pervasive worldwide and, both in terms of numbers participating and financial return to the providers, has demonstrated remarkable expansion. However, while the overall growth in numbers of people accessing online learning material has been spectacular, the number of those doing so in order to obtain a degree has been more modest, and it is particularly clear that it is

---

20  National Center for Education Statistics (NCES), 'Undergraduate Enrollment', Condition of Education, US Department of Education, Institute of Education Sciences, 2023, <https://nces.ed.gov/programs/coe/indicator/cha>.

those studying for accredited degree programmes that account for the most substantial revenues to the online providers (see Figure 9.1). The largest providers are now in China, followed by the US (see Table 9.1), probably reflecting the 'local' markets available and the language constraints associated with delivery. It will be interesting to see whether artificial intelligence (AI) will enhance the quality of delivery (pace and individuality – see Chapter 4) and make translation sufficiently accurate to mean that language of origin becomes irrelevant.

The growth in higher education throughout the world over the last fifty years has been enormous. It has been encouraged by national governments' policies recognising the benefit that a tertiary education brings to productivity and prosperity, and by the self-interest of individuals (and their parents) who recognise the economic and non-economic benefits of higher-level education. Nonetheless, there are many unanswered questions regarding the future of higher education enrolment. Predictions that MOOCs would sound the death knell for the campus university appear to have been premature. No doubt though that even if the shape of higher education changes, demand for it will remain strong. It has been estimated that global enrolment to higher education will rise from 216 million (2016) to 380 million by 2030, 472 million by 2035, and more than 594 million by 2040, with the greatest growth in East Asia and the Pacific. Much of the growth in numbers will be associated with population growth, but there is also likely to be increased percentage participation within the growing population. It is difficult to predict how many universities will be needed to cater for the projected increased student numbers. Currently in western countries there are about two universities for every million of the population, however there is a great range in size, from large multi-faculty to small specialist institutions. Universities may get bigger and more of the teaching may be digital – requiring less teaching space, they may become more international, with some countries becoming education hubs, or there may simply need to be more of them. Since tertiary education has itself an impact on population growth – with lower population growth in more educated populations, it is likely that the greater the participation in tertiary education – the sooner the planet will reach a steady state population (where the number of births equal the number of deaths) and the lower that population number will be. Many of the questions and uncertainties impacting universities will be explored in the subsequent chapters. These consider in more detail the development of universities in the UK and the major academic and operational activities and policies which affect them.

# CHAPTER 2
# British Universities: Development and Growth

Following the establishment of Oxford, Cambridge and the Scottish 'ancients', the last of which was Edinburgh in 1583 (and an abortive attempt to establish a university in Northampton) it took a further two hundred and forty-three years before Britain could truly claim a new university. University College London (1826) is generally considered to be the first genuinely secular university in the United Kingdom to which students were accepted regardless of religion[1] and makes a claim (which is contested by the University of Bristol) to be the first to have admitted women. The federal Victoria University, with its principal college, Owens College, in Manchester garnered royal charter in 1880 and was the first civic university in the UK. It incorporated colleges in Liverpool and Leeds and, together with several Victorian institutions in Birmingham, Bristol and Sheffield that had taught medicine or engineering, gained independent university status between 1900 and 1909. These became known as the 'Red Brick' universities because of their architectural design.[2] Several other civic universities emerged after the First World War, but it was not until the 1960s that the

---
1  N.B. Harte and J.A. North, *The World of UCL, 1828–2004* (London, 2004), pp. 29–32.
2  E.A. Peers, 'Redbrick University Revisited: Autobiography of Bruce Truscot', in A.L. MacKenzie and A.R. Allan (eds), *E. Allison Peers Lectures* (Liverpool, 1996).

University Grants Committee (UGC) established a group of universities generally carrying county names (Essex and Kent among them) which followed the tradition of architectural description by becoming the 'Plateglass' universities.[3] The UGC had been set up in 1918 on the recommendation of the Haldane committee to rationalise the system of direct treasury grants for universities which had operated up to that time.[4] The UGC had responsibility to advise government on the distribution of grant funding to universities and later to support the development of new universities.[5] By 1960 there had been some growth in the number of school-leavers going to university, but it was still a small percentage (4%), male-dominated and largely reflected a privileged portion of the population (by 1962 5.6% of men and 2.5% of women of the school-leaving cohort attended university). At that time more than half of students going to university in England received support for fees and living costs from their own local authority. The number of students supported and the amount of support they received varied for different authorities. The British government commissioned Lord Robbins to lead a review of higher education, which reported in 1963 and was made famous by its central principle that universities 'should be available for all those who are qualified by ability and attainment to pursue them and who wish to do so'. To enact this principle, Robbins recommended expansion of universities and in particular that colleges of advanced technology (CATs) should be given university status.[6] This created a further ten universities including Aston, Loughborough, Brunel and Bath. Running in parallel with the growth of universities was the growth and creation of polytechnics. Originally established to deliver applied education in vocational subjects, many evolved to deliver the broad range of

---
3  M. Beloff, *The Plateglass Universities* (London, 1968).
4  *Haldane Report*, Report of the Machinery of Government Committee (London: HMSO, 1918).
5  M. Shattock, *The UGC and the Management of British Universities* (Buckingham, 1994).
6  *Robbins Report*.

subjects familiar to most universities. Some of the polytechnics date back to the early nineteenth century – the London Polytechnic, now the University of Westminster, was founded in 1838. However, most were established in the 1960s and offered degree-level programmes originally validated by The University of London and later by the UK Council for National Academic Awards (CNAA).

The appetite for tertiary and particularly university education continued to grow, and the number of graduates produced by Britain's universities burgeoned from about 4000 in 1920 to 22,000 in 1960 to 68,000 in 1980.[7] The Conservative governments of Margaret Thatcher and John Major wrestled with the growth, initially pressing for greater efficiency – more students but without a proportionate increase in funding. The unit of resource (i.e. the amount of funding per student) fell by about 40% between 1976 and 1996[8] and the ratio of academic staff to students fell from 1:12 in 1983 to 1:22 by 1995.[9] The growth could not be fully absorbed by the existing universities – and the distinction between universities and polytechnics, the 'binary divide', grew blurred. In 1992, in a transformational change in legislation, the Further and Higher Education Act 1992[10] conferred university status on the polytechnics, which now acquired increased autonomy and their own degree-awarding powers. The thirty-five new universities created the capacity for continued higher-education expansion and by 2000, 243,000 students were acquiring first degrees each year.[11] Although apparent 'efficiencies' had been gained, these came at a cost:

---

7 P. Bolton, 'Education: Historical Statistics', House of Commons Library SN/SG/4252, 28 November 2012.
8 *Dearing Report*, Reports of the National Committee of Inquiry into Higher Education (London: HMSO, 1997).
9 P. Maitlis, 'The Revolution in England's Universities 1980–2000', May 1998, <https://warlight.tripod.com/ MAITLIS.html>; UNESCO Institute for Statistics (UIS), 'Pupil-Teacher Ratio, Tertiary', The World Bank, February 2020, <https://data.worldbank.org/indicator/SE.TER.ENRL.TC.ZS>.
10 Further and Higher Education Act 1992, c. 13.
11 Bolton, 'Education'.

the decreased student-to-staff ratio is likely to have had an impact on the quality of delivery – even accepting that the relationship between class size and quality is not straightforward. Furthermore, universities were struggling to upgrade their facilities, traditionally a call on capital grants from government – but now, with autonomy, needing a financial model which permitted the creation of reserves for such investment. By 2004 there was an estimated £4 billion of 'deferred' capital infrastructure costs across the sector.[12]

The national trends in growth and development sit alongside historical differences in the education systems in the four nations of the UK (England, and what are referred to as 'the devolved nations' of Scotland, Wales and Northern Ireland). Each have had independent textures of their own, perhaps best exemplified by variations in school-leaving qualifications which in Scotland comprise a greater number and diversity of subjects, usually culminating in a maximum of five 'higher' examinations, with the option of university at age seventeen or eighteen. Whereas in the other nations, leaving examinations comprise fewer and more specialised A-levels taken at eighteen. This has enabled universities in England, Wales and Northern Ireland to award three-year degrees, while those in Scotland (and in countries such as the US) generally require four years of study. The historic differences in educational systems were largely based on educational philosophy, heritage and practicalities, up until 1988, when devolution Acts of Parliament gave Scotland, Wales and Northern Ireland further independent political powers, and from 2000, when major divergence in funding mechanisms for higher education in the different nations were codified (see Chapter 10). Since then, the complexion of higher education in each of the nations of the UK has been dramatically influenced by political doctrine. In England, the number of registered higher education providers increased from 131

---

12  Universities UK (UUK), *Achieving our Vision: Universities UK 2004 Spending Review Submission for England and Northern Ireland* (London, 2004).

to 416 between 2002 and 2022, although those with university status have only increased to around 150. This increase has been encouraged by Conservative governments, wishing to increase competition, and in doing so, improve value for money for students. Such growth has, by necessity, required revision of the accreditation processes needed to gain degree awarding powers (DAP). Nor is it clear that it has been successful, since the most intense competition for places by the consumer is still for the institutions embracing the traditional idea of a university. In Scotland and Wales, by contrast, there has been no increase in the number of higher education providers, and although the numbers in Northern Ireland have increased to four, it was from a small base of just two.

There are also considerable differences in growth in recruitment to universities across the UK nations. Until 2015 the number of undergraduate students that each university in England could recruit was capped, in part to control the cost of government investment in grants and then loans. In Scotland, there remains an annual cap on the number of Scottish students who can access university places funded by the Scottish government.

Interestingly, despite removing the numbers cap on UK home-based undergraduates, the numbers in England and Wales have only increased by 15.3% and 16.6% respectively, between 2001/02 and 2021/22, whereas those in Scotland and Northern Ireland have increased by 22.2% and 17.3%,[13] despite the necessity of numbers caps to control expenditure, which comes from the budgets of the Scottish government and Northern Ireland executive. Of course, the absolute number of undergraduate students has grown by 189,000 in England, compared to 31,000 in Scotland, and the total number of home undergraduate students in the UK has increased from about 1.5 million in 2001/02 to about 1.7 million in 2021/22. During that same period, the number of international students (both undergraduate

---

13  Carasso and Plume, 'To Measure is to Know'.

and postgraduate) in the UK has increased from 243,000 to 680,000, an almost three-fold increase. A further legislative change in England saw the removal of financial support for equivalent or lower-level qualifications (ELQs). This meant that support would no longer be available for someone already holding a bachelor's degree wishing to do another.[14] The number of part-time students fell from 34% of the total to 12% between 2008 and 2020.[15]

Perhaps the other key difference between the home nations of the UK with regard to universities relates to their governance. In 2017, a Higher Education and Research Act (HERA) was passed by Westminster, and brought to life in 2018 a new regulatory system for universities in England: the Office for Students (OfS). The OfS has been established as the market regulator and protector of students' interests, and unlike its predecessor, the Higher Education Funding Council for England (HEFCE), has no real role in the wellbeing of the institutions themselves, other than where that might impact the service provided to their customers, the students. The devolved nations retained their governing instruments through the Scottish Funding Council, the Higher Education Funding Council for Wales (which has been replaced by the Commission for Tertiary Education and Research), and the Department for the Economy in Northern Ireland. Universities in the devolved nations retained the rather more benign regulatory environment, whereby the 'regulator' was still able to exert its will, but did so through the actual or implicit distribution of funding. On the other hand, the tangible impact of the OfS has been seen in the way English universities are regulated compared to the other devolved nations. Objective measurements of continuation, completion and progression (graduate jobs – perhaps earnings in the

---

14  Innovation, Universities, Science and Skills Committee, *Withdrawal of Funding for Equivalent or Lower Level Qualifications (ELQs)*, 17 March 2008, HC 187-I 2007–08.
15  C. Millward, 'What happened to the Masterplan? The Relationship between Government and Higher Education', in Carasso (ed.), *UK Higher Education*.

future) are key areas covered in the 'conditions for registration' with the OfS (condition B3) and within the Teaching Excellence Framework (TEF), with a score in TEF providing the reputational incentive to improve. The HERA required a 'designated quality body' to complement the role of the OfS, but the Quality Assurance Agency (the QAA), who fulfilled this role from 2017, stepped down from 1 April 2023 as it believed the OfS's requirements of it conflicted with international standards in quality assurance. The OfS has taken on responsibility in this area. A further major effect of the 2017 Act was to create United Kingdom Research and Innovation (UKRI) which brought together the seven Research Councils of the UK under one authority. It has responsibility for the distribution of competitive or response-mode research funding to the whole of the UK, and for some more specific funding, such as Higher Education Innovation Funding (HEIF), in England.[16]

The organisation of the university sector in England, and to some extent in the devolved nations, is further complicated by the government departments to which they are answerable. In 2007, responsibility for universities in England was moved from the Department for Education (DfE) to the Department for Innovation, Universities and Skills, which subsequently became the Department for Business, Innovation and Skills (BIS) in 2009. This reflected the role which government perceived that universities had in stimulating and supporting the economy through their research and their role in enhancing human capital (the knowledge, skills and experience held by an individual which are valuable to the country). In 2016, the responsibility for universities was split between the DfE and the Department for Business, Energy and Industrial Strategy (BEIS), which has since morphed into the Department for Science, Innovation and Technology (DSIT).

---

16 Response-mode funding is funding made available on a competitive basis, in response to a specific call for research in a specific area or into a particular subject.

Over the thousand years that universities have existed (as conceived of in 'western' society), they have grown in size and also greatly in complexity. Perhaps the apparent difficulty in deciding how best to organise, govern or regulate universities, exemplified by the UK, is an inevitable result of that complexity, or perhaps it adds to the diversity of the organisations themselves and will contribute to further divergence over the next millennia.

# CHAPTER 3
## Access and Equity: Entry

University education confers substantial advantage on individuals in terms of earnings and enlightenment, and the number of applicants has generally risen year on year, creating intense competition, particularly for the most prestigious places. It is clearly important to the applicants that the system of selection is fair, and democratic societies should wish to create a system which is just to everyone.

In the UK, we have by most measures (applicants achieving their university of choice, low numbers of non-completers of those accepted by international standards[1] and excellent employment rates for graduates) a good admissions system, but is it truly fair? The assessments on which admissions depend, for instance, A-levels (in England), are large, summative examinations, usually administered at the end of an instructional course, and chiefly designed to test assimilation of content, much of which can now be accessed instantly. Many applicants are accepted on predicted and not actual grades, and while the predictions offer some basis for selection, they are clearly less certain than actual results.

---

1  Organisation for Economic Co-operation and Development (OECD), Graduation and Entry Rates, <https://stats.oecd.org/Index.aspx?DataSetCode=EAG_GRAD_ENTR_RATES>.

The prior educational context of an applicant is not uniformly or robustly considered in the application process. Since it is likely that those who have been previously disadvantaged will perform above average in their studies relative to those with a history of educational advantage arriving with similar qualifications at entry, the process should select for future potential as well as proven ability.[2]

While it is essential that the admissions process is fair to the applicant, it should also be fair to employers, who require graduates with the appropriate knowledge, skills and behaviours to contribute productively to their enterprise, and to society, which will bear a substantial part of the cost of graduate education and might expect a return in the form of both revenue and improvements to the social fabric.

The 2022 UCAS (Universities and Colleges Admissions Service) end-of-year data[3] indicate that approximately 206,000 students entered UK universities with A-levels, the largest cohort of entry, although substantial numbers (49,000) now enter with alternatives such as BTEC (Business and Technology Education Council) qualifications. It has been suggested that the British (English, Welsh, and Northern Irish) fixation on the A-level as the gold standard entry qualification has had a detrimental influence on depth over breadth, and that this is the fault of the university admission system.[4]

Undoubtedly the general requirement by many universities for three A-levels does mean that A-level students specialise at a much earlier age than students applying to university in most other countries, and that it has the undesirable effect of narrowing educational focus – generally *either* in the sciences *or* in the humanities. This

---

2  University of Bristol, Contextual offers, <https://bristol.ac.uk/study/undergraduate/entry-requirements-qualifications/contextual-offers/>.
3  Universities and Colleges Admissions Service (UCAS), Undergraduate end of cycle data resources, 2022, <https://www.ucas.com/data-and-analysis/undergraduate-statistics-and-reports/ucas-undergraduate-end-cycle-data-resources-2022>.
4  D. Willetts, *A University Education* (Oxford, 2017).

polarisation is only worsened within the university, where the student will be required to dedicate all their energies towards a disciplinary outcome (usually in a narrow subject area). Joint Honours were developed to overcome this division, but the complexity of administration (timetabling and assessment) and the focus of the educators in each discipline – each subject academic tends to want *their* part of the 'joint' qualification to match in stringency and depth the equivalent single-honours qualification – have meant a decline in joint honours degrees in many universities. There are of course some benefits to the depth of learning that an A-level delivers. Students are well-prepared for the intensity of study required at university, and for the UK (Scotland excepted), this generally means a three-year degree. Furthermore, it is argued by academics immersed in their own discipline that the growth of subject-specific knowledge means that students need more prior learning and need to dedicate even more time and energy to their subject. In reality, much of the subject knowledge required for a degree (or to have the competence to start a job) is readily available and instantly accessible on the internet. Academics should be reviewing their curricula regularly to manage 'knowledge growth' and ensure that their students can access and assess the knowledge critically. Nevertheless, the English (and Welsh and Northern Irish) entry system means that we have students and graduates with a narrower view of the world, who are less likely to be able to bring broader perspectives into the workplace and indeed into their communities and societies. We have fewer scientists who can happily converse with their international peers in a foreign language, and we have fewer humanities graduates who can confidently comment on the merits of vaccination or electric cars. Those countries with broader university entry requirements and often broader early-years university curricula, such as Scotland and the US, might (arguably) be expected to have a more enlightened population. The counter-arguments that employers expect 'oven-ready' graduates, with detailed knowledge and understanding, and that a three-year degree is more resource-efficient (Scotland and the US still have general four-year degrees) and confers an extra year of 'useful' employment on graduates, are no doubt true, but rather utilitarian.

Furthermore, early specialisation imposed by the A-level results in not just polarisation but creates actual hostility between the science and humanities graduates, and, since this is not a new phenomenon, is likely to be deeply entrenched in the cultures of UK graduates.[5] A report into UK education, commissioned by *The Times* newspaper, identified the deficiencies of the A-level model and recommended instead a baccalaureate, with academic or vocational options. The academic track would comprise three major and three minor subjects, covering both sciences and humanities, with critical thinking, communication, creativity, and digital skills woven in throughout. Those on the vocational track would combine learning with work experience.[6] Undoubtedly, the demands of university admissions systems, and particularly the Oxbridge admission systems, have contributed to the emergence and dominance of the A-level. The present situation is, however, further exacerbated by the demands of employers, who have the 'ear' of government with regards to graduate employability, and by professional, statutory and regulatory bodies (PSRBs), who impose strict requirements on courses which they accredit, some would say in order to enhance their own disciplinary stature.

Whatever the previous educational experience or prior qualifications obtained by those applying to university, at the point of application the system should be fair to all. If the English fixation on specialisation were only or largely the fault of the university admissions system, as Willetts suggests, it is surprising that the Scottish

---

5 C.P. Snow, *The Two Cultures and the Scientific Revolution*, The Rede Lecture (Cambridge, 1959).
6 *Times Education Commission: Bringing out the Best*, 2022, <https://www.thetimes.co.uk/society/education/education-commission>.

system, where universities have similar autonomy with regard to admissions, has not fallen into line.[7] Furthermore, it is clear that successive Education Secretaries, who have the authority to make change, are also culpable and in the future will be required to demonstrate political resolve if change is to happen.

The premium gained in lifetime earnings for graduates amounts to about £170,000 for men and £250,000 for women and has remained relatively constant over the last twenty years in real terms, despite the increase in graduate numbers and the imposition of increased tuition fees (see Chapter 6).[8] There is therefore a real economic advantage in getting into university. The advantage to the individual extends beyond wealth: graduates drink less alcohol, exercise more, suffer less depression and live longer.[9] They are also given an opportunity to devote time to discovering the joy of learning and the wonder of knowledge. Competition for the most prestigious universities is highly intense, and on graduation these universities confer additional advantage in terms of initial graduate earnings,[10] however, this is insignificant if corrected for father's income and educational attainment, and after seven years has disappeared. Thus a degree from most UK universities confers similar earnings benefits.[11] It is also true that despite the very substantial increase in the number of people going to university, there are still more applications than acceptances of offers for places. In 2020 there were about 730,000 applicants, of which about 570,000 were accepted. Furthermore, there are a number

---

7   Willetts, *A University Education*.
8   I. Walker and Y. Zhu, 'The Impact of University Degrees on the Lifecycle of Earnings: Some Further Analysis', Department for Business Innovation and Skills (BIS) research paper 112, August 2013, pp. 44–6.
9   Willetts, *A University Education*.
10   I. Walker and Y. Zhu, 'University Selectivity and the Relative Returns to Higher Education: Evidence from the UK', *Labour Economics*, 53 (2018), pp. 230–49, <https://doi.org/10.1016/j.labeco.2018.05.005>.
11   K. Purcell and P. Elias, *Seven Years On: Graduate Careers in a Changing Labour Market* (Manchester, 2004).

of universities for which application numbers greatly exceed their capacity, and as a limited resource in high demand, finding a fair way of selecting those students for admission is essential. For very high-cost courses such as medicine, where the state carries much of the financial burden, it would be unaffordable and impractical to accept all candidates who meet minimum requirements.

Beyond the acquired benefit to the individual, and the competitive nature of the process, there are also issues of natural justice in creating a system of admissions which is seen to be as fair as possible to the greatest number of applicants.

By some measures, a simple lottery of all applicants for a particular course could be seen as perfectly fair. Each applicant has an equal chance, and no partiality is shown. It is unlikely though that it would be perceived as fair by applicants who have worked hard and are appropriately gifted and wish entry into those courses which might give them greatest lifetime earnings, or for which they have a particular passion. A simple lottery would also present concerns for highly prestigious institutions which may wish to attract the 'best' students, or at least those with some proven record, which might make them suited to a particular course of study. It is also likely that society would hesitate to support a system whereby future doctors were selected randomly, or where employers might have limited confidence in the abilities of the graduate pool available. Semi-random selection may be more attractive, particularly for heavily oversubscribed subjects such as medicine, where there are many more applicants with the proven record of achievement than are needed to fill the course. Semi-random selection based on 'adequacy', or a weighted lottery based on grades achieved, rather than open competition, is used in admission processes in some countries, for example, in the Netherlands, often with selection happening at a later stage in the academic journey. This has the advantage of creating a larger initial pool of recruits, but the disadvantage that a later 'cull' is likely to be wasteful in resource, and similarly viewed by those not selected to progress as a waste of their time and effort. A semi-random process is likely to appear fair only to those chosen to proceed.

The question remains, what do we mean by *fair*, and can a system of admissions be created which would be considered fair by most people? In considering assessment, Nisbet and Shaw determined several measures of fairness: the process should be valid and reliable, it should meet the legitimate expectations (of the candidate among others), it should be impartial, and it should consider the context of the candidate (for instance, previous educational advantage).[12]

If the validity and reliability of the admissions process should be robust and appropriate, as Nisbet and Shaw's first pillar requires, a lottery is unlikely to be considered a valid process for selecting recruits to a medical course, although it could no doubt be done in a reliable way, and indeed semi-random selection has been shown to deliver as good predictive validity as other systems of selection.

It is important to consider what universities are selecting candidates for – they may be selected on the basis that they might successfully complete the course, or 'success' may be measured by whether they are likely to achieve a 'good' degree (a 2:1 or First). We may select for students who might become the most accomplished scientists, mathematicians or historians, or the most likely to progress to postgraduate study, or we may be selecting for future professional achievement, those who might become the best teachers, engineers or doctors. We might also be selecting for those who will make the 'best' citizens, or those for whom university might make the biggest difference. There are universities, and indeed applicants, that desire each and often several of these goals. The selection criteria should be sufficiently flexible to accommodate each potential outcome for different courses and universities.

---

12   I. Nisbet and S. Shaw, *Is Assessment Fair?* (London, 2020) <https://dx.doi.org/10.4135/9781529739480>.

## Selection methods

Once we have decided on our goals, it is instructive to look at the validity of different methods of selection. School or college-based qualifications deploy a range of different assessment methods. Terminal summative (end of course) examination processes, such as A-levels, may not be as valid as qualifications which comprise assignments and continual assessment such as BTECs (Business and Technology Education Council qualifications) if university assessment is also continual in nature, or if subsequent graduate jobs require skills, knowledge or behaviours better assessed by assignments or the like rather than summative examinations. Qualifications associated with traditional disciplines (maths, English, history etc.) may not be as valid as those with vocational content (business, engineering, information technology etc.) although it is likely that numeracy and literacy still form an important bedrock of most university assessment processes or later job requirements. The International Baccalaureate (IB) has some benefits in terms of breadth of study and mixed modes of assessment, which might give confidence during the university admissions process. It also has the advantage of wider international recognition and historic legitimacy. In Scotland, students may take up to five Highers as national school-leaving-certificate exams, thus providing greater breadth to their learning. However, this is normally as a prelude to a four-year undergraduate university degree, subsequently allowing greater depth of learning in the chosen subject matter. It may be appropriate to have uniform or standardised admissions tests, such as the SATs (Scholastic Aptitude Tests) used in some US college admissions systems, although these may be best suited as preparation for the liberal arts early years (when students spend time improving their critical thinking and study skills) embraced by US universities. More specific tests, such as the BMAT (Bio Medical Admissions Test), have been developed to support the admissions process for medical, dental and veterinary schools, and are designed to identify an aptitude for specific courses.

The validity of the assessment process may go beyond the sense that it is an appropriate process to assess someone's basic potential to succeed and may also test the individual's aptitude for a particular vocation, for instance by assessing a portfolio of material to determine artistic merit, requiring a presentation for entry to a performing arts programme, or an interview to assess empathy and other appropriate characteristics in the caring professions.

## Interviews

The reliability of an interview process may be enhanced by embracing a standard structure, although it is acknowledged that this can suppress the spontaneity which often differentiates candidates. Interviews are also criticised because they tend to result in the selection of candidates in the likeness of the interviewers. While selecting recruits who may have the same attributes as a previous generation of highly competent and successful practitioners may be a perfectly valid goal, it could though also exclude candidates with different but equally useful attributes, nor is it likely to enhance diversity, unless some sort of affirmative action is taken to select diverse interviewers. Bias at interviews (or even without interview) has been apparent in some professions historically. Currently approximately 80% of recruits to veterinary medicine are women and this broadly reflects applicant numbers. In 1949, 70% of applicants to veterinary medical courses were women, yet only 12% were recruited – it is inconceivable that the qualifications of women applicants were so woefully poorer than those of men that this disparity could be justified.[13] A call to interview can also present barriers to applicants from lower-income households, who may simply not be able to afford the travel or have the technological resources for a virtual interview. In these circumstances universities may wish to offer small bursaries to support low-income students.

---

13  M. Aitken, 'The Rise of Women in the Profession', *In Practice*, 25/5 (2003), pp. 292–4.

## Personal statements

Up until 2024 applicants to universities in the UK were required to include a 4000-character personal statement, indicating their ambition to undertake a particular course and the skills and experience that made them suitable for the course. The use of personal statements – with the intention to determine whether an applicant has enthusiasm for, and understanding of a course of study – is a worthy aim, but the likelihood that it had been substantially influenced by tutors or career advisors from school, if not largely composed by the applicant's mother or father, must be considered. It is also likely that the personal statement expanded the disadvantage gap, whereby more disadvantaged applicants were likely to receive the poorest support in creating the statement and were unlikely to have acquired the social capital conferred by visits to potential workplaces and supporting extracurricular activities, which strengthen personal statements. The UCAS website carried some useful tips for completing a personal statement, in which they suggested the candidate 'talks about their motivation, demonstrates enthusiasm and relevance and outlines their ideas clearly', however there is little good research evidence to show how valid or useful personal statements were, and much of the research available is old and based on limited numbers of applicants or statements.[14] Personal statements are not used in all countries; some, such as China, do not use them at all, and others, such as some US colleges, use personal essays rather than statements, which are written in response to a specific question relating to the candidates' experience or background. In reviewing and adding to the research into personal statements, Fryer et al. indicate that applicants from state schools were likely to provide personal statements with more grammatical mistakes and were less likely to be able to reflect on work experiences (2.66 experiences) than those from independent schools

---

14  T. Fryer, S. Westlake and S. Jones, 'Reforming the UCAS Personal Statement: Making the Case for a Series of Short Questions', HEPI Debate Paper 31, November 2022.

(5.42 experiences).[15] Overall, applicants from state schools were less likely than those from independent schools to be accepted into Russell Group universities (a group of large UK research-intensive universities), even if they were applying with the same grades, suggesting that personal statements give more privileged applicants an advantage.[16] In proposing options for reform, Fryer et al. consider compliance with the Universities UK (UUK) and GuildHE's 'Fair Admissions Code of Practice', which is based on the principle that admissions processes protect and prioritise the interests of applicants, that they are transparent and should enable universities to select students able to complete a course and that they are reliable, valid and explainable.[17] They should also minimise barriers and address inequalities.[18] Fryer et al. conclude that a series of short-response questions, with a clear focus, considering valid and reliable traits that relate to an applicant's potential to complete the course, and which address inequalities, would comprise the best alternative to the personal statement.[19] They give exemplar short questions:

1. Please describe one topic that is related to your course. Please discuss what you have learnt about this topic through exploring this outside of the classroom.
2. Please describe one experience and explain how this demonstrates you have the skills to thrive on your course.

These questions are expanded to describe how the applicant may evidence the answer, through books, articles, blogs, work experience and so on.

---

15  Ibid.
16  V. Boliver, 'How Fair is Access to More Prestigious UK Universities?', *The British Journal of Sociology*, 64/2 (2013), pp. 344–64, <https://onlinelibrary.wiley.com/doi/full/10.1111/1468-4446.12021>.
17  Fryer et al., 'Reforming the UCAS Personal Statement'.
18  UUK/GuildHE, 'Fair Admissions Code of Practice', 2022, <https://www.universitiesuk.ac.uk/what-we-do/policy-and-research/publications/fair-admissions-code-practice>.
19  Fryer et al., 'Reforming the UCAS Personal Statement'.

Fryer et al. point out that the short-response questions are likely to assess baselines like basic level of interest, rather than predict differential achievement, and that more advantaged applicants could still receive more support than those with less advantage.[20] Nevertheless, they make a strong case that the short-response question format would be more in line with the UUK and GuildHE's Fair Admissions Code of Practice than the previous system of personal statements.

UCAS produced a report on the 'Future of Undergraduate Admissions' reflecting the sentiments outlined by Fryer et al. and indicating that from 2024 (at the earliest) it will change the personal statement to a series of structured questions.[21] It identified six areas likely to be addressed, including motivation, preparedness for course and for study, preparation through experience, extenuating circumstances, and preferred learning styles.[22] In July 2024, UCAS published the structured questions which will be asked of applicants from September 2025. These are:

1. Why do you want to study this course or subject?
2. How have your qualifications and studies helped you to prepare for this course or subject?
3. What else have you done to prepare outside of education, and why are these experiences helpful?[23]

## Validity

In considering validity, both objective and subjective (qualitative) methods of assessment could be justifiably and fairly utilised as criteria for admissions to university. However, the range of qualifications and admissions processes used does raise the question – are they all equally valid or reliable?

---

20  Ibid.
21  UCAS, 'Future of Undergraduate Admissions', MD-8018, January 2023, <https://www.ucas.com/file/672901/download?token=VccObZXZ>.
22  Fryer et al., 'Reforming the UCAS Personal Statement'.
23  'UCAS to Reform University Personal Statements', BBC News, 18 July 2024, <https://www.bbc.co.uk/news/articles/cger11kjk1jo>.

The question of reliability applies to all methods of assessment for admission; indeed, a lottery could be made quite reliable, given an adequate number of applicants and a suitably randomised method of selection. From a more analytical perspective, reliability could be considered in terms of precision and repeatability. How precise is the method of assessment? Is a candidate who scored 65% in the assessment distinctly better than one who scores 64%, or does the imprecision of the method mean that a grade boundary of say 5% (between 62.5 and 67.5) is a more appropriate level of granularity for selection? It is also important that the assessments are likely to give the same results if repeated. Giving a candidate the same test or a test of similar difficulty should produce a similar outcome on more than one occasion, although it is accepted that candidates can have 'off' days, and adjustments may be made for illness or disruption to the candidate. It is more likely that fairness will be questioned if the same piece of assessment work is marked on different occasions or by different assessors and produces very different marks. This has been addressed in some university assessments, by double marking and accepting the average mark or, when the marks differ by more than say 10%, having a third marker. It is also possible to derive some confidence in the reliability of the test if a statistically valid number are double marked, and any differences are found to be acceptably low. A-levels are likely to be about 98% reliable only to one grade either way.[24]

## Pre-qualification predictions

In the UK, more than 97% of eighteen-year-olds who apply to university do so before their assessment results are known. They are able to do so on the basis of predictions of what grades they might be expected

---

[24] S. Rhead, B. Black and A. Pinot de Moires, 'Marking Consistency Metrics', Ofqual/18/6449/2, November 2018, <www.gov.uk/ofqual>; Education Committee, *The Impact of COVID-19 on Education and Children's Services*, HC 254 2020, <https://committees.parliament.uk/event/1755/fomral-meeting-oral-evidence-session/>.

to get, made by their teachers. The accuracy of predicted grades is low, with only about 50% of individual predicted and actual grades matching exactly. Where predictions are made on best three A-level results (assuming students sit three A-levels) the predictions are even less accurate, with only 16% alignment. While it is self-evident that using actual grades would be more accurate than using predicted grades, that is not the whole story. Teachers are actually somewhat consistent in making predictions, but for a variety of reasons they consistently over-predict. Based on best three A-levels, 75% are over-predicted and only 8% underpredicted.[25] Over-prediction amounting to about 2.1 points (where an A* is 6 points, an A is 5 points, and a B is 4 points and so on).[26] This is hardly surprising since judgement of their teaching quality may depend upon the examination outcomes of their students. The small number of underpredictions by teachers present a significant impediment to fair access for the students affected.[27] Nevertheless, university admissions systems have become highly capable of 'compensating' for the more common over-predictions as they offer places to applicants. Moreover, it has been claimed that basing offers on predicted grades could disadvantage more disadvantaged students, presumably on the assumption that those in advantaged areas or schools are likely to be given relatively higher predictions. However, if account is taken of different predicted grade distributions between those from advantaged and disadvantaged backgrounds, the data does not indicate that using predicted grades harms equality generally. Indeed, for most disadvantaged groups, using predicted grades is positive.[28] It is also true that teachers who create the predicted

---

25  L. Macmillan and G. Wyness, 'Should we stop using predicted A-level grades in university applications?', *Economics Observatory*, 3 September 2020, <https://www.economicsobservatory.com/should-we-stop-using-predicted-level-grades-university-applications>.
26  M. Corver, 'Predicted Grades and University Admissions', in R. Hewitt (ed.), *Where Next for University Admissions?*, HEPI report 156 (Oxford, 2021).
27  OECD, Graduation and Entry Rates.
28  Corver, 'Predicted Grades and University Admissions'.

grades will have an intimate knowledge of the students in their care and are likely to contextualise to some extent the grades which they award, presumably to the benefit of the applicant, although there is a view, particularly in the US, that Black students are hampered by the low expectations of their (White) teachers.

Given the relatively poor precision of most assessment processes on one hand, and the fairly consistent over-prediction of A-level results on the other, together with the sophistication of university adjustments used in admissions, it is likely that the use of predictions is less unfair than might be imagined and is unlikely to disadvantage applicants greatly. In its present form, the use of predictions also has the advantage of greater time between application and recruitment (provided that 'conditional unconditional offers' are not made – see below) which allows the applicant to engage with their institution of choice, develop a relationship and reflect on their decisions. Nevertheless, it is self-evident that the use of actual results must be more accurate than the use of predicted results, and furthermore, using actual outcomes must provide a more transparent platform for the legitimate expectations of applicants and, more broadly, society. This underpins the second pillar of fairness proposed by Nisbet and Shaw, that of legitimate expectation.[29]

## Legitimate expectation

The legitimate expectation of applicants to university has changed as a result of evolving government policy and university expansionism. In the UK in 1950, only 3.4% of school leavers went to university; by 2014 that had increased to 48%. It would be fair to assume that success in the process is the legitimate expectation of many more applicants than it was in 1950, and this is probably reflected in the number of people applying, which has grown accordingly. Legitimate expectation is also influenced by published information. If a university publishes

---

29  Nisbet and Shaw, *Is Assessment Fair?*

entry requirements for a particular course as AAB, and an applicant achieves AAB, then they will have a legitimate expectation of a place. This raises a secondary question around the transparency of information provided, both in terms of extent and accuracy, and this is now more robustly legislated for by both the OfS and the Competition and Markets Authority (CMA). From an institutional perspective, published information has become important in a competitive sense – since entry grades offer a proxy for quality – with some universities apparently inflating their advertised minimum entry requirements to create a brand image of quality and thus attract a larger number of applicants, but then accepting students with grades below those advertised. In terms of fairness and transparency, there is a strong argument that institutions should publish the actual grades at which they recruit, accepting that this may have to be retrospective, and this has been embraced by UCAS who now make retrospective data available.

There are also, of course, legitimate expectations from employers and society that graduates will have acquired the knowledge, skills and behaviours essential to their jobs. In this regard, more academically demanding careers such as medicine could legitimately expect higher grades to be demanded for entry to university. It is important to balance this against the unnecessarily high-grade expectations of some PSRBs which might be perceived as creating 'closed shops' (perhaps to encourage demand-driven salary premia for those already 'in post'). Since expectations are tempered by information, it is important that universities produce sufficient, unambiguous and easily accessible information, advice and guidance for prospective students, and that schools provide sufficient and competent careers advice to their students. Obligations consequent on the information provided become substantially more rigorous once an offer has been made to an applicant, since this forms the basis of a contract between provider and applicant.³⁰

Providing high-quality information and advice could present a problem if a system of post-qualification admissions were implemented, whereby recruitment was compressed into a shorter period at the end of the summer, when many teachers and other careers advisors may be on holiday. I will return to post-qualification admissions later (see p. 55).

## Impartiality

Nisbet and Shaw's third pillar of fairness relates to impartiality, or ensuring that all individuals applying for a particular course are treated alike. It is important that at the point of admission all cases with the same qualifications or equivalent qualifications (for instance, using reliable conversion to a standard tariff) are treated the same.

To compare assessment outcomes, particularly where qualifications from different countries or under different examination authorities are being considered, a centralised system has been developed. When the UK was in the European Union it used the National Academic Recognition Information Centre (NARIC).³¹ This has changed to the UK National Information Centre for the recognition and evaluation of international qualifications and skills which is a wider European (beyond EU) title for national recognition agencies.³²

Universities in the UK pride themselves on impartiality, but this has not always been the case here or elsewhere. In the US, some universities have historically embraced explicit donor-preference schemes, whereby the children of large donors were given preferential access, and children of alumni may have received preferential

---

30 Competition and Markets Authority (CMA), 'UK Higher Education Providers – Advice on Consumer Protection Law', CMA 33, 12 March 2015, <https://assets.publishing.service.gov.uk/government/uploads/system/uploads/attachment_data/file/428549/HE_providers_-_advice_on_consumer_protection_law.pdf>.
31 National Academic Recognition Information Centre (NARIC), <www.naric.org.uk>.
32 The UK National Agency for International Qualifications and Skills (UK ENIC), <enic.org.uk>.

treatment. For privately funded institutions this may be acceptable, if unpalatable. Indeed, if a large donation from a wealthy parent allows several scholarships for less advantaged students this could even be perceived as a kind of natural justice.

Where higher education is supported by the state (in the UK largely through the 'subsidy' on the student loan scheme) it is considered inequitable to give advantage based on anything beyond the merit of the candidate. This does not mean that every individual applicant will be treated in exactly the same way in every university. Each university has its own character, prestige and capacity. The Oxbridge examination and interview system may look for different academic characteristics to a redbrick or post-92 university with a more technical or professional focus. The important thing is that Oxford will treat all its applicants the same and a post-92 university will treat all its applicants the same. In the US there has been controversy over the use of 'affirmative action' in the selection and recruitment of students to universities. Affirmative action in respect to race, and more specifically for potential Black students, has been used in many US universities as part of their diversity policies, to encourage a greater proportion of Black, Asian and Minority Ethnic (BAME) students entry to their programmes. Legal cases have been taken out against universities using affirmative action, on the basis that it may disadvantage other students gaining access. Some states (for instance California) have banned the use of affirmative action and in 2023 the US Supreme Court considered whether race-based admissions processes are lawful, concluding that they are not.

### Anonymised applications

Concerns are often raised at the relatively low number of recruits to Oxford or Cambridge, and some other pre-92 universities, from ethnically diverse backgrounds and from state schools.[33] It could be argued that impartiality would be enhanced if applications were anonymised and information such as their school or college removed. There are mixed views on the benefit of anonymised recruitment more generally. Outside of academia, it has been shown to improve gender mix in, for example, the Boston Symphony Orchestra, when auditions were held behind a screen. However, ascribing a woman's name to a name-blind CV in the Australian civil service increased the chance of the applicant making it to interview by 2.9%, contrary to the perception that bias might be shown in favour of male candidates.[34] In gathering data for the UUK review of fair admissions in 2019/20, only a small minority of Black, Asian or Minority Ethnic students who were asked thought that anonymisation would support impartiality, the majority did not, or had no opinion on the question. Anonymisation could support impartiality if it were combined with overt contextualisation (taking the candidates' historic educational disadvantage into account), otherwise it could have the opposite effect to that desired, since it is possible that there is already some unsolicited contextualisation happening on the basis of race or school. Some universities are encouraged to attract disadvantaged students.

The Commission on Race and Ethnic Disparities begins its section on Education and Training by stating that 'Education is the single most emphatic success story of the British ethnic minority experience' and goes on to show that while Black African children still perform less well at GCSE level than White British children, Chinese and Indian children achieve highest attainment up to and including A-levels.[35]

---

33  H. Connor, C. Tyers, T. Modood and J. Hillage, 'Why the Difference? A Closer Look at Higher Education Minority Ethnic Students and Graduates', Department for Education and Skills (DfES) research report 552, June 2004.
34  A. Makoff-Clark, 'Is Blind Recruitment the Secret to the Perfect Hire?', *People Management*, 24 January 2019.
35  Commission on Race and Ethnic Disparities, 'The Report', March 2021, <https://assets.publishing.service.gov.uk/government/uploads/system/uploads/attachment_data/file/974507/20210331_-_CRED_Report_-_FINAL_-_Web_Accessible.pdf>.

Research quoted by the commission demonstrates that differences in socio-economic background, such as the qualifications attained by a child's parents, can have a larger impact on educational attainment than ethnic group. Indeed, an Indian girl with professional parents who had a degree-level education and a high family income would have a substantial advantage over a Black Caribbean boy whose parents had manual jobs, no qualifications and low family income.[36] Data on entry to universities derived from pupils from state schools in England is reassuring in terms of access for ethnic minority groups. Chinese (71.7%) and Asian (53.1%), Black (47.5%) and mixed (39.0%) race groups are all more likely than White students (32.6%) to go to university.[37] Attracting students from diverse backgrounds will enhance the education and experience of all students at university and, in a survey carried out by the Schwartz review, was considered beneficial by 96% of respondents (one third of which were from higher education institutions) and compelling by the US Supreme Court, which recognised the 'educational benefits that flow from a diverse student body'.[38]

## Contextualisation

Nisbet and Shaw's fourth major pillar of fairness relates to context, and, as far as university admissions are concerned, to previous educational advantage. Complete impartiality on the basis of A-level (or equivalent) results is not fair to a student who carries a legacy of

---
36  S. Strand, 'Ethnic, Socio-economic and Sex Inequalities in Educational Achievement at Age 16', Report for the Commission on Race and Ethnic Disparities (CRED), 3 February 2021, <https://www.gov.uk/government/publications/the-report-of-the-commission-on-race-and-ethnic-disparities-supporting-research/ethnic-socio-economic-and-sex-inequalities-in-educational-achievement-at-age-16-by-professor-steve-strand>.
37  UCAS, 'Entry into Higher Education', 16 February 2021, <https://www.ethnicity-facts-figures.service.gov.uk/education-skills-and-training/higher-education/entry-rates-into-higher-education/latest>.
38  S. Schwartz, 'Fair Admissions to Higher Education: Recommendations for Good Practice', Admissions to Higher Education Review AHER3, DfES, 2004, <www.admissions-review.org.uk>.

educational disadvantage prior to sitting their A-levels. In this regard it is useful to consider issues of equality, deservedness and merit.

From an equality perspective, a compelling argument can be made to compensate individuals who have been historically disadvantaged, since the qualifications that they bring to the admissions process reflect their previous educational (and, more broadly, social) context, and not their future potential. Research has shown that a male student from a local education authority (LEA or state) school is 6.5% more likely to get a good degree (2:1 or First) than an equivalent-grade student from an independent school.[39] Indeed, the more expensive the independent-school tuition fees are (as a proxy for educational advantage at school), so the likelihood of a good degree declines for equivalent grade school qualification students – by about 1% for each £2000. The effect of social background on attainment begins at the age of two[40] and is easy to understand when it becomes apparent that a child from the most deprived cohort is likely to have heard 30 million words fewer than one from the most advantaged by the age of three.[41]

The question then arises how best to determine the level of disadvantage to the individual and therefore how much to compensate or adjust. There is no right answer to this, and, in an ideal world, each applicant would be considered as an individual, with a battery of metrics ranging from parental income, family circumstances, location of home and historical achievement of their school, among many others. Ideally a similar range of metrics would be embraced by all universities, such that there was equal compensation.

---

39 R. Naylor and J. Smith, 'Schooling Effects on Subsequent University Performance: Evidence for the UK University Population', Department of Economics, University of Warwick Economic Research Paper 657, 2002, p. 7.
40 Education and Skills Committee, *The Future of Higher Education*, 23 June 2003, HC 425-I; DfES, *Widening Participation in Higher Education* (London: HMSO, 2003).
41 'Child Development: In the Beginning was the Word – How Babbling to Babies can Boost their Brains', *The Economist*, 22 February 2014, <https://www.economist.com/science-and-technology/2014/02/20/in-the-beginning-was-the-word>.

This is well beyond the current admissions systems in subtlety and complexity; nevertheless, in Scotland, universities have embraced a robust and workable system, using the government's Scottish Index of Multiple Deprivation (SIMD). The SIMD is based on seven domains: income, health, employment, education, housing, crime and environment. In Scotland, universities use the lowest (SIMD 20) or two lowest (SIMD 20 and SIMD 40) quintiles of deprivation as priority cohorts for contextualisation. Each university sets a minimum entry requirement for each programme, which should allow successful recruits to complete their course. Applicants from SIMD 20 (or SIMD 20 and SIMD 40), who achieve the minimum entry requirement, are offered a place and accepted on to the course outside the general competitive entry process. Since each university sets the minimum entry requirements of each of their programmes, these differ between universities.[42] There has been some criticism of the system in Scotland, where some courses have apparently been entirely filled by students from less socio-economically advantaged backgrounds, but this could also be a feature of number caps imposed by the funding scheme in Scotland.[43] Despite the general embrace of contextualisation in Scotland, the numbers (or percentage) of those from state schools proceeding to university is lower, and has declined both in absolute terms and relative to England, where universal contextualisation has not been adopted. In Scotland, in 2002/03, the proportion of young entrants to full-time first-degree courses from state-schools was 87.5%. By 2020/21, this had dropped to 86.4%. In England on the other hand, the percentages rose from 86.4% in 2002/03 to 90.1% in 2020/21.[44] This apparent paradox probably had nothing to do with contextual

---

42 The author is most grateful to Aoife Keenan (Senior Policy Officer) and Sally Mapstone (Principal) from St Andrews University for explaining the Scottish system.
43 C. Stewart, 'Middle Class Pupils missing University Place will see Reform', *The Herald*, 13 January 2023, https://www.heraldscotland.com/opinion/23247308.middle-class-pupils-missing-university-place-will-see-reform/>.
44 Carasso and Plume, 'To Measure is to Know'.

applications and more to do with larger grants/loans being available to cover living expenses in England than Scotland (see Chapter 10). It is also interesting that the growth in state-school recruits to university in England happened during the time that higher tuition fees were introduced.

In England, the Index of Multiple Deprivation (IMD) ranks population areas of around 1500 inhabitants, with 1 being the most deprived, through to 32844, the least deprived. Areas can then be allocated to deciles or quintiles (e.g., lowest 10% or 20%) and this measure used to contextualise the admission.

The IMD is sufficiently granular to give a reasonable picture of likely deprivation. Other measures, such as whether the applicant received free school meals, or whether they were in care during their school education, are likely to be even more appropriate since they focus on the individual, but the data on these is not universally available, and is subject to data-protection legislation.

In the US, the state of California has a provision which means that any student meeting index-eligibility – placing in the top 9% of their high-school-graduating cohort, is automatically guaranteed a place in the University of California system.[45] This by its nature corrects for overall school deprivation but not within-school advantage.

In most US schools and universities and some UK universities, the traditional UK degree award (a First, 2:1 or 2:2 etc.) is replaced or supplemented by a grade point average (GPA), which gives an outcome based on assessment throughout the course, rewards steady achievement throughout, and offers a future employer a measure of effort and ability. At the point of entry to university it is also likely that the BTEC and IB systems, with some reflection on assignment and coursework, support the more consistent applicants. Graduates who

---

45 'Tips for Applying to the University of California System', *IvyWise*, <https://www.ivywise.com/ivywise-knowledgebase/resources/article/tips-for-applying-to-the-university-of-california-system/>.

gained admission to university with a BTEC have better employability outcomes than graduates who gained admissions with A-levels.[46]

Somewhere beyond equality and deservedness there is merit. Although deservedness and merit are often used interchangeably, deservedness can be distinguished by being rightfully earned, whereas merit may be associated with inherent good or worthiness. Whether assessed over a period of time or by summative examination, it is likely that candidates who are both diligent and have ability will score well and will be considered worthy or will merit admission. The idea of a meritocratic society, in which those who are worthy succeed, is rather more widely accepted now than when the term was first coined by Alan Fox in 1956, describing it as 'a society in which the gifted, the smart, the energetic, the ambitious and the ruthless are carefully sifted towards their desired positions of dominance'.[47] Indeed Nisbet and Shaw[48] devote considerable energy to debating the value of merit from the perspective of fairness in assessment, eventually rejecting it on the basis that it does not account for social context and that it is likely that the applicant's merit will be greatly influenced by the merit of their parents. For university admissions, however, merit potentially brings together many of the elements of fairness already discussed: it conforms to many principles of natural justice; it can be used to discriminate for competitive processes or to determine adequacy; it is fair (context excepted) by way of impartiality to the individual, the provider, the ultimate employer and to society. Used together with contextualisation (compensation) for previous educational disadvantage offering a form of restorative justice, merit emerges as the most appropriate measure for admission to university. It is also likely that a system of admission based on merit will select or recruit students

---

46  London Economics, 'The Outcomes Associated with the BTEC Route of Degree Level Acquisition: Report for Pearson', May 2013, <www.londoneconomics.co.uk>
47  A. Fox, 'Class and Equality', *Socialist Commentary*, May 1956, p. 13.
48  Nisbet and Shaw, *Is Assessment Fair?*

able to succeed in their course. The validity and reliability of the measure of merit can be tested by retrospective analysis of success rates (completion statistics, good degrees – Firsts or 2:1s, and employability and earnings data) at university.

## Admission of international students

Concern has been expressed about whether the admissions process for international students to the UK is fair and in particular whether admission is simply a backdoor to migration. It is suggested in the popular media that universities have been favouring applicants from overseas over UK applicants, since international recruits pay higher tuition fees.

There are several checks and balances in place to prevent unfair admission of international students. Firstly, international students require a CAS (Confirmation of Acceptance for Studies), which is necessary for gaining a student visa, and which holds information on the qualifications used to assess eligibility, confirmation that the course represents academic progress (for those who have already studied in the UK) and confirmation of English language ability, among many financial and other requirements. Academic equivalences are normally determined from UK NARIC[49] and the UK government website for international qualifications.[50]

English language proficiency is determined by success (minimum standards) in one of a number of recognised examination systems, the best known of which are IELTS (International English Language Testing System), TOEFL (Test of English as a Foreign Language) and CAE (Cambridge Advanced Certificate in English). There will be some differences in the requirements of different universities and for different courses, but minimum standards are required by the UK

---

49  www.naric.org.uk
50  https://www.gov.uk/government/publications/overseas-degree-equivalency-table-and-methodology

government to obtain a CAS. A further concern has been raised about the use of agents to attract international students, since the agents receive substantial payments for their services and could offer inducements or provide misleading information to international students, for instance relating to how much the students might be able to earn from part-time work in the UK while studying for their degree.

The vast majority of UK universities have signed up to the Agent Quality Framework to ensure that international (and home based) agents adhere to ethical standards and provide accurate data to prospective students. It is likely that the Agent Quality Framework will become mandatory for universities wishing to use agents.

The final area of concern regarding the fair admission of international students relates to the International Foundation or Year 1 courses offered by universities and their feeder colleges. It is suggested that international students access these courses with lower qualifications than UK recruits progressing directly onto undergraduate courses. This is of course true, and it is the precise intention of the Foundation or Year 1 course to bring the students' learning up to a standard equivalent to the undergraduate entry requirement. It is in essence no different from UK students undertaking a UK Foundation course, or for that matter additional A-Levels at a further education college, in order to gain access to university.

The suggestion that student visas might be a back door entry to the UK through the graduate-route visa by which international graduates can work in the UK for two years after graduation was contested by the Migration Advisory Committee, which found no abuse of the graduate-route visa and identified that international graduates were earning roughly the same as their UK equivalents after their graduate-route period. They concluded that the existing graduate-route visa, whereby international graduates may work for two years after graduation in the

UK, should be retained.⁵¹ In response to the concerns raised about International Foundation and Year 1 courses, UUK and the Russell Group commissioned the QAA to review these courses. Its report found that international programme providers were following their published entry requirements, and that entry requirements were broadly equivalent, that academic standards on international pathway courses are of expected standard in the vast majority of cases, but that the sector should consider improving consistency in the description of programmes to ensure that stakeholders understand their nature. The reports of the MAC and QAA into the admissions process and requirements for international students were greatly reassuring and give confidence in the recruitment processes.

## Admissions in practice

Having considered the basic elements of a fair admissions system, it is now worth considering how these could be embraced in a workable system for UK undergraduate applicants. I concluded the previous section by suggesting that the most appropriate measure of an individual for entry to university is merit and that merit can be judged on previous educational attainment, contextualised for previous educational disadvantage.

## Standardisation

There is a strong argument for standardised testing, with the complexion of the test designed to select individuals potentially suited for their course of choice (such as the BMAT for medical courses). This could be extended to common interviews or other additional requirements, such as a creative performance or portfolio. It does seem unnecessary to have a candidate applying to five different nursing schools then being subjected to five interviews – not to mention the cost and

---

51  Migration Advisory Committee (MAC), 'Rapid Review of the Graduate Route', May 2024, <https://assets.publishing.service.gov.uk/media/6641e1fbbd01f5ed32793992/MAC+Rapid+Review+of+Graduate+Route.pdf>.

effort required to undertake the task. The arguments for and against common systems of assessment and common interviews are similar: it would be fairer if everyone was subjected to the same entrance assessment process – at least for particular courses or groups of courses – and to the same interview or assessed performance.

More generalised standardisation, such as a general standard test for all university applicants, would potentially fail the validity test – could the test be equally valid at determining aptitude for chemistry and modern languages for example? While it could no doubt discriminate on some universally desirable attributes, such as critical thinking, it could fail on the required competency and aptitude in numeracy for a mathematics course, or the required creativity for an arts course.

Universities are also very diverse institutions and an interview for a veterinary place at Glasgow, which has a strength in cattle medicine and pathological research, might with good reason be different from an interview for the Royal Veterinary College in London, which has strength in small animal medicine and surgery and research in animal locomotion. The diversity of assessment process also prevents tunnel vision in teaching and learning, and since most candidates work towards their assessment – a variety of assessment methods allow, within the limits of validity and reliability, some 'experimentation' in teaching and assessment methods, without which progress would be inhibited. There is also a strong argument that the institutional interview process gives the candidate a chance to assess the institution and determine if it would fit with their character, values and expectations. The development of a relationship between candidate and institution should not be underestimated and is undoubtedly supported if the candidate visits and meets the faculty, a relationship enhanced by the interview. Historically there has been limited enthusiasm by government to radically change school or college assessment methods and given the fiercely autonomous institutional character of UK universities, it seems unlikely that standardised measures of merit will be created or accepted in the admissions process. That said, things may change: Rishi Sunak, when Prime Minister, suggested an overhaul of the A-level system at the 2023 Conservative Party conference. There is a compelling argument, and indeed individual, if not collective, willingness to consider some greater standardisation – for instance in determination of educational disadvantage and compensation thereof. This has been shown to work in Scotland and should be embraced in the rest of the UK and elsewhere.

## Post-qualification admissions

Having previously considered the advantages and disadvantages of the use of predicted grades in relation to fair process, and despite some strong arguments in support of predictions, I concluded that in terms of validity and reliability, and in the best interests of transparency and expectation, the use of actual results was more appropriate. From a practical perspective in the UK this presents a challenge. A-level (and other level 3) assessment results are made available to candidates and universities in the middle of August. For students to get their results, apply to a selection of universities (currently they can apply to five), perhaps undergo an interview or several interviews, receive an offer from these universities, decide which offer to accept, and complete the recruitment process, would make it virtually impossible to start at the beginning of October. Certainly, interviews could be done in advance of results, but this would mean interviewing many candidates who had no reasonable chance of success. It would be possible to change the school timetable or the university timetable, although neither sector seems enthusiastic to do this. It has been proposed that the university start date be moved to the January following the A-level (and other qualification) results day, but this would mean candidates spending about six months in limbo – a time too short to get useful employment or to have a worthwhile gap year experience, but much too long to recover from the 'trauma' of A-levels or other examinations. Indeed, it is just about the ideal time to allow eighteen-year-olds to engage with antisocial behaviours, or to sink into idle despair. It has been suggested that during a prolonged break between school and university young people might be 'offered' a sort of short-term national service, similar to the conscription embraced in Norway. It would be interesting to determine the popularity of such a proposal in the UK.

A more workable proposal was made by UUK, who reviewed fair access to universities and proposed that candidates make their applications in the current time cycle. From the January before the September/October start date, they would engage with their universities of choice and undertake any extra required processes – DBS (Disclosure and Barring Service) checks, financial-aid checks, portfolio submission, and even performance assessment and interview. When their assessment results are released, universities make an offer if the candidate is deemed suitable, and the candidate then decides from the offers which they have received which university to accept. There would also be a Clearing system, much as now, to pick up candidates whose results fall below expectations and who do not receive an offer from any of their chosen universities, or for those who achieve at or above the grades expected and necessary but change their mind later in the cycle. This process has been modelled by UCAS and would allow time for all processes to be complete by the current September/October start dates of most universities.

However, there are challenges with this approach; critically, any shift in cycle would require a shift in parallel support and advice processes so that candidates were appropriately equipped in their decision making, either by school/college or national advisers. In the current 'predicted results' system, most students (more than 70%) get their first-choice university and there is no reason to anticipate that this would reduce opportunity if offers were made later in the cycle, based on achieved results. Furthermore, for those students who fail to gain any of their applied places and seek to be placed in the Clearing process, they would be in no worse position.

From a standpoint of fairness and considering practicality, a post-qualification offer system is the compelling option. The idea of offers being made on actual rather than predicted grades is not new – it was recommended for development by Schwartz and his colleagues when they reviewed fair admissions in 2004.[52] That it has not happened is down to self-interest and inflexibility on the part of the actors involved and lack of commitment or courage by successive Education Secretaries.

The second radical reform required to enhance fairness in the admissions process to universities is a more reliable and uniformly applied system of contextualisation, which adjusts for previous educational disadvantage. Using the data available on success at university, appropriate adjustments can be made to reset the likely success of applicants according to both their assessment outcomes and educational disadvantage. Support for contextualisation is not universal; doubters, perhaps those who have invested heavily in their children's education to create advantage, or vocal political detractors, who considered such adjustment 'abhorrent discrimination',[53] should be reassured that it could be moderated to limit the number of students that would benefit and therefore the number of advantaged students who might be displaced. Indeed, in England, where there are no number caps, the admissions could simply grow to absorb these students. The great majority of those with advantaged educational backgrounds will continue to happily carry that advantage into university, should they wish to do so.

The Scottish system described earlier is sufficiently pragmatic, yet

---

52  Schwartz, 'Fair Admissions to Higher Education'.
53  Iain Mansfield quoted in, 'Contextual admissions "as abhorrent as racism" – ex-DfE adviser', *Times Higher Education*, 3 October 2022, <https://www.timeshighereducation.com/news/contextual-admissions-abhorrent-racism-ex-dfe-adviser#:_:text=In%20an%20apparent%20reference%20to,as%20abhorrent%20as%20discrimination%20on>.

sufficiently flexible to give confidence that institutional autonomy is not compromised and candidates who are likely to succeed in their courses are selected, although the capped numbers in Scotland make the Robbins principle of availability to all qualified by ability and attainment who wish to attend more difficult to achieve.[54] The Scottish higher education sector is now ahead of its 2030 targets, with 16.7% of full-time first-degree entrants from the Scottish Index of Multiple Deprivation (SIMD 20) lowest quintile background.[55] A system of contextualisation utilising the IMD should be adopted in England and should embrace at least the lowest two deciles of disadvantaged applicants, and each independent higher education provider should be able to select its own minimum-entry grades, at which applicants in the lower IMD deciles would be recruited (other criteria such as successful interview/portfolio excepted). Alternatively, a pre-calculated and universally agreed tariff uplift could be applied to those applicants in the lower deciles – this could be graded across a number of the lower deciles. If the supplementary tariff takes the applicants above the institute's published minimum tariff, those applicants should be offered a place.

The University of Bristol has been a pioneer of this sort of approach and has shown that students accepted from disadvantaged backgrounds with lower tariffs do almost exactly as well as the general intake with regard to good degree outcomes. Sensible contextualisation is likely to enhance widening access to universities and is important since a higher education provides the most effective way of navigating the social, cultural and economic barriers in societies. Oxbridge are often unfairly criticised for their intake, but as two of the most prestigious universities in the UK and globally, it is right that they attract the brightest students. Using the current assessment systems, the brightest students apparently come from independent

---

54  *Robbins Report.*
55  UUK, *Our Universities: Generating Growth and Opportunity* (London, 2022).

schools – furnishing 38% and 31% respectively of students for Oxford and Cambridge, from a general proportion of only 7% of the population. Only with a fair system of contextualisation is this likely to change, and only if 'potential' can be measured effectively enough to give confidence in the process.

## Unconditional offers

The post-qualification offers system proposed earlier would remove any concerns regarding the use of unconditional offers, since offers would only be made on the basis of actual assessment results and could only be made when the results became available. Unconditional offers are a normal part of the admissions cycle for those who have already received their results prior to the cycle underway, for instance mature students, or those having taken a gap year. There are also institutions, such as the Open University and the University of London, whose distance learning programmes do not carry a minimum entry requirement, and for whom it would be appropriate to continue to make offers outside the annual results day cycle. If a post-qualification offers (or admissions) system is not adopted, then there is a strong argument that so-called 'conditional unconditional offers' should not be made. These are unconditional offers made to candidates on the basis of predicted results, *but* dependent on the candidate making the offering institution their destination of first choice. The argument put forward for conditional unconditional offers is that they give the candidate security and the certainty of a place, thereby reducing anxiety and allowing a more robust relationship to develop between applicant and institution prior to joining. There is a more compelling rationale for the offering institution – that it provides a competitive advantage over other universities who do not make their offers conditional. This forced their use by many institutions who were philosophically opposed to them, but who recognised that it would be competitive suicide not to do so. The percentage of conditional unconditional offers made to applicants increased from 1.1% in 2013 to 34.4% made in 2018. The arguments against conditional unconditional offers are that they are made too early in the cycle, reducing the time the applicant has to consider their options, and that they restrict applicants' opportunities to change their mind at a time when many options lie open to them, and as their own ideas about a future career mature. However, they allow candidates to take their 'foot off the gas' as they approach critical assessments such as A-levels. This not only weakens the underpinning platform of learning which they will carry into their university programme but may also deflate their assessment results – and since many future employers use both degree level and A-level (or equivalent) results in their recruitment process, this would be to the applicant's long-term disadvantage. In a pre-qualification admissions system, there is still a place for unconditional offers, for instance when the offer is dependent upon a portfolio, performance or interview, but these should not be conditional on the applicant making the institution their preferred option, which could be interpreted as naked coercion.

The OfS banned the use of conditional unconditional offers during the pandemic[56], and in response to the recommendations of the UUK Fair Admissions Review[57], UUK has produced a Fair Admissions Code of Practice, which puts into practice the recommendations relating to conditional unconditional offers, and to which the majority of UK universities have committed[58], meaning their use has largely stopped.

## Complexity of diversity

Universities are diverse, and for some their recruits are equally diverse in ethnicity, nationality, age and mode of study (such as part-time

---

56  OfS, 'Regulator Bans Controversial "Conditional Unconditional" Offers during Pandemic', 3 July 2020, <https://www.officeforstudents.org.uk/news-blog-and-events/press-and-media/regulator-bans-controversial-conditional-unconditional-offers-during-pandemic/>.
57  UUK, *Fair Admissions Review June 2019 – November 2020* (London, 2020).
58  UUK/GuildHE, *Fair Admissions Code of Practice* (London, 2022).

or apprenticeships) and even time of entry (with January and other entry dates being variously used). Many of the principles of admission already described apply, no matter the nature of the recruit. However, for some cohorts, for instance mature students who have gained substantial work experience, processes such as the Accreditation of Prior Experiential Learning (APEL) can greatly enhance the admissions process and should be more broadly embraced. For international students, the UK has remained remarkably attractive despite historic negativity in the visa system (whereby post-study work visas were not automatic but depended on job offers), and much less reliance on a centralised admissions process. Given UK university success in the international market, supported by the marketing and recruitment processes developed by individual universities, it would seem unnecessary to radically reform the system currently in place. The enthusiasm of UCAS to engage in the international process no doubt represents an opportunity for expansion of its own market, but also it appears to be creating a solution which is looking for a problem.

## More means better

The economic argument for increasing the number of people going to university is made very persuasively by David Willetts.[59] He demonstrates that individuals attract higher lifetime earnings – even accounting for the cost of tuition fees and the opportunity costs of going to university for at least three years, when the alternative might reap the reward of work and earnings. The contribution to the economy is boosted by higher tax contributions throughout the working life of a graduate, which exceed the individual benefit they receive and there is a boost to national productivity associated with increased graduate numbers. Graduates also cost the state less by being healthier (probably by doing more exercise) and being less likely to engage in crime. He argues that the benefits to individual and state have not

---

59 Willetts, *A University Education*.

diminished with increasing numbers, since there has been growth in the number of jobs suited to those with graduate education which has, if anything, exceeded the growth in graduate numbers. While the arguments made by Willetts are compelling in terms of absolute numbers and need, there is a lurking suspicion among some that more means worse. Kingsley Amis bluntly asserted that by taking a larger cohort there must be people recruited with lower ability and intelligence.[60] This of course depends on the cohort selected in 1960 being those of greatest ability and intelligence, and fails to factor in the likely influence of previous educational advantage.

Even *if* the 4% of school-leavers going to university in 1960 were those with the highest Intelligence Quotients (IQs), there is an argument for substantial growth associated with improvements in IQ. James Flynn demonstrated improvements in IQ of about 3 IQ points per decade in populations tested.[61] These improvements are probably associated with greater sensory stimulus from the great expansion in human communication and interaction. IQ tests are adjusted to normal distributions within a population around a median of 100, so at any particular time the proportion of the population scoring say 130 remains reasonably constant. Nevertheless, in an absolute sense the Flynn effect will have resulted in an 18-point improvement in IQ since 1960, and this alone will have brought at least a further 15% of the population of school-leavers into the IQ catchment which would have captured the 4% 'brightest and best' in Amis's time. Furthermore, the IQ of an individual is not static and is likely to change over time. Positive changes are mostly associated with stimulation, and it is likely that the learning environment of a university would have a positive impact, but whether this is related to increased basic

---

60  K. Amis, 'Lone Voices', *Encounter*, July 1960, pp. 6–11.
61  J.R. Flynn, 'The Mean IQ of Americans: Massive Gains 1932 to 1978', *Psychological Bulletin*, 95/1 (1984), pp. 29–51, <https://doi.org/10.1037/0033-2909.95.1.29>; J.R. Flynn, 'Massive IQ Gains in 14 Nations: What IQ Tests really Measure', *Psychological Bulletin*, 101/2 (1987), pp. 171–91, <https://doi.org/10.1037/0033-2909.101.2.171>.

intelligence, or because some individuals are better able to use the intelligence they are born with, is not clear. None of the discussion above is meant to suggest that selection for university on the basis of IQ scores would be a good idea, rather it is used to challenge the perception that more means worse. Indeed, since 37.3% of eighteen-year-olds entered higher education in 2002, about half of the total increase in numbers since 1960 could be attributed to improved IQ alone at that time.

It is unlikely that a university admissions system could ever be created which would appear fair to all applicants, universities, future employers and society. The system we have in the UK is by many measures good, but from the perspective of reliability, legitimate expectation and restorative justice, it could be improved. A post-qualification offers system, with more uniform contextualised adjustments for previous educational disadvantage, would be fairer, more transparent and more just – we owe it to future generations to embrace such a system and to make it work. It is the unambiguous conclusion of this chapter that schools, universities, the Department for Education and the Secretary of State for Education should adopt these recommendations without delay.

# CHAPTER 4
## Illuminating Minds: Education

The fundamental reason for universities to exist is to educate. The way that they do so has been both remarkably conservative and extraordinarily innovative. Delivery of the didactic lecture has been the backbone of higher education for at least two millennia, yet curricular design and technological innovation have, in more recent times, added diversity and complexity to university programmes. Courses may now offer flexibility of place, pace and mode of delivery, and in the near future are likely to be substantially personalised by the embrace of artificial intelligence.

Much of what and how higher education has been delivered reflects the evolution of knowledge and learning itself. The purpose of universities for most of history was to create or support those destined for high office, usually office of state or religion. Yet even in ancient times the wonder of the universe captured the imagination of educators, who explored astronomy and mathematics together with logic and law. Literacy, numeracy, and broader education remained the confine of the privileged. With the emergence of the European university in medieval times, medicine and the humanities expanded. It is likely though that the methods of teaching and learning did not change much, and students would have been expected to learn by assimilation from the wisdom of the teacher presenting on the stage, much as Aristotle no doubt presented in the Lyceum. Discussion, debate and interrogation would have enlivened and enriched the learning experience and progressed the subject, but until the nineteenth century even in the vocational subjects like medicine, practicals would have been largely observational.

## Curriculum

The term curriculum has been used since the sixteenth century to describe the plan of study and learning experience. At that time, the curriculum would have described subjects including arithmetic, geometry, astronomy, grammar, rhetoric and logic, which would have been recognised by Aristotle. The emergence of the professions and expansion of knowledge through discovery meant a requirement for more structured curricula – still largely subject-based, in order that the graduate could claim sufficient competence in their chosen discipline.

In 1949, Ralph Tyler proposed a more ordered approach to curriculum design, based on the general purpose of the curriculum and considering what experiences might meet that purpose.[1] His proposals considered effective organisation of the curriculum and how to determine the outcomes of the learning experiences. The general overall structure of contemporary curricula differs between North American universities and those in Europe and elsewhere. The US model is built on a liberal arts foundation, normally taught over two years, the purpose of which is as much to teach the student how to learn and how to think critically as it is to assimilate content. This intellectual training may use historically proven texts which encourage inquiry and insight into human purpose and improvement.[2] The

---

1  R.W. Tyler, *Basic Principles of Curriculum and Instruction* (Chicago, 1949).
2  Education Encyclopaedia, 'Higher Education Curriculum – Traditional and Contemporary Perspectives', <https://education.stateuniversity.com/pages/1895/Curriculum-Higher-Education-TRADITIONAL-CONTEMPORARY-PERSPECTIVES.html>.

idea of knowledge for its own sake is not new and formed the basis of the educational philosophy of Cardinal Newman (an English theologian and scholar who was instrumental in the founding of what became University College Dublin). The US system provides for more specific disciplinary and professional instruction by way of a subsequent 'major'. These have become more segmented and specialised as subject matter has expanded and become more detailed.

The European model progresses more directly towards subject specificity, although earlier years often offer broader choice or range of subject matter. Most member-countries of the European Higher Education Area[3] have agreed to the Bologna accord,[4] which was designed to ensure comparability of higher education qualifications, whilst not dictating any specific curriculum at course level. The Bologna accord recognises three cycles of higher education qualification within its framework, and roughly quantifies the learning required in each using the European Credit Transfer and Accumulation System (ECTS) whereby an academic year normally equates to 60 ECTS or 1500–1800 hours of study.[5] The cycles comprise a bachelor's degree (180–240 ECTS credits) normally taking at least three to four years, a master's degree (60–120 ECTS credits) taking up to two years and a doctoral degree (normally 120–420 ECTS credits) which may take up to four years and is normally undertaken under close supervision of a competent mentor.

In many disciplines the expansion of knowledge has resulted in greater specialisation and subdivision of subject. Curricular design has of necessity involved a reductionist approach towards more

---

3  *European Education Area*, official website of the European Union, <https://education.ec.europa.eu>.
4  M.C. Van Der Wende, 'The Bologna Declaration: Enhancing Transparency and Competitiveness of European Higher Education', *Higher Education in Europe*, 25/3 (2010), pp. 305–10, <https://doi.org/10.1080/713669277>.
5  Directorate-General for Education, Youth, Sport and Culture (European Commission), *ECTS Users' Guide 2015*, <https://data.europa.eu/doi/10.2766/87192>.

manageable 'packages'. For many areas, longer programmes (the five/six-year medical programme or four-year integrated master's engineering programme) became essential and now the basic requirement for employment in some jobs is the master's or doctorate degree rather than the bachelor's degree.

The twentieth century saw a dramatic increase in the study of learning and teaching itself and, as a consequence, the evolution of the curriculum.[6] This progressed beyond subject-related curriculum development to learner-focused curricula and methodological-based curricula. A greater understanding and appreciation of the way people learn has also allowed curricula to adapt in more learner-focused ways. The five-year medical and veterinary courses historically taught basic subjects such as chemistry and anatomy in the first year, physiology and biochemistry in the second year, pathology, bacteriology and virology in the third year and so on, through to the clinical subjects in the fourth and final year. This rather left the student with a distant recollection of anatomy when they started surgery and long-forgotten acid-base concepts when kidney function became important. Spiral curricula, which revisit and build on basic and more advanced concepts in each succeeding part of the course, provide the reflective opportunities for deeper learning and understanding, integrate the different material more effectively and give the student a greater appreciation of the importance of basic concepts.

Problem-based learning was introduced in McMaster University in Hamilton, Canada as an active learning, student-centred approach to medical education.[7] In problem-based curricula the student learns by working around and trying to solve complex, real-life problems. Like the spiral curriculum, this brought relevance to the learning in

---

6   R. Murray (ed.), *The Scholarship of Teaching and Learning in Higher Education* (Maidenhead, 2008).

7   H.S. Barrows, 'Problem-based Learning in Medicine and Beyond: A Brief Overview', *New Directions for Teaching and Learning*, 68 (1996), pp. 3–12, <https://doi.org/10.1002/tl.37219966804>.

the earlier years of the medical course. It encourages the acquisition of knowledge in a collaborative environment, within which students also develop the skills and attributes essential to the medical practitioner. Problem-based learning has since been used to enhance teaching in many different subject and discipline areas beyond medicine and is often used in a scaffolded programme, where it complements delivery of material which may be more effectively delivered by other means, and which forms a 'scaffold' of learning, supporting and enhancing the approach to problem-solving.

Principles of good curriculum design have been crystalised by the thematic Peer Group report of the European University Association.[8] Just as Tyler began by considering the purpose of the curriculum[9], the Peer Group begin by proposing that the attributes required of the graduate are defined from the purpose of the course. At an institutional level, attributes can be defined in a way which characterises the university, although differentiating from other institutions with similar strategic goals may prove challenging, and developing a curriculum which enhances a chosen attribute may also require imagination. At programme level, attributes appropriate to a particular profession may be defined and are more easily embraced in the curriculum. Curricula should balance subject-specific competencies with what the Peer Group call 'transversal' skills, including communication and professional skills, and those skills reflected in societal values such as ethical and cultural attributes. They point out that while many universities include critical thinking as a transversal skill, few define how it is taught or assessed. Coherence of the curriculum is considered essential and may be achieved by ensuring that all elements of the curriculum link back to intended learning outcomes and perhaps the learning required to deliver the graduate

---

8  O. Vattori, 'Curriculum Design', Learning and Teaching Paper 8, Thematic Peer Group Report, European University Association, 2020, <www.eua.eu.info>.
9  Tyler, *Basic Principles*.

attributes. Spiral curricula and problem-based courses embrace this desired coherence.

It is also important to consider outcomes that go beyond those explicitly defined in the curriculum. For instance, cultural inclusion may be enhanced implicitly by the internationalisation of the university. Teachers should utilise a variety of didactic approaches, where these might be appropriate to the material being taught and the different learning styles of students. Many universities utilise external stakeholders, such as employers, to inform the curriculum design, and for some delivery, for instance degree apprenticeships, this is a requirement and may be particularly rewarding for professional and vocational courses. It may be possible to enhance student-centred learning by engaging with the students themselves in the creation of the curriculum. This has the additional benefits that students then have 'ownership' and responsibility for the curriculum. Given the turnover of student cohorts, it may be necessary to hold end of semester/year discussions or round tables to create effective dialogue with the student body. Student-centred learning encourages a focus on the students' abilities and learning styles and supports the teacher to facilitate learning rather than simply deliver material. The Peer Group consider there to be a great advantage in communication among teachers on a programme, not only by supporting and adapting good teaching practice, but also by sharing research outcomes which enhance, renew and invigorate the curriculum content. Finally, they encourage continual reflection to augment the curriculum design and content.

## Technology

The development of curricula in higher education has been driven by content and the way the material is organised and delivered, and informed by a desire to enhance the learning experience of the student. It has also been greatly influenced by technological evolution: radio, television, computers and the telephone have all played a part in educational design. Distance delivery is not new; the University of London has been offering degrees by distance learning since 1858. Nevertheless, distance delivery was really only able to offer engagement with faculty (albeit that it was on receive mode only) when the Open University began to offer degrees in 1969. Now computers and phones offer a facility for synchronous interaction and asynchronous delivery, and can be used to deliver whole degree programmes fully online. It is also now possible to cater for the different preferences, behaviours and abilities of individual learners, as well as the different capabilities of the teacher and characteristics of the learning material, by blending face-to-face and digital material toward optimal delivery for the greatest number of students.

## Blended learning

'Blended learning' is now broadly accepted to apply to technology-enhanced learning (which usually means digitally enhanced in practice). There are many examples which demonstrate that specific technology-enhanced interventions can improve student engagement and success. However, taken overall, there is little, if any, data to suggest that blended-learning approaches significantly improve outcomes compared to face-to-face learning.[10] Nevertheless, a blended approach can be utilised to more effectively cater for different learning preferences and, used wisely, can deliver in ways best suited to the subject or discipline being taught, and can play to the strengths of the teacher. In 1987, Chickering and Gamson identified seven principles of good pedagogy which have been widely used in

---

10   M.J. Jacobson, 'Educational Complex Systems and Open, Flexible, and Distance Learning: A Complexity Theoretical Perspective', *Distance Education*, 40/3 (2019) pp. 419–24, <https://doi.org/10.1080/01587919.2019.1656152>; G. Veletsianos, 'Best Evidence on Supporting Students to Learn Remotely', 2020, <https://educationendowmentfoundation.org.uk/guidance-for-teachers/covid-19-resources/best-evidence-on-supporting-students-to-learn-remotely>; M. Loon, 'Flexible Learning: A Literature Review 2016–2021', 1 March 2021, <advance-he.ac.uk/news-and-views/flexible-learning-literature-review-2016-2021>.

educational development and curriculum design.¹¹ According to them, good pedagogy 1) encourages contact between students and faculty, 2) develops reciprocity and cooperation among students, 3) uses active-learning techniques, 4) gives prompt feedback, 5) emphasises time on task (students learning to use their study-time well), 6) communicates high expectations and 7) respects diverse talents and ways of learning. These principles have not changed fundamentally even as a greater range and depth of technological modes of delivery have come on stream. Indeed, technology has been demonstrated to enhance the implementation of the seven principles in supportive ways.¹² Since the blend of learning comprises both technology-enhanced delivery and face-to-face interaction, it is unlikely that a well-constructed blended approach will offer substantial cost efficiencies when compared to a conventional programme. Indeed, as material is being devised and prepared, it may be more expensive. Nevertheless, the utilisation of film or recordings to deliver some material may free up time to strengthen smaller group interactions and thus greater engagement. It is also axiomatic that today's students will use many of the technologies used in a blended approach to teaching when they enter the workplace, and having exposure to them is going to enhance their employability and is likely to make them more productive. It is also likely that, as technologies improve, they will be utilised in a blended approach ever more effectively, with adaptive technology allowing greater personalisation of the education experience. Artificial intelligence will enhance assessment and support adaptive teaching, data analytics will improve student support, and haptics (sensory experience) technology will create more realistic simulated activities.

---

11  Chickering and Gamson, 'Seven Principles'.
12  A.W. Chickering and S. Ehrmann, 'Implementing the Seven Principles: Technology as Lever', *AAHE Bulletin*, 49 (1996), pp. 3-6, <https://sphweb.bumc.bu.edu/otlt/teachingLibrary/Technology/seven_principles.pdf>.

In October 2022, the OfS commissioned a review of blended learning on the back of which it based its code of practice and related conditions of compliance.[13] The review used Sir Michael Barber's definition of blended learning as 'teaching and learning that combines in-person delivery and delivery in a digital environment'[14] as its starting point but noted that 'thoughtful integration'[15] and achieving greatest educational ambitions[16] had also been proposed in variations of the definition. Using experiences from six higher education institutions of different size and shape, the review began by emphasising that face-to-face and digital did not equate to on campus and at home, indeed that students did not compartmentalise learning in that way; rather, they used technology to access learning on campus, and this could lead to a greater requirement for appropriate spaces. For instance, library or social learning spaces which were sufficiently individualised and sound-proofed to allow engagement with synchronous or hybrid delivery and to watch recorded lectures. In surveys a substantial majority of students claim to value the campus experience (63% of students are satisfied with their timetabled contact hours and 70% are satisfied with the learning spaces on campus)[17], and the post-Covid 'bounce', whereby our campuses became busier and more vibrant than

---

13  S. Orr, M. Highton, N. Lieven, D.S.P. Thomas and M. Lawson, 'Blended Learning Review Report of the OfS-appointed Blended Learning Review Panel', OfS, October 2022.
14  M. Barber, L. Bird, J. Flemming, E. Titterington-Giles, E. Edwards and C. Leyland, 'Gravity Assist: Propelling Higher Education towards a Brighter Future', Report of the Digital Teaching and Learning Review, OfS, 1 March 2021, <https://www.officeforstudents.org.uk/digitalreview/>.
15  D.R. Garrison and H. Kanuka, 'Blended Learning: Uncovering Its Transformative Potential in Higher Education', *The Internet and Higher Education*, 7/2 (2004), pp. 95–105, <https://www.researchgate.net/publication/222863721_Blended_Learning_Uncovering_Its_Transformative_Potential_in_Higher_Education>.
16  D. Laurillard, 'Thinking about Blended Learning. A Paper for the Thinkers in Residence Programme', in G. Van der Perre and J.V. Campenhout (eds), *Higher Education for the Digital Era; A Thinking Exercise in Flanders* (Brussels, 2015), p. 10, <https://discovery.ucl.ac.uk/id/eprint/1549749>.
17  J. Neves and A. Brown, 'Student Academic Experience Survey 2022', Advance HE and HEPI, <https://www.hepi.ac.uk/wp-content/uploads/2022/06/2022-Student-Academic-Experience-Survey.pdf>.

ever, suggests that students are voting with their feet. Yet Orr and colleagues found that, while students said that face-to-face lectures helped motivate them and that they valued the social contact and peer-and-teacher interaction of the lecture, the authors also found low attendance at learning events on campus.[18] They referred to this as the attendance paradox. It may be that students are coming on to campus for the 'experience' but accessing their learning through digital technology from the library or elsewhere, rather than face-to-face in the lecture or seminar room.

The OfS review group were struck that universities often failed to communicate adequately with their students about the reasons and rationale for the blended approach or about the resources available to them, such as laptop loans, bursaries for equipment purchase and e-book reading lists. Students may ask for digital access to a face-to-face lecture in real-time, but this hybrid approach was not then rated highly by them and indeed it might be seen as offering the least good educational option, although the review points out that as equipment and technologies improve, hybrid delivery might also be enhanced. Where online lectures are offered as part of the blended approach they offer the advantages of flexible opportunity for access and revision, they can utilise expert contributors from overseas and from industry and they can be 'chunked' into more manageable learning quanta with breaks appropriate to periods of effective concentration.[19] Material being delivered should be regularly reviewed and updated, and where it may have not changed over the course of a year, previous lectures may be re-used, but they should be future-proofed without reference to potentially confusing out-of-date assessment deadlines for example. The group recognised the importance

---

18  Orr et al., 'Blended Learning Review Report'.
19  Joint Information Systems Committee (JISC), 'Student Digital Experiences Insights Survey: Higher Education Findings', 2021, <Jisc.ac.uk/reports/student-digital-experience-insights-survey-2021-22-higher-education-findings>.

of skills needed by academics to create high-quality digital resources and recommended that they should be supported to 'edit, caption, create podcasts, online quizzes and use creative digital tools'. They also recognised that students needed support to effectively use online material. Only 41% of students received guidance on digital skills and it was recommended that blended-learning support should be built into course induction.[20]

## Flexible learning

Technology has also supported greater flexibility in university education. Through the medium of television, the Open University championed flexibility in learning, and more recently MOOCs have made educational material available at a grand scale. Both offer limited delivery of some of Chickering and Gamson's principles, for instance contact with faculty, reciprocity and feedback, and MOOCs suffer from a lack of financial return, since in their original incarnation they were offered free, despite the cost of production. Nevertheless, technologies now offer a variety of modes of delivery and permit flexibility of place, pace and time of learning. The place of study may be at home or at university, in residences, libraries, learning resource centres, social learning spaces or in corridors or on the grass. Wi-Fi is used on many bus and train services and has become an essential requirement for students who work and socialise while in transit. The pace of delivery is also now flexible: law degrees can be completed in two or three years, and part-time students and apprenticeship learners are supported to complete their degrees in a wide variety of timelines in many universities. The pace of learning will also be impacted by artificial intelligence systems, permitting adaptive processes whereby the rate of learning can be accelerated or decelerated depending upon the capacity and success of the individual student. The mode of teaching will also become more flexible with face-to-face, distance and

---

20   Ibid.

blended learning, and with the use of technology enhancements, film, audio recordings, simulations, practical labs and work experience.

The opportunity for flexibility of work location does challenge the value of the university campus, and although the campus will still be important for practical, laboratory and some simulated experience, and for work-based placements, the workspace is less important as the place of learning for digital material. It is likely that the social, cultural, sporting and counselling framework of a university campus will retain its value and attraction. Surveys of students during the Covid pandemic, when all teaching had moved online, suggested that 92% still valued a face-to-face experience, which substantially reduces the flexibility of place, pace and time. Where universities have tried to offer greater flexibility in the past through, for instance, modularisation, it has quickly become apparent that there are resource limits to the extent that flexibility can be delivered. For example, when students are offered free choice of which modules and when to study them, popular topics and time quickly become overwhelmed and less popular options unviable. Within the constraints of Chickering and Gamson's principles this will also be true, utilising current and likely future technology, for instance, encouraging contact between student and faculty. Nevertheless, for the commuting student, or those constrained by part-time work, caring responsibilities or indeed for those studying from the workplace, and for those who simply enjoy its convenience, flexibility in learning is a win-win outcome.

Online delivery provides the backbone of much flexible learning, and while flexibility of place can be accorded by both synchronous and asynchronous (accessed at the time of delivery or available to access anytime) online delivery, a more flexible approach to time can best be achieved using asynchronous delivery material. Adaptive technologies will undoubtedly enhance our approach to pace, allowing and encouraging students to progress at a pace best suited to their own ability. Hybrid delivery will also enhance the flexibility of place, where synchronous delivery is important. Flexibility is constrained for those subjects which demand a substantial content of practical and laboratory instruction. These are often also under constraints from professional bodies, which may stall progress in the name of perceived quality, if the benefits of alternative learning through, for instance simulation, are not made sufficiently clear. For example, in medical education, where human (cadaver) dissection may be perceived to be better than simulated anatomy instruction.

Technological evolution has been fundamental to the revolution which has occurred in higher education. Laptops and Wi-Fi emerged as the exception, quickly became common then pervasive, then an expectation and now offer the benchmark below which we recognise digital poverty. The evolution of Virtual Learning Environments (VLEs) also brought together many structural and operational facilities in a digital format and could act as a repository for teaching materials and provide platforms for engagement and delivery. Universities developed their own VLEs during the early 1990s and this provided an excellent starting point to develop and utilise digital technologies. They were used for online discussion groups and to deliver and engage in tutorials, and acted as a signpost to, and facility for, student support, both academic and pastoral. They provided access to electronic resources for student education and acted as an archive for recorded lectures which were produced and deposited as podcasts.[21] The cost and time required to maintain and upgrade a unique institutional VLE however were untenable. Furthermore, the commercially available alternatives were improving faster, becoming relatively more affordable and acquiring greater connectivity with other existing and essential academic and business platforms and systems. Most universities have moved their VLEs onto commercial platforms, which form the anchor for their digital learning pedagogy.

---

21   JISC, 'Effective Practice in a Digital Age', 2009, <https://www.Jisc.ac.uk/practice>.

In the early 2000s, the Higher Education Funding Council of the UK funded a competition within the higher education sector, to develop Centres for Excellence in Teaching and Learning (CETL), one of which was won by the University of Hertfordshire.

## Establishing a Blended Learning Unit (BLU)

In order to kick-start the blended approach to learning, the University of Hertfordshire utilised capital funding, which had been made available, to extend its wireless network to 300 teaching rooms, many of which were upgraded with interactive whiteboards and audio-visual connectivity. All academic staff were provided with laptop computers, thus enhancing their digital resource, as well as incentivising them to invest in the digital elements of a blended approach to teaching. Many utilised their laptops to facilitate electronic voting for formative assessment, and podcasting either as a supplementary teaching resource or for revision and reflection on face-to-face activity. During the four years of support for the CETL, 25 academic staff received substantive secondments within the unit and became BLU teachers. They were subsequently expected to lead on the evolution of the blended approach to learning but were also expected to disseminate their outcomes and champion the methodology.

A Curriculum Design Toolkit was produced as an important resource for academics wishing to adapt and develop the curricula for their subject in a more blended way. Dissemination was also enhanced by an internal workshop series open to all academics and access to relevant external seminars through virtual classroom technology. Within the overall programme, groups undertook more specific projects, including researching the learner experience, developing multimedia, determining best practice in assessment and utilising audio support for learning. Special interest groups were established to progress podcasting for pedagogy, evaluation of the learner experience, engagement of students through in-class technology, and enhancing and assuring quality. Each year an internal conference was held to assimilate and disseminate the learning across the institution.

The project was evaluated using Higher Education Academy (HEA, a precursor to Advance HE) benchmarking methods. This demonstrated that 82% of all academic staff had benefitted in one way or another from the project, and of those actively participating 91% expressed an improvement in their learning technologies, teaching styles and educational culture. Furthermore, 85% of all staff indicated that they were more confident to utilise the technologies associated with a blended approach to learning. During the evaluation of the BLU there was a substantial increase in the use of the university's VLE, StudyNet, with logins rising from 4.8m (2004/05) to 9.3m (2008/09). While this could represent the evolution of student digital engagement independent of a blended-learning approach, it is highly likely that much of the traffic was encouraged by the changed methods of teaching. The BLU also developed an online journal dedicated to the subject, called *Blended Learning in Practice*. This acted as a repository for the research outcomes of the project and received external submissions of relevant material, thus enhancing communication. External communication was no doubt supported through the *Blended Learning in Practice* journal articles, which are included in the 332 peer-reviewed outputs relating to the work of the BLU. It was also enhanced through an annual International Blended Learning Conference, which hosted leading international figures to deliver keynote papers on the topic, and which attracted delegates in person and virtually from around the world. Sustainability was ensured by the cultural change associated with colleagues who became disciples of the approach, and whose behaviours and success encouraged others.

It is perhaps surprising that blended-learning approaches have not been more widely adopted across the higher education sector, or that academics are not embracing the available technology to its greatest potential. This is likely a feature of individual intransigence or insecurity. In a sector-wide survey in the early period of Covid restrictions, only 21% of teachers were very confident that they had the skills to design and deliver digital teaching and learning.[22] There are also obstacles associated with the many professional body accreditations, whereby the accrediting bodies often demand specific in-contact or in-person teaching, where the flexibility to utilise technology-enhanced learning is limited. It would seem obvious that a blended approach to learning is best adopted when the technologies and face-to-face are complementary or indeed synergistic. Well-structured blended courses are likely to create this added value, however if they do not, there is little advantage over only digital or face-to-face teaching.

## 2020 paradigm shift

Many universities in the UK had identified the possibility of disease outbreak in their risk register before 2020 and were also very conscious of the danger associated with a highly infectious coronavirus in a globally interconnected world. They had also followed the spread of the disease following its emergence in China. Despite all these warnings and a three-month 'lead-in' period, they had not radically changed their teaching provision, a substantial proportion of which was delivered in conventional face-to-face classroom or practical settings, before the first lockdown. The reasons that direct action, in relation to teaching methods, was not taken earlier are many. Academics were mid-semester, dedicating all their time to actual teaching and with no headroom to start developing new approaches to material. The government response was unknown and the potential for a full lockdown uncertain until the scale, pace and hospital capacity (incapacity) became apparent. When the first lockdown was imposed, many universities gave all the students a 'reading week' in order to give staff an opportunity to put teaching material online. The imposition

---

22   Barber et al., 'Gravity Assist'.

of 'emergency' online provision was of course radically different from a pedagogically motivated blended approach. Indeed, much of what had been taught face-to-face was simply produced as a recording with a slideshow for online delivery. Nevertheless, the effort required to continue to teach more than 2.5 million students across the UK in all 140 universities should not be underestimated, nor the success of the transition. In the higher education sector in the UK at the time of the lockdowns, 58% of students and 47% of teaching staff had no experience of digital teaching, yet by December 2020 92% of students were learning mostly online.[23]

Those universities which already had some blended learning were in a very favourable position when the lockdowns occurred. Libraries of recordings were instantly available and those with well-developed VLEs were able to utilise them for delivery. It was also a pleasant surprise that many academics were able, through necessity, to overcome their apprehensions about the technologies and methodologies required for online delivery. Full online delivery has its limitations beyond the pedagogical – many subjects depend on practicals and laboratories to develop skills, enhance knowledge, and encourage imagination and creativity. Indeed, many accrediting professional bodies demand practicals and laboratory experience as part of their professional education programme. It was greatly impressive to see how our academics produced opportunities for their students to have practical experiences from their home environments – some developing simulated activities, others producing practical kits which were sent to students, who could then experiment from home. In a survey of students in UK universities during the Covid lockdown, 67% were content with their digital teaching.[24]

During the first two years of the Covid pandemic the opportunities for face-to-face teaching varied as the waves of infection waxed

---

23   Ibid.
24   Ibid.

and waned, from full lockdown with all students learning online, to Covid 'safer' environments, with greater (1.5–2.0 m) spacing between students, cleaning and disinfection between teaching sessions, enhanced ventilation and mask wearing, to variations on this theme and finally back to 'normal'. During this period academics were able to improve the online material which they were using, and to adapt and enhance their own skills at digital delivery. Many universities saw the opportunity for a step change in their pedagogic approach and decided to move to a universal, high-quality, blended, flexible pedagogy for all programmes.

Sadly, during this period politicians and the media chose to make political gains at the expense of educational progress. As we emerged from the pandemic, our Secretaries of State for Education and Ministers for Higher Education in the UK encouraged students to demand compensation if they were not receiving the face-to-face teaching which they 'had anticipated' on application to university. Not surprisingly this had the effect of stimulating discontent among students across the sector. It was a surprising and disappointing volte-face on the part of our government, who had been demanding that we utilise technology more effectively in the years preceding the pandemic. Their rationale was that universities were utilising online delivery as a 'cheap' alternative to returning to face-to-face, and that students were not receiving good value for money. This fails to acknowledge that high-quality blended learning offers many opportunities for face-to-face engagement and is not cheaper than conventional, didactic teaching. Indeed, it is likely to result in engagement with smaller student cohort sizes, thus making it more expensive. It also fails to acknowledge the evidence which has shown that a reduction in classroom time, substituted with online learning of between 30% and

79%, did not adversely affect learning outcomes[25] and that blended approaches are at least as effective in terms of outcomes as face-to-face teaching.[26] Furthermore, the myopic view of some politicians failed to appreciate that the pandemic had merely accelerated the embrace of digital technology in education, which had been evolving over the previous two decades.

As we emerged from the Covid pandemic in 2022, many universities saw a 'spike' in the number of students failing to complete their courses. Provisional feedback data from some of these students suggests that this was because a proportion of the student body had enjoyed the facility to study from home and that being 'forced' back to face-to-face teaching by government instruction was sufficiently unpopular to cause them to leave their programmes. It is interesting to note that students themselves report in the Student Academic Experience Survey, sponsored by the Higher Education Policy Institute, that their contact hours have changed very little over time, and post-Covid are about the same as they were in 2006. They reported that in 2006 their contact hours were 13.7 per week, and their total learning time of contact hours and private study were 25.7 hours per week, which compare to 13.4 and 26.1 hours in 2022.[27] The spike in non-completions is likely also associated with a crisis in cost of living. Student maintenance grants or loans have failed to keep pace with inflation, forcing more students to do more part-time work to cover their living expenses – at the notable

---

25  C. Müller and T. Mildenberger, 'Facilitating Flexible Learning by Replacing Classroom Time with an Online Learning Environment: A Systematic Review of Blended Learning in Higher Education', *Educational Research Review*, 34 (2021), p. 100394, <https://doi.org/10.1016/j.edurev.2021.100394>.

26  R. Owston, D. York and S. Murtha, 'Student Perceptions and Achievement in a University Blended Learning Strategic Initiative', *The Internet and Higher Education*, 18 (2013), pp. 38–46, <https://doi.org/10.1016/j.iheduc.2012.12.003>; H.M. Vo, C. Zhu and N.A. Diep, 'The Effect of Blended Learning on Student Performance at Course-level in Higher Education: A Meta-analysis', *Studies in Educational Evaluation*, 53 (2017), pp. 17–28, <https://doi.org/10.1016/j.stueduc.2017.01.002>.

27  B. Bekhradnia, 'Foreword: The Early Years', in Carasso (ed.), *UK Higher Education*.

expense of their learning time and consequently impacting their assessments and completion.

History suggests that it is difficult to stop progress, and it has been argued that flexible learning is now an inevitable reality.[28] The political and media debate on teaching methodology made it clear that the descriptors used were poorly understood and often misinterpreted, with many of the commentariat failing to appreciate the small group face-to-face components generally delivered in a blended-learning programme. It also polarised a subject which was in reality much more subtle, graduated and integrated. The evaluation of curricula has been supported by the Advance HE framework, which has four dimensions covering technology-enhanced learning, pedagogic approaches (integrated and balanced approaches), employment, and institutional systems and structure.[29] Flexible-learning approaches may appeal to any student but are likely to be most attractive to those who have part-time employment, or caring responsibilities, are more mature, or have a commute to get to their university campus.[30] Successful outcomes of any flexible approach to learning have been highlighted by Barnett and include acquiring a qualification, embracing self-directedness, interacting with other students and tutors, receiving prompt and informative feedback, having access to counselling and careers advice, being inclusive and academically sound, offering a ladder of progression,

---

28  B. Whalley, D. France, J. Park, A. Mauchline and K. Welsh, 'Towards Flexible Personalized Learning and the Future Educational System in the Fourth Industrial Revolution in the wake of Covid-19', *Higher Education Pedagogies*, 6/1 (2021), pp. 79–99, <https://doi.org/10.1080/23752696.2021.1883458>.

29  N. Gordon, 'Flexible Pedagogies: Technology-enhanced Learning', The Higher Education Academy, January 2014, <https://www.advance-he.ac.uk/knowledge-hub/flexible-pedagogies-technology-enhanced-learning>; L.M. Leon, 'Flexible Learning in Higher Education', Advance HE, 2021, <https://www.advance-he.ac.uk/guidance/teaching-and-learning/flexible-learning>.

30  M.S. Andrade and B. Alden-Rivers, 'Developing a Framework for Sustainable Growth of Flexible Learning Opportunities', *Higher Education Pedagogies*, 4/1 (2019), pp. 1–16, <https://doi.org/10.1080/23752696.2018.1564879>.

being cost effective, challenging, and allowing students to complete their programmes.[31]

Many studies have demonstrated the learner benefits of a flexible approach to learning and it will be interesting to see if the evolving UK assessment of teaching quality will reflect these benefits.[32]

## The future of assessment

Assessment is a critical part of the learning process. It has been used to determine whether and what level of credential might be awarded, give confidence that candidates have reached a particular standard of achievement, and contribute to assurance of quality of learning provision. It may allow future employers or professional bodies the facility to judge the likely competence of new recruits, and has even contributed to the metrics used in league tables of universities and thereby to their reputation. Assessment can also be used very effectively to enhance the learning process and give feedback to students on their progress.

Changes in technology have created opportunities to enhance assessment and make it more efficient, but have also given opportunity for plagiarism and cheating. Looking to the future, the Joint

---

31  R. Barnett, 'Conditions of Flexibility: Securing a more Responsive Higher Education System', Advance HE, 2014, <https://www.advance-he.ac.uk/knowledge-hub/conditions-flexibility-securing-more-responsive-higher-education-system>.

32  S. Cook, D. Watson and D. Vougas, 'Solving the Quantitative Skills Gap: A Flexible Learning Call to Arms!', *Higher Education Pedagogies*, 4/1 (2019), pp. 17–31, <https://doi.org/10.1080/23752696.2018.1564880>; M.-D. González-Zamar, E. Abad-Segura, A. Luque de la Rosa and E. López-Meneses, 'Digital Education and Artistic-visual Learning in Flexible University Environments: Research Analysis', *Education Sciences*, 10/11 (2020), p. 294, <https://doi.org/10.3390/educsci10110294>; A.J. Jeffery, S.L. Rogers, K.L.A. Jeffery and L. Hobson, 'A Flexible, Open, and Interactive Digital Platform to Support Online and Blended Experiential Learning Environments: Thinglink and Thin Sections', *Geoscience Communication*, 4/1 (2021), pp. 95–110, <https://doi.org/10.5194/gc-4-95-2021>; C.-M. Lo, J. Han, E.S.W. Wong and C.-C. Tang, 'Flexible Learning with Multicomponent Blended Learning Mode for Undergraduate Chemistry Courses in the Pandemic of COVID-19', *Interactive Technology and Smart Education*, 18/2 (2021), pp. 175–88, <https://doi.org/10.1108/ITSE-05-2020-0061>; Loon, 'Flexible Learning'.

Information Systems Committee (JISC) produced an expert report in 2020 outlining five principles of good assessment.[33]

*Principle one: Authentic assessment*

Assessment is best done in a way which prepares students for their future employment or vocation, and is realistic and motivating. They may be asked to create or edit videos, build websites, work in teams, or use social media, if these are relevant to their future employment. It is also likely that a digital examination will more realistically reflect their future work practice than a written assessment.

*Principle two: Accessible assessment*

Inclusivity is important to ensure everyone gets a fair and even chance in assessment. Digital technologies which allow change in font size or colour, or voice to text and text to voice, as well as refreshable braille displays, all enhance inclusivity and should become universally available.

*Principle three: Appropriately automated assessment*

The enormous growth of higher education over the last fifty years, and the appreciation of the role of assessment in learning has meant that educators spend a large proportion of their time marking assessments and that students expect high-quality feedback from the process. Dissatisfaction with feedback has been a consistent feature across the higher education sector in national student feedback surveys. Multiple choice questions, with automated feedback based on model answers, can be used, and tools are available to give spelling and grammar support for essays. Adaptive comparative judgement uses technology to compare very good or very bad scripts, allowing more human effort to go into assessing those that more closely match a given standard. This can help determine grade boundaries. Automated assessment

---

33  JISC, 'The Future of Assessment: Five Principles, Five Targets for 2025', 2020, <https://repository.jisc.ac.uk/7733/1/the-future-of-assessment-report.pdf>.

should of course be used appropriately and should not diminish the student/academic interaction essential to good teaching.

*Principle four: Continuous assessment*

The evolution of knowledge (see Chapter 12) means that learning now must become a lifelong activity. Assessment throughout a course (without overassessment) may be more appropriate than delivery of large summative assessment processes at end of year or end of course. It may become possible to develop assessment on demand, to reflect the 'readiness' of the student, and learning analysis systems are likely to make this a reality. Formative assessment processes also allow students to take risks and learn from mistakes.

*Principle five: Secure assessment*

Studies suggest a substantive rise in the number of students cheating.[34] Essay mills, whereby it is possible to pay someone to write or produce an essay of sufficient quality to achieve a high mark in an assessment, have been made illegal in many countries, and direct plagiarism can often be picked up using technologies such as Turnitin. Good assessment design, perhaps with an element of personalisation, can help reduce cheating, and technologies are now available which make cheating much more difficult. The Indian National Testing Agency, which carries out assessment at scale for entrance to leading educational facilities in India, utilise a range of technologies to prevent cheating. Students access the examination with an e-card containing their thumbprint and a photo, the computers on which the students take their assessment are not online, and question papers are encrypted until the candidate starts. Multiple choice questions are randomised, such that adjacent students cannot copy, and real-time analytics, which identify cheating patterns (working too quickly or

---

34   R. Harper, T. Bretag, C. Ellis, P. Newton, P. Rozenberg, S. Saddiqui and K. van Haeringen, 'Contract Cheating: A Survey of Australian University Staff', *Studies in Higher Education*, 44/11 (2018), pp. 1857–73, <https://doi.org/10.1080/03075079.2018.1462789>.

too slowly) are employed. These also identify two students providing similar answers. The whole process is scrutinised with a live CCTV feed.[35] It is unlikely that cheating will ever be completely eradicated, however it is possible that processes can be devised which make the effort of cheating greater than that required to perform well in assessment, thereby substantially reducing the incentive.

Assessment processes are extremely important in higher education, and as technologies advance it is likely that they can be used to improve the learning experience and more effectively ensure reliability.

## Post-Covid evolution

It is apparent that the embrace of different teaching methods during Covid have given many universities the incentive needed to review their curricula and learning designs in the immediate post-Covid period.[36] In doing so, universities have taken a strategic approach to curriculum change at programme level. On-campus and on-campus/blended provision are the dominant delivery modes, although some providers are actively exploring micro-credentials, which will comprise smaller packages of learning, with assessment which can be certified, perhaps towards reskilling or upskilling. There is recognition that the desired changes to curriculum will require review of staff workload allocation, staff reward and investment in staff development. Universities are cautious about fully online or hybrid delivery.

The links between quality assurance, quality enhancement and staff engagement with learning design are explicit. The assessment of the quality of educational delivery is being radically changed in England. The system which historically existed relied on internal processes of programme revalidation, embracing best practice, and focusing on quality enhancement with external validation, assured

---

35  JISC, 'The Future of Assessment'.
36  S. MacNeill and H. Beetham, 'Approaches to Curriculum and Learning Design across UK Higher Education', JISC, November 2022, <https://repository.jisc.ac.uk/8967/1/approaches-to-curriculum-and-learning-design-across-uk-higher-education-report.pdf>.

through the oversight of external (to the institution) examiners and QAA visitations. With the creation of a regulatory agency, the OfS, a more quantitative method, the Teaching Excellence Framework (TEF), was introduced in 2017. This initially used data on student satisfaction, employment outcomes and student continuation, together with a statement from the institution. It was judged by an independent panel and institutions awarded bronze, silver or gold awards. This system has evolved more specific and objective metrics, utilising outcome data relating to progression from year 1 to year 2 of a course, numbers successfully graduating and numbers going on to acquire 'graduate-level' jobs.

It remains to be seen whether a blended approach to learning or more flexible learning provision will enhance the quality as measured by the outcomes data above. It is likely though that the quality of the provision, whether conventional, blended or flexible, will have greatest impact on outcomes, whether they are measured objectively or subjectively.

The most critical elements in the delivery of quality education are undoubtedly the competence, energy, imagination and interest of the academic staff delivering it. There has been a remarkable improvement in the development of academic staff in the UK over the last 40 years. In the 1980s initial 'training' of academics might have involved as little as a two-day course on presentation skills, with the junior appointee expected to pick it up as they went along – compare this to the several years of education and training required to become a primary or secondary school teacher. Now almost all universities have well-structured programmes for the development of early career academics and most provide specific continuing professional development to upskill and reskill in particular aspects of pedagogy. Universities also offer teaching academics the opportunities to gain recognised qualifications which enhance their abilities and may contribute to their promotion and progression. Perhaps the most universally recognised of these qualifications are the fellowships awarded or accredited by Advance HE. There are four levels – associate fellow, fellowship, senior and principal fellowship – available and these have recently been revised into an updated Professional Standards Framework which provides the dimensions and descriptors around the professional values, core knowledge and activities necessary to support talent development and which might support the career progression of individual academics.[37]

It seems unlikely that the didactic lecture will ever be completely consigned to history. It has the virtue of efficiency for the campus-based timetable and the attraction of flamboyant entertainment when done well. The masters of the 'art' can also adjust pace and complexity according to the receptivity of the audience. Nevertheless, it will largely remain a facility to transmit content. The use of technology is progressive and its broader embrace inevitable. It will support the flexibility of place and pace and, done well, will enhance the educational experience. A blended approach will assist the engagement between teacher and student and support the appeal and sustainability of the campus university.

---

37  Advance HE, 'Professional Standards Framework for Teaching and Supporting Learning in Higher Education 2023', <www.advance-he.ac.uk>.

# CHAPTER 5
## Beyond the Curriculum: The Experience

The teaching or, more broadly, education which students receive and embrace while at university is the fundamental part of the experience of being at or engaged with a university. It is though only part of the much broader university environment and community, every part of which impacts their perception, enjoyment and development as students. The place itself – if indeed there is a physical place – will impart feeling and create belonging. The lecture theatres, laboratories, libraries or learning resource centres, seminar rooms and common rooms, refectories, bars and sports halls, as well as digital and virtual spaces, and perhaps most of all the cafes and social learning spaces all contribute to the 'feel' of a university. The extracurricular 'offer' is, for many students, the thing which generates esprit de corps, where lifelong friends are made, and which provides the most vivid and lasting memories. The debating society, political club, dance or cooking forum, together with sport and games societies, are now legion in most universities and often provide facilities beyond anything available outside the university campus. Students' transport needs are also supported through designated bus services, subsidised train tickets and bicycle clubs. They also receive support with finance, insurance and accommodation. They have access to counselling, mental-health support, medical services and careers advice, and they are offered guidance, support and advice while doing work placements and volunteering. For those entering university directly from school, the provision of university residences may provide a safe accommodation environment from which to transition into independent living, and the halls' communities may make indelible memories and multicultural friendships, and are places where partners are found and deeper friendships formed.

For the most part, students consider their university experience to be very positive and consistently score their satisfaction levels highly. In the UK, the National Student Survey (NSS) asks questions related to the course that a student has undertaken and is completed by students in their final year. Overall satisfaction across the UK in the 2021 survey was reported as 75% and this was the lowest satisfaction score since 2006, when the score was 80.3%. The 2021 score was no doubt affected by the Covid-related lockdowns, which prevented students receiving the full on-campus experience normally available. The NSS asks a series of teaching- or learning-related questions and so may not reflect the satisfaction that students feel in relation to the non-teaching part of their course. However, in the 'overall satisfaction' question it is inconceivable that other aspects of the whole university experience are not being judged. In a recent review of the NSS, the OfS has chosen to remove the overall satisfaction score in England (although it was retained in Scotland and Wales under different regulators), despite sector support for the question. Arguably, the high NSS satisfaction scores make it difficult for a regulator to criticise universities and for government to cast aspersions on the value derived by students, as the Conservative government did in 2023 in its campaign against 'low-value' degrees; when pressed, ministers were unable to identify any examples. Despite the absence of an overall satisfaction score in the 2024 survey, the positivity measures for each individual question improved compared to the previous year.[1]

The impact which the broad university experience has on human capital is difficult to quantify. It is clear that work placements, whether an integral part of the curriculum or as a voluntary extracurricular activity, have a positive impact – not only on the ultimate employability of students, but also on their degree outcome.[2] It is also undeniable that many senior politicians have honed their skills in the debating halls and political societies of our universities (approximately 85% of the UK's members of parliament went to university), just as many of our Olympic athletes and professional sports people developed their prowess on university sports fields.[3] At the Rio Olympics, 28 athletes came from Loughborough University alone and this is a picture replicated in many countries, including the US, where 29 of their athletes had attended Stanford University. Perhaps even more impressively, 34 former or present Stanford athletes won medals at the Paris Olympics in 2024.

## Extracurricular activities

Activities in which students engage outside the academic curriculum but broadly associated with the university are termed extracurricular and include an extraordinary range of clubs, societies and sport activities. It is common now for universities to have more than 100 such organisations, ranging from Nepalese cookery and salsa dancing to debating and rugby. These act as an attractive currency to prospective students with particular interests and can confer substantial reputational kudos on the university – more than 270,000 people turn up

---

1  D. Kernohan, 'National Student Survey 2024', Wonkhe, <https://wonkhe.com/blogs/national-student-survey-2024/>.
2  R. Brooks and P.L. Youngson, 'Undergraduate Work Placements: An Analysis of the Effects on Career Progression', *Studies in Higher Education*, 41/9 (2014), pp. 1563–78, <https://doi.org/10.1080/03075079.2014.988702>.
3  'MPs and their Degrees: Here's Where and What our UK Politicians Studied', *Studee*, 2019, <https://studee.com/media/mps-and-their-degrees-media/>.

to watch the Oxford–Cambridge boat race live each year and it is viewed by a television audience of more than 6 million. It is self-evident that immersing oneself in an extracurricular activity to the notable exclusion of curricular activity could be counterproductive, but the time-management skills required to do both effectively are of themselves useful employability attributes. In the US, universities often impose mandatory GPA hurdles, which the student's academic performance must clear in order to be allowed to participate in extracurricular activities.[4]

Extracurricular activities also enhance attributes which might be expected outcomes of a university experience, and the soft skills which employers and society more broadly might expect of university graduates.[5] That students are able to perform well at Olympic-level sport and also acquire their degrees is a testament to their time management. In the survey by Buckley and Lee the attributes which students themselves most strongly associated with their extracurricular activities were self-confidence and teamwork and of course these are attributes sought by employers and businesses.[6] Participation in clubs and societies also encourage individuals to grow in leadership roles, to deal with difficult personalities and to enhance their general problem-solving and communication skills.[7] Participation in sports clubs also improves physical health and those who participate report improved mental-health benefits as well.

---

4  P.S. Seow and G. Pan, 'A Literature Review of the Impact of Extracurricular Activities Participation on Students' Academic Performance', *Journal of Education for Business*, 89 (2014), pp. 361–6.

5  P. Buckley and P. Lee, 'The Impact of Extra-Curricular Activity on the Student Experience', *Active Learning in Higher Education*, 22 (2021), pp. 37–48.

6  Buckley and Lee, 'Impact of Extra-Curricular Activity'.

7  R.W. Larson, D.M. Hansen and G. Moneta, 'Differing Profiles of Developmental Experiences across Types of Organized Youth Activities', *Developmental Psychology*, 42/5 (2006), pp. 849–63; G. Clark, R. Marsden, J.D. Whyatt, L. Thompson and M. Walker, '"It's everything else you do…": Alumni Views on Extracurricular Activities and Employability', *Active Learning in Higher Education*, 16/2 (2015), pp. 133–47; Buckley and Lee, 'Impact of Extra-Curricular Activity'.

Beyond the benefits to the individual, which might enhance their academic and softer skills, clubs and societies create strong social networks within which students make acquaintances, often becoming lifelong friends, and they strengthen their bonds with their host university, becoming more engaged alumni. Buckley and Lee also suggest that engagement with clubs and societies early in the student lifecycle may help with the transition from school or college, and may offer a pillar of support which improves the retention of students within their educational programme.[8]

## Beliefs and behaviours

The broader university experience undoubtedly influences the evolution of students' beliefs and politics. Critics often accuse universities of being too political and most often too left-wing in their doctrine. It is no doubt true that academics have historically leant to the left, but whether that informs their teaching is not proven – and indeed for the vast majority of university subject matter, political doctrine is unlikely to be relevant at all. That most students have left-of-centre views is undeniable, but that is a general feature of younger voters and has less to do with their attendance at university than it does with the demographics of their age. As John Curtice, Professor of Politics at Strathclyde University, points out, it is older people who vote Tory. To engage younger voters, then, politicians might be advised to enact policies which are persuasive to them and not to criticise the student electorate for not thinking as they ought.

Universities have been citadels of debate, discussion, disagreement, exploration and occasional consensus since their creation. Their initial incarnation in medieval Europe stole the idea of the academy from the ancient Greek philosophers who spoke freely and challenged orthodoxy. Given a history where academics and their students have been the principal advocates of free speech stretching over more than two

---

8  Buckley and Lee, 'Impact of Extra-Curricular Activity'.

millennia, it is extraordinary that they should have been challenged on their commitment to freedom of speech by politicians and journalists in recent years. The challenge has been based on the apparent no-platforming of controversial speakers at some universities, perhaps most notably Germaine Greer, a writer and feminist, who, when invited to the University of Cardiff, had 3000 students sign a petition supporting cancellation of her invitation. University authorities ensured that she was allowed to speak freely and indeed the incidences where freedoms have actually been curtailed are vanishingly few. In 2019/20, six events out of 10,000 (0.06%) involving external speakers to student unions were cancelled and, of those, four were for administrative reasons.[9] Numbers of recorded incidences of no-platforming have nevertheless increased since then, with 193 incidences reported out of a total of 19,407 university speaking events in academic year 2020/21. The numbers are not directly comparable since the more recent report includes events put on by the whole university body, not just the student unions. Several of the reported cancellations (47) were the result of concerns raised under the 'Prevent' legislation, designed to prevent individuals being drawn into terrorism, and several for administrative reasons (no doubt someone forgot to book the room). Given the core belief of the overwhelming majority of the university community in freedom of speech, and the remarkably small number of events which have ever been cancelled, it seems absolutely extraordinary that the then Conservative government felt compelled to pass a specific Higher Education (Freedom of Speech) Act in 2023. It is reassuring to note that the Labour government, elected in 2024, postponed the implementation of and considered repeal of parts of the Act, since the burden of bureaucracy which it carries for universities

---

9   J. Lewis, 'Free Speech in Universities; What are the Issues?', House of Commons Library, 19 March 2021, <https://commonslibrary.parliament.uk/free-speech-in-universities-what-are-the-issues/>.

substantially outweighs the actual risks that universities are likely to curtail free speech. Indeed, universities are the most ardent defenders of freedom of speech and offer the most robust challenge to those who dissent from such freedoms.

Freedoms of speech, and indeed other expression such as freedoms in what we wear and how we behave, have been challenged by student groups. Extreme right- and left-wing provocateurs are regularly challenged by students with opposing views, but only where the provocations incite violence or overtly support terrorism are they justifiably and lawfully denied a platform. One only has to walk through a university campus in the UK to appreciate that most students wear what they like, and where there are cultural sensitivities around dress, these should be rightly addressed by self-censure. The verbal onslaught against the Yale academic Erika Christakis in 2016, for proposing a liberal approach to dress which drove her from the university, is simply unacceptable. It challenges both freedoms of speech and expression. The flash of tartan in Alexander McQueen or Vivienne Westwood designs should not cause a highland rebellion.

There may be a place for what have become known as trigger warnings, where students are warned that the material that they are about to be exposed to may be disturbing. This should not though allow students to absent themselves from material essential to their development in the subject area of concern. Academics can of course support students by approaching difficult material in a sensitive way, and by building on previous material to increase the resilience of those being exposed. Academics can also present material in a way which resonates most powerfully with a diverse student body, and using a broad range of literature, particularly from indigenous scholars, may be useful in challenging assumptions of colonial historians. More inclusive curricula may also help address the attainment gap, which primarily exists between Black male and other ethnic groups.

It is greatly reassuring to note that most of the issues now characterised by journalists as 'wokeist' are genuine attempts by students to strive towards a better and fairer world. It is disappointing that the popular press use a term ('woke') originally defined as a sensitivity to social and political injustice in a derogatory way and deride today's students who campaign for a sunnier future.

It is the more radical views of our students which will draw us to think with greater depth and embrace or reject their ideas, leading to a more inclusive society, just as preceding generations argued for emancipation, equality and inclusivity, against prevailing orthodoxy.

## Mental ill-health

Universities in the UK have faced criticism for not doing enough to support students with mental health challenges and there have been some tragic examples reported in the press, leading to changes in university policy and practice. The number of home students prepared to disclose mental ill-health in England increased seven-fold from less than 1% in 2010/11 to more than 5% in 2020/21. This could of course be substantially influenced by reporting bias and still represents a relatively low proportion of the 1.8 million home students in English universities.[10] It is important to consider mental ill-health in universities in the context of overall mental ill-health in the population at large. According to NHS figures, severe mental ill-health has increased from 6.9% in 1993 to 9.3% in 2014. The increase and total numbers are higher in women than men with one in five women and one in eight men suffering from some form of mental illness. The reasons for the overall increases in mental ill-health have been attributed to economic uncertainty and unrealised expectations of what life might offer, together with unrelenting and often negative media exposure

---

10   J. Lewis and P. Bolton, 'Student Mental Health in England: Statistics, Policy and Guidance', House of Commons Library, 30 May 2023, <https://commonslibrary.parliament.uk/research-briefings/cbp-8593/>.

and in particular omnipresent social media. The problem is more severe in young people, with three-quarters of mental health issues established by the age of 24. While there has been justifiable concern about the number of suicides amongst university students, the proportion of students committing suicide in 2015 was approximately 0.006% of the student population, which is lower than the 0.01% suicide rate of the general population in 2016. It is likely that the numbers of suicides in young people in the all-age general population will be higher than this. While general mental ill-health is increasing, particularly in young women, the number of men committing suicide is higher still. Thankfully the total number of suicides in the population decreased from 14.8 per 100,000 of the population in 1981 to 10.1 per 100,000 in 2016, although worryingly in students the number of women committing suicide increased between 2001 and 2015 (this may in part reflect the increased number of women going to university). Clearly the number of students and other young people with mental health issues is a cause for deep concern.

It has been suggested that the increase in young women with mental ill-health could be associated with the type of aggressions commonly dealt out by women to other women. These are often associated with language and exclusion which are easily imposed and amplified by the relentless online bombardment now experienced by young people, surrounded by social media and part of an 'always on' generation.[11]

The Student Academic Experience Survey of 14,000 students in 2019 suggests that student wellbeing is lower than wellbeing in the general population, and that anxiety among students had increased from 2018.[12] Exploring the data in more detail, Blackman demonstrated

---

11   J. Haidt and G. Lukianoff, *The Coddling of the American Mind: How Good Intentions and Bad Ideas are Setting up a Generation for Failure* (London, 2019).
12   J. Neves and N. Hillman, 'Student Academic Experience Survey 2019', Advance HE and HEPI, <https://www.hepi.ac.uk/2019/06/13/student-academic-experience-survey-2019/>.

that dissatisfaction with life was higher in ethnic Bangladeshi, Black and Pakistani students than in other minority groups, and was lowest in White students.[13] Black students on the other hand were least anxious, while White, Bangladeshi, Chinese and Pakistani students had progressively higher anxiety scores, in that order. Students from POLAR1 cohorts (areas with low participation in higher education and generally higher deprivation) were most dissatisfied with life and most anxious.[14] Students living at home and with long commutes, often those in POLAR1, were also more dissatisfied with life than those in POLAR5. The POLAR1 students were also most likely to work more than 12 hours a week in paid employment, and Blackman had previously demonstrated that this was likely to have a negative effect on the hours that students devoted to independent study, and to their self-reported learning gain.[15]

In a further analysis of the impact of teaching and feedback on anxiety and dissatisfaction with life, Blackman demonstrated a statistically significant relationship between anxiety and satisfaction and teaching and feedback, with students reporting greatest anxiety and life dissatisfaction when teachers were least helpful and gave least useful feedback. While there could be other factors at play, he concludes that the data suggests a wellbeing gain from improving teaching and feedback measures.[16] The 2024 Student Academic Experience survey showed little material change compared to the 2022 and 2023 data, but higher scores for life

---

13 T. Blackman, 'What Affects Student Wellbeing?', HEPI policy note 21, February 2020, <https://www.hepi.ac.uk/wp-content/uploads/2020/02/HEPI-Policy-Note-21-What-affects-student-wellbeing-13_02_20.pdf>.
14 OfS, 'Young Participation by Area: About POLAR and Adult HE', 30 September 2022, <https://www.officeforstudents.org.uk/data-and-analysis/young-participation-by-area/about-polar-and-adult-he/>.
15 T. Blackman, 'What Affects how much Students Learn?', HEPI policy note 5, January 2018, <https://www.hepi.ac.uk/wp-content/uploads/2018/01/HEPI-Policy-Note-5-What-affects-how-much-students-learn08_01_17.pdf>.
16 Blackman, 'What Affects Student Wellbeing?'

satisfaction, happiness and lower anxiety than in the immediate post-Covid 2021 survey.[17]

Students today have many more challenges than they had in the past and broadly rise to them extremely well. They do work harder, and achieve more, than previous generations. They graduate better prepared and are just as ambitious as their forebears. They are powered by intentions to create a more compassionate and more just world, which bodes well for our future.

---

17  J. Neves, J. Freeman, R. Stephenson and P. Sotiropoulou, 'Student Academic Experience Survey 2024', Advance HE and HEPI, <https://www.hepi.ac.uk/wp-content/uploads/2024/06/SAES-2024.pdf>.

# CHAPTER 6
# Earnings and Happiness: The Benefits

There are good reasons for countries to want lots of graduates. They are likely to enhance prosperity and happiness. Even across borders, graduates appear to be helpful, they are generally more peaceful, they enhance trade, and they are likely to promote sustainability and embrace climate-change-mitigation behaviours. At an individual and societal level, graduates are healthier, more productive and more law-abiding. In most things which make up human capital, it is generally good to have acquired a university education.

Education may have a general pacifying effect. Perhaps it does not seem so, but the global number of deaths in conflicts has been in general decline, from 23.5 deaths in state-based conflicts per 100,000 of the population in 1950, to 0.63 deaths per 100,000 of the population in 2020[1] and during that period there has been a substantial growth in school- and university-level education.[2] It is not possible to draw conclusions from any correlations between the two, since there have been many other factors which have changed: the presence of

---
1  Data updated to 2020 so does not include the conflicts in Ukraine, Gaza, Lebanon or Sudan.
2  M. Roser, J. Hasell, B. Herre and B. Macdonald, 'War and Peace', *ourworldindata.org*, 2016 (updated to 2020 and accessed in 2023), <https://ourworldindata.org/war-and-peace>.

the nuclear deterrent, change in weapon systems and ways of fighting, better emergency treatment of injured combatants and so on. Nevertheless, more granular work suggests that education does lead to pacification, with some disturbing exceptions such as terrorists and genocide-perpetrators who tend to have above-average levels of education.[3]

Higher education, and particularly international and transnational education, is likely to increase the soft power of a nation by spreading its values to those travelling or living elsewhere (see Chapter 9). It is inconceivable that this does not enhance the trade between countries. International trade has grown to a record high of $28.5 trillion in 2021[4] and international trade has been generally growing since the early nineteenth century, with some shorter-term decreases during the world wars and global recessions.[5] International trade barriers are also for the most part coming down and international trade is driven by productivity and comparative advantage.[6] Domestic innovation and the cross-border spread of technology from other countries both contribute to productivity and comparative advantage, with domestic innovation being more important in high-income countries, and foreign-technology spread conferring greater benefit in low-income countries. This is apparent from the benefits of increased research and development spend, where a 1% increase in the log R&D spend improves productivity by 0.49% in high-income countries, but by

---

3  G. Ostby, H. Urdal and K. Dupuy, 'Does Education Lead to Pacification? A Systematic Review of Statistical Studies on Education and Political Violence', *Review of Educational Research*, 89/1 (2019), pp. 46–92, <https://doi.org/10.3102/0034654318800236>.

4  United Nations Conference on Trade and Development (UNCTAD), 'Global trade hits record high of $28.5 trillion in 2021, but likely to be subdued in 2022', <https://unctad.org/news/global-trade-hits-record-high-285-trillion-2021-likely-be-subdued-2022>.

5  E. Ortiz-Ospina, D. Beltekian and M. Roser, 'Trade and Globalisation', *ourworldindata.org*, 2018, <https://ourworldindata.org/trade-and-globalization>.

6  A.M. Santacreu and H. Zhu, 'Which Countries and Industries Contributed the Most to the Decline in Trade Barriers Around the World?', *Economic Synopses*, 26 (2018), <https://doi.org/10.20955/es.2018.26>.

only 0.12% in low-income countries.[7] The impact of higher education on innovation is very positive (see Chapter 8). It is also likely to enhance technology spread and adoption, and consequently play a major positive role in enhancing international trade.

Investing in education in general is likely to have a positive impact on the global challenges of climate change. It has been suggested that providing universal education and consequent family planning, which reduces birth rate, could reduce harmful emissions by between 69 and 120 billion tons by 2050.[8] Furthermore, it is suggested by the World Bank that graduates are more climate conscious than the general population.[9] Graduates are likely to affect global warming by their own individual behaviours, and as the numbers of graduates grow globally, so too will their potential positive impact. They are also likely to make a very significant impact by developing innovative technologies and through social-science research into ways that human behaviours can be adapted to reduce emissions.

Beyond the very big global issues outlined above there are some characteristics of highly educated countries, which by their consistency suggest that higher education is a good thing (Table 6.1). The data from Erudera – a global academic search platform (its name derived from erudite and era) – demonstrates fairly convincing relationships between the number of people in the population with tertiary-level education and prosperity (GDP per capita), employment and happiness.[10]

---

7   A.M. Santacreu and H. Zhu, 'Domestic Innovation and International Technology Diffusion as Sources of Comparative Advantage', *Federal Reserve Bank of St. Louis' Review*, Fourth Quarter (2018), pp. 317–36, <https://doi.org/10.20955/r.100.317-36>.
8   Drawdown, 'Table of Solutions', 2023, <drawdown.org/solutions/table-of-solutions>; 'How Education as a Human Right is Changing the World We Live in', *University of the People*, 8 December 2023, <https://www.uopeople.edu/blog/how-education-as-a-human-right-is-changing-the-world-we-live-in/>.
9   The World Bank, 'Higher Education', 22 October 2021, <worldbank.org/en/topic/tertiaryeducation>.
10  Erudera, 'World's Most Educated Countries and their Main Common Characteristics', 5 October 2022, <https://erudera.com/resources/worlds-most-educated-countries-their-main-common-characteristics/>.

In his excellent book, *A University Education*, David Willetts considered the value of a university education to the individual or to society and considered whether those benefits were economic or non-economic.[11] It is worth revisiting these benefits to see if his general conclusions, that a university education benefits both individuals and society in both economic and non-economic ways, still stand.

Table 6.1
What the world's most educated countries have in common.

|  | Share of people with tertiary education | GDP per capita (2020) | Happiness level as a score (out of 10) | Annual expenditure (state and private) on higher education per student | Unemployment rate |
| --- | --- | --- | --- | --- | --- |
| Canada | 59.96% | $43,241.62 | 7.1 points | $24,498 | 5.4% |
| Japan | 52.68% | $40,048.93 | 5.9 points | $19,309 | 2.6% |
| Luxembourg | 51.31% | $115,873.60 | 7.3 points | $47,694 | 4.6% |
| South Korea | 50.71% | $31,489.12 | 5.8 points | $11,290 | 2.5% |
| Israel | 50.12% | $43,610.52 | 7.1 points | $12,336 | 5.05% |
| USA | 50.06% | $63,543.58 | 6.9 points | $34,036 | 3.7% |
| Ireland | 49.94% | $83,812.80 | 7 points | $17,125 | 6.6% |
| UK | 49.39% | $40,284.64 | 7 points | $29,911 | 3.6% |
| Australia | 49.34% | $51,812.15 | 7.1 points | $20,647 | 3.5% |
| Finland | 47.87% | $49,041.34 | 7.8 points | $18,170 | 6.7% |

Source: Erudera, 'World's Most Educated Countries and their Main Common Characteristics', 5 October 2022, <https://erudera.com/resources/worlds-most-educated-countries-their-main-common-characteristics/>.

## Economic benefits to the individual

The 2021 government statistics indicate that the median salary premium for graduates over non-graduates was £10,000 per annum and that the median salary for graduates was £36,000 and for

---

11 Willetts, *A University Education*.

non-graduates £26,000.[12] Assuming a working life of 45 years (graduate) or 48 years (non-graduate) and subtracting the tuition fee costs (in England) of a degree (3 x £9250), the lifetime graduate premium would be about £344,000. This is a very rough calculation since some non-graduates may start work at a younger age than 18 (so may have more working years) and it is not possible to predict accurately how graduate and non-graduate earnings will grow over the next 48 years, although it is true that the trajectory of earnings tends to be steeper for graduates than non-graduates and the number of graduate jobs is increasing faster than those of non-graduates (see Chapter 12). The figures are even more impressive for post-graduates, who have median salaries of £42,000 and therefore an annual post-graduate premium of £16,000 compared to a non-graduate. The data also indicates that the employment rates for working-age graduates (86.7%) and post-graduates (88.2%) were well above those of non-graduates (70.2%). Using the tax and student loan system in place in 2019, the Institute for Fiscal Studies estimated an earnings premium of £130,000 for men and £100,000 for women, a gain in net lifetime earnings of 20% for men and women.[13]

The results above could simply reflect the relative abilities of those who do or do not go to university, independent of the contribution actually made by the university. In other words, it is a selection of the population – those with required entry qualifications against those who do not necessarily have those qualifications. Older data suggests that when using Net Present Value (essentially the current value of future income streams) and correcting for A-level attainment, there is still a large positive benefit of going to university.[14] These earning

---

12 'Graduate Labour Market Statistics', 9 June 2022, <explore-education-statistics.service.gov.uk/find-statistics/graduate-labour-markets/2021>.
13  Institute of Fiscal Studies, 'The Impact of Undergraduate Degrees on Lifetime Earnings', 29 February 2020, <https://ifs.org.uk/publications/impact-undergraduate-degrees-lifetime-earnings>.
14  Walker and Zhu, 'The Impact of University Degrees on the Lifecycle of Earnings'.

premia appear to be a common feature of university education and apply in other countries too. In the US those with bachelor's degrees are half as likely to be unemployed and earn on average $1.2 million in additional earnings over a lifetime than those with high-school-only qualifications.[15] Many of the studies show differential graduate premia depending on the university, the course of study or the level (2:1 or First) of degree which the graduate achieves, but that might be expected, and it would be rather surprising if the reputation of the institution, job or vocation chosen, and evidence of achievement, did not affect earnings. Economists and doctors are likely to earn more than English teachers and nurses. There is a further economic benefit to the individual beyond higher earnings and employment achieved during non-recessionary periods of the economy, since, at least for male graduates, their earnings continue to grow during a recession (female graduates' earnings flatten out[16]).

In the US, it has been estimated that individuals with a bachelor's degree are 72% more likely to have a retirement plan (pension) and their pensions are 2.4 times higher than those without a degree, and they can earn on average 4.9 times more than those without a degree from their assets, all of which contribute to individual economic benefit.[17]

It has been suggested that much of the increased earning commanded by graduates is a result of 'signalling'[18], and that what

---

15  Association of Public & Land-Grant Universities (APLU), 'How Does a College Degree Improve Graduates' Employment and Earnings Potential?', 2022, <https://www.aplu.org/our-work/4-policy-and-advocacy/publicuvalues/employment-earnings>.
16  J. Britton, L. Dearden, N. Shephard and A. Vignoles, 'How English Domiciled Graduate Earnings vary with Gender, Institution Attended, Subject and Socio-economic Background', Institute for Fiscal Studies (IFS) working paper W16/06, 13 April 2016, doi.10.1920/wp.ifs.2016.1606.
17  P. Trostel, 'It's Not Just the Money, The Benefits of College Education to Individuals and to Society', Lumina issue papers, Lumina Foundation, 14 October 2015, <https://www.luminafoundation.org/resource/its-not-just-the-money/>.
18  A. Wolf, *Does Education Matter? Myths About Education and Economic Growth* (London, 2002).

people learn at university does not increase human capital that much. In other words, access to a university demonstrates that you are bright and worth employing, and access to an elite university demonstrates that you are really bright. There is no doubt some truth in that, but it is certainly not the whole story. If we consider the evidence produced by Britton et al., using tax returns to determine salaries, the three highest-earning graduate jobs were medicine, economics and law.[19] Clearly graduating in medicine from Oxford would signal high intelligence, but the graduate would still have had to demonstrate knowledge, ability and competence in the very rigorous medical-degree course, as would medical graduates from every other medical school in the UK. Indeed, the professional body overseeing medicine (the General Medical Council) ensures that very high minimum standards are maintained throughout the UK. The salaries commanded by doctors reflect our willingness to pay for someone who has acquired a great deal of subject knowledge and related skills, and not simply because they are bright. The subject competencies associated with economics and law similarly reflect higher human capital, which is in demand across society.

A university degree may offer an employer the facility to select who to employ, and employers may rank universities according to their own perceptions of institutional reputation. That does not mean that employers will not be selecting individuals with enhanced human capital as a consequence of their university learning and experience. Wolf argues that the increased earnings of graduates, from which productivity data is derived, need not necessarily be associated with enhanced human capital; it is though, a great leap of faith to deny that it might be. She does infer that there are some skills crucial to the labour market, particularly mathematical and linguistic skills, and

---

[19] J. Britton, L. van der Erve, C. Belfield, A. Vignoles, M. Dickson, Y. Zhu, I. Walker, L. Dearden, L. Sibieta and F. Buscha, 'How much does Degree Choice Matter?', *Labour Economics*, 79 (2022), <https://doi.org/10.1016/j.labeco.2022.102268>.

that higher competence in these is likely to enhance an individual's productivity, whatever course of study they take. Given that numeracy and literacy are important for most university courses, and arguably are enhanced in most courses beyond those focusing on mathematics and language, it is likely that this will enhance the productivity gain associated with a university education. The cumulative evidence, or at least the correlations at individual, national and international level, make a compelling case for the positive impact of university education on human capital, and, consequently, on productivity.

## Economic benefit to society

The most obvious economic benefit to society cascading from higher earnings is in higher tax returns. It has been suggested that UK graduates are being taxed at a disproportionate rate compared to non-graduates, when student loan repayments are factored in, with graduates who earned more than £27,295 paying tax of 42.25% (20% income, 13.25% National Insurance and 9% loan repayment) whereas non-graduates earning up to £50,270 pay 33.25%. For a graduate earning more than £50,270, the marginal tax rate is 52.25%, while a non-graduate earning up to £100,000 pays 42.25%.[20] While these figures show an apparent enhanced 'per-earnings' bonus to the economy, they do include the loan repayments, which is not, in the true sense, a tax. Nevertheless, if the tuition fees are subtracted from the lifetime annual graduate premium, it is fair to include the repayment of them in returns to the state. It is also important to appreciate that interest is being accrued on those loans and has been repaid at variable rates (now RPI – see Chapter 10). It would be fair in these calculations to include the Resource Accounting and Budgeting (RAB) charge as

---

20   G. Eaton, 'How the Tax System Squeezes Graduates', *The New Statesman*, 8 September 2021, <https://www.newstatesman.com/economy/2021/09/how-the-tax-system-squeezes-graduates>. Since these calculations were made the salary above which loan repayments begin has changed to £25,000, and the calculations are based on tax and national insurance rates at the time.

a disbenefit to society (the proportion of the total student loan debt which will never be paid back) because some graduates will simply never earn enough to do so. The total loan book stood at £333 billion (2021/22) and for the 2021/22 fulltime undergraduate cohort the RAB charge was estimated to be 44% on borrowing of about £24 billion for that year. Changes in repayment terms introduced in 2022/23 mean that the percent RAB charge is forecast to come down to 28% in 2023/24.[21] Despite the RAB charge, the overall sum gained to the exchequer for an undergraduate degree exceeds that paid, by about £110,000 for men and £30,000 for women over their lifetime.[22]

A second substantial positive impact is made to the economy by graduates through increased human capital and productivity. In the UK, it has been shown that higher-level skills account for the largest contribution to labour productivity during both high growth and periods of recession. In the run up to the 2008 financial crisis, upskilling in the UK's workforce accounted for 20% of total labour-productivity growth.[23] Putting this into the context of university education, Holland et al. found that a 1% rise in the share of the workforce with a degree raises the level of productivity by 0.2–0.5% over the longer term.[24] Higher education may impact productivity by producing graduates who invent or develop new technologies, products or ways of doing things and this is most often associated with scientists and

---

21  'Student Loan Forecasts for England Financial Year 2021–22', 14 July 2022, <https://explore-education-statistics.service.gov.uk/find-statistics/student-loan-forecasts-for-england/2021-22>.
22  J. Britton, L. Dearden, B. Waltmann and L. van der Erve, 'Most students get a big pay-off from going to university – but some would be better off financially if they hadn't done a degree', IFS, 29 February 2020, <https://ifs.org.uk/news/most-students-get-big-pay-going-university-some-would-be-better-financially-if-they-hadnt-done>.
23  A.R. Aznar, J. Forth, G. Mason, M. O'Mahony and M. Bernini, 'UK Skills and Productivity in an International Context', BIS research paper 262, BIS/15/704, December 2015, <www.gov.uk/bis>.
24  D. Holland, I. Liadze, C. Rienzo and D. Wilkinson, 'The Relationship between Graduates and Economic Growth across Countries', BIS research paper 110, August 2013, <www.gov.uk/bis>.

engineers. Graduates may also enhance the exploitation of technologies which already exist and thereby improve business productivity.[25]

There is compelling evidence that improving human capital through education does enhance productivity, and that this is true for primary, secondary and tertiary education. The impact of tertiary education is more substantial than primary or secondary education in OECD countries, and is greater in OECD countries than in developing countries. A one-year increase in education raises the level of output per capita by greater than 1% or between 3% and 6% (depending on the growth theories used).[26] Globally it is suggested that returns on tertiary education are the highest of all levels of education and increase earnings by an estimated 17% (compared with 10% for primary and 7% for secondary education) but, unlike the OECD figures, the World Bank estimates that returns on tertiary education are even higher in sub-Saharan Africa at 21%.[27]

It has been suggested by Willetts that the returns to the state through taxes from graduates substantially exceed (by £300,000 over a lifetime earnings) those from non-graduates.[28] However, specific recent data on tax differentials are hard to find and, by their nature, are retrospective. In a recent study using tax data (pay as you earn [PAYE] and self-employment records) to determine annual earnings for people who finished secondary school in England between 2002 and 2007, and were paying tax between 2005/6 and 2016/17, Britton et al. show that average earnings, and by direct inference tax paid, is greater in university graduates from all types of university, and even greater by female graduates in most types of university.[29] They also

---

25  B.A. Lundvall and B. Johnson, 'The Learning Economy', *Journal of Industry Studies*, 1/2 (1994), pp. 23–42.
26  B. Sianesi and J. Van Reenen, 'The Returns to Education: Macroeconomics', *Journal of Economic Surveys*, 17/2 (2003), pp. 115–226, <https://onlinelibrary.wiley.com/doi/abs/10.1111/1467-6419.00192>.
27  The World Bank, 'Higher Education'.
28  Willetts, *A University Education*.
29  Britton, 'How much does Degree Choice Matter?'

show, however, that the subject studied makes a big difference, with medicine, economics and law making the highest returns, and social care and creative arts the lowest. The selectivity (based on GCSE at entry) of the university has little effect across most universities, but a profoundly positive impact in the highly selective elite universities in the UK. The data indicate the strong benefit to the UK state in terms of tax returns, and since tax data is calculated before student loan repayments are taken, this is a direct additional benefit to the state. The data also shows that for some subjects, including nursing and education, income (and tax) are lower, but for graduates in these subjects the return to society is likely to be very high in non-economic terms. In the US, it has been estimated that graduates with a bachelor's degree contribute $381,000 more over their lifetime in taxes than they receive in benefit (in the US this includes medical care, food stamps, school lunches, energy assistance and housing subsidies). This compares with a net gain of $26,000 for those with just high-school education.[30]

The economic effects of education at all levels extend beyond earnings and tax receipts. In England, the negative impact on health from a poorer education has been estimated to cost about £32 billion in productivity losses, on top of healthcare costs of £5 billion and increased welfare payments and lower tax revenues.[31]

## Non-economic benefits to the individual

Higher education has a positive impact on health, but the reasons are not straightforward nor associated with a single factor such as doing more exercise. It has been suggested that there are economic, social and behavioural relationships between education and health. These allow people to access healthcare and solve health-related problems, recognise symptoms, and embrace behaviours, activities and lifestyle

---
30  Trostel, 'It's Not Just the Money'.
31  S. Meriouma, 'The Role of Education in Reducing Health Inequalities', Health Action Research Group, July 2021, <https://www.healthactioncampaign.org.uk/tackling-obesity/the-role-of-education/>.

choices which improve health. Policies which improve education have knock-on effects, reducing population growth, smoking and obesity. Utilising data from the OECD and the World Bank from between 1995 and 2015, Raghupathi and Raghupathi demonstrate a clear correlation between increased education (particularly tertiary education) and reduced infant mortality rates, increased life expectancy at birth, a drop in years of life lost, and increased take-up of child vaccination.[32] They also demonstrate positive relationships between high tertiary-education levels in countries and higher overall health expenditure. The health:education gradient, that is the positive relationship which exists as education improves, has been studied in China between 1991 and 2006. The strongest relationship exists between resources (as education improves there is more money available to spend on nutrition and healthcare) and health, and between the improved knowledge and information associated with a more educated population. There was a limited relationship between behaviours and health, suggesting that in low-income countries the gradient is likely to be associated with fundamentals such as nutrition, and only when resources reach a certain level are they likely to substantially influence health behaviours.[33] In the US it is estimated that people with a bachelor's-level degree are almost four times less likely to smoke, and are less likely to be obese or to drink heavily.[34]

It has been estimated that the global economic burden of physical inactivity amounts to $65–$145 billion.[35] Higher education has been

---

32  V. Raghupathi and W. Raghupathi, 'The Influence of Education on Health: An Empirical Assessment of OECD Countries for the Period 1995–2015', *Archives of Public Health*, 78 (2020), <https://doi.org/10.1186/s13690-020-00402-5>.
33  H. Zhong, 'An Over Time Analysis on the Mechanisms behind the Education–Health Gradients in China', *China Economic Review*, 34 (2015), pp. 135–49, <https://doi.org/10.1016/j.chieco.2015.04.003>.
34  Trostel, 'It's Not Just the Money'.
35  D. Ding, T. Kolbe-Alexander, B. Nguyen, P.T. Katzmarzyk, M. Pratt and K.D. Lawson, 'The Economic Burden of Physical Inactivity: A Systematic Review and Critical Appraisal', *British Journal of Sports Medicine*, 51/19 (2017), pp. 1392–409.

associated with increased physical activity, and in a study of young people in Finland, each additional year of education led to a 0.62 unit (units were composite measure of overall physical activity, intensive activity, total steps, aerobic steps and years of education) of higher overall physical activity, which comprised 0.26 hours of intense activity per week, 560 more steps per day and 390 more aerobic steps per day.[36] This may be part of a positive cycle, since high frequency of leisure-time physical activity results in improved academic performance.[37] It is also likely that those doing physical activity do so because they enjoy it, and there is a clear positive relationship between physical activity and happiness.[38] Education also has a positive impact on participation in, and consumption of, art and cultural activities[39] and these also enhance life satisfaction.[40] Given the very positive relationships between health, life expectancy, exercise and cultural participation on the one hand, and increasing educational achievement on the other, it would be expected that there would be an overall positive relationship between level of educational attainment and happiness, and this does appear to be the case. Nevertheless, it is unlikely that this is only due to the non-economic benefits of education, since there is also a relationship between earnings and happiness. Utilising

---

36 J.T. Kari, J. Viinikainen, P. Böckerman, T.H. Tammelin, N. Pitkänen, T. Lehtimäki, K. Pahkala, M. Hirvensalo, O.T. Raitakari and J. Pehkonen, 'Education Leads to a more Physically Active Lifestyle: Evidence based on Mendelian Randomization', *Scandinavian Journal of Medicine and Science in Sports*, 30/7 (2020), pp. 1194– 204, <https://doi.org/10.1111/sms.13653>.
37 S. Aaltonen, A. Latvala, A. Jelenkovic, R.J. Rose, U.M. Kujala, J. Kaprio and K. Silventoinen, 'Physical Activity and Academic Performance: Genetic and Environmental Associations', *Medical Science Sports Exercise*, 52/2 (2020), pp. 381–90, <https://doi.org/10.1249/mss.0000000000002124>.
38 Z. Zhang and W.A. Chen, 'A Systematic Review of the Relationship Between Physical Activity and Happiness', *Journal of Happiness Studies*, 20 (2019), pp. 1305–22, <https://doi.org/10.1007/s10902-018-9976-0>.
39 A. Reeves, 'Neither Class nor Status: Arts Participation and the Social Strata', *Sociology*, 49/4 (2015), pp. 624–42, <https://doi.org/10.1177/0038038514547897>.
40 L.C. Lin, G.W. Lee, H.C. Hung and N.M. Shih, 'The Influence of People's Cultural Activities, Participation and Sense of Gain on Life Satisfaction', *Leis Soc Res*, 17 (2018), pp. 75–84, <http://lawdata.com.tw/tw/detail.aspx?no=336194>.

biennial survey data from the Bank of Italy on Italian household incomes between 2004 and 2014, Ruiu and Ruiu demonstrate both improved incomes and increased happiness in those with higher levels of education (Table 6.2).[41]

Table 6.2
Mean values over the years 2004–14 with income expressed in 2015 values using Istat currency revaluation coefficients.

| Educational Level | Happiness Score (out of 10) | Income (Mean) |
| --- | --- | --- |
| Elementary | 6.3 | 12.6 |
| Secondary | 6.9 | 14.4 |
| Vocational | 7.2 | 15.0 |
| High School Diploma | 7.3 | 17.0 |
| Graduate | 7.5 | 22.4 |
| Postgraduate | 7.7 | 29.5 |

Source: Adapted from G. Ruiu and M. Ruiu, 'The Complex Relationship Between Education and Happiness: The Case of Highly Educated Individuals in Italy', Journal of Happiness Studies, 20/8 (2019), pp. 2631–53, <https://doi.org/10.1007/s10902-018-0062-4>.

They point out that the happiness figures are somewhat reduced by greater 'expectation frustration' in those with higher education, who believe that their level of education should confer *even* higher income outcomes.

Degree-level graduates in the US are 47% more likely to have health insurance through their employment compared to non-graduates, and are more likely to be safe at work (workers' compensation is 2.4 times lower, since graduates make fewer claims). They are also 21% more likely to be married and 61% less likely to be divorced.[42]

---

41   G. Ruiu and M. Ruiu, 'The Complex Relationship Between Education and Happiness: The Case of Highly Educated Individuals in Italy', Journal of Happiness Studies, 20/8 (2019), pp. 2631–53, <https://doi.org/10.1007/s10902-018-0062-4>.
42   Trostel, 'It's Not Just the Money'.

## Non-economic benefits to society

People benefit in a very direct and largely non-economic way by having doctors, nurses, teachers, scientists, engineers, lawyers and even politicians, among the many other graduates who create the fabric of society. Having access to people with appropriate knowledge, training and skills to ensure that we can function effectively as individuals, families and communities is critical to the way that modern society works.

Many studies have shown that increasing educational attainment is associated with decreased crime rates[43] and some have shown an additional impact of education beyond school, and associations between reduced criminality and college- or degree-level education.[44] US Census Bureau reports show reduced violent crime rates for those with college or university education compared to those with only high-school diplomas.[45] States with higher educational attainment have lower crime rates, and those that make bigger investments in higher education have better public-safety outcomes. It has been estimated that the average annual cost to the state of educating a student in the US is $12,643 whereas to house a prison inmate costs $28,323, and that increasing male high-school-graduation rates by 5% would save the state of California $2.4 billion in crime-related spending and add $200 million in earnings.[46] The reasons for decreasing criminality in those with higher education are not entirely clear; there are direct

---

43  R. Hjalmarsson and L. Lochner, 'The Impact of Education on Crime: International Evidence', CESifo DICE Report, *ifo Institut – Leibnizinstitut für Wirtschaftsforschung an der Universität München*, 10/2 (2012), pp. 49–55.
44  J.A. Ford and R.D. Schroeder, 'Higher Education and Criminal Offending over the Course of a Lifetime', *Sociological Spectrum*, 31/1 (2010), pp. 32–58, <https://doi.org/10.1080/02732173.2011.525695>; R.R. Swisher and C.R. Dennison, 'Educational Pathways and Change in Crime Between Adolescence and Early Adulthood', *Journal of Research in Crime and Delinquency*, 53/6 (2016), pp. 840–71, <https://doi.org/10.1177/0022427816645380>.
45  A. Page, A. Petteruti, N. Walsh and J. Ziedenberg, 'Education and Public Safety', The Justice Policy Institute Report, 30 August 2007, <www.justicepolicy.org>.
46  B. DeBaun and M. Roc, 'Saving Futures, Saving Dollars: The Impact of Education on Crime Reduction and Earnings', Alliance for Excellent Education, 2013, <www.all4ed.org>.

associations with IQ, and because brighter and more highly educated people tend to earn more, there are also associations with prosperity. Correlations do not prove cause and effect, and it is likely that criminality and education have a complex and multifactorial relationship. Having higher education gives people more choice, and, in particular, the choice not to engage in crime. Those with higher earnings associated with increased education also have more to lose. Education may also give people the ability to consider the future consequences of their actions and may allow them to more effectively weigh up the potential negative impact of the more immediate gratification of criminal activity. The data may also be biased by the fact that more highly educated people commit different types of crimes, such as fraud, and they may be better at avoiding the criminal-justice system.

In the US it has been estimated that people with a bachelor's degree annually contribute more than four times ($1300) the value in volunteer work than non-graduates. They also give 3.4 times ($900) as much to charities, participate almost twice as much in schools, civic and religious organisations, and attend 2.6 times as many community activities. They are more likely to vote and engage significantly more with neighbours.[47]

## Benefits of the university 'business'

The major contributions which universities make are through their graduates, as described above, their research (Chapter 7) and their engagement with business and industry (Chapter 8). They are though themselves major businesses, although some educational purists reject the description. In the UK, in 2018/19, universities contributed £95 billion to the economy, with an estimated GDP value of £52 billion.[48] By 2021/22, the economic benefit of universities to the UK economy

---

47  Trostel, 'It's Not Just the Money'.
48  D. Popov, 'Large Economic Contribution of Universities in England', *Frontier Economics*, 29 September 2021, <https://www.frontier-economics.com/uk/en/news-and-articles/news/news-article-i8785-large-economic-contribution-of-universities-in-england/>.

had grown to £265 billion,[49] and they employed 385,500 full-time equivalent staff directly and supported a further 382,500 jobs throughout the wider economy.[50]

Many of the benefits identified as a consequence of degree-level education in this chapter are tangible and measurable, although it can be argued why they come about. Other benefits are implied by corelations at population level, and it is possible to debate whether the associations are directly related to university education. It is though simply inconceivable that the broader associations between university and positive outcomes are not real, and the compelling conclusions are that, for the individual and for society, universities are very good things.

---

49  London Economics report quoted in, 'New Report Reveals Key Role Universities Play in Boosting Growth and Productivity Across the UK', UUK, 6 September 2024, <https://www.universitiesuk.ac.uk/latest/news/new-report-reveals-key-role-universities#:~:text=The%20London%20Economics%20report%20also,will%20be%20involved%20in%20crime.>.
50  J. Booth, J. Miller, M. Halterbeck and G. Conlon, 'The Impact of the Higher Education Sector on the UK Economy', Summary Report for UUK, August 2023.

# CHAPTER 7
## The Triumph of Discovery: Research

The evolution of research methods has catalysed an extraordinary growth in knowledge over the last 400 years. It has been calculated that knowledge (accumulated and transmitted in text and now digitally) approximately doubled every century up until 1900[1], by 1945 it was doubling every 25 years and now each day, with the expectation that it will double every 12 hours in the near future.[2] The impact of research has been profound on areas such as productivity, health, policies, education, culture, global warming and communication, and it is only through research that planet earth will reach a sustainable equilibrium with its human inhabitants. Research is undertaken in institutes, universities and businesses, with different objectives and outcomes. It is measured in many ways and forms the basis of competition for reputation and funding.

All human progress has been made on the back of observation and discovery. The creation of tools, the cultivation of wheat and the use of the wheel almost certainly required observation, trial and error and

---
1   R. Buckminster Fuller, *Critical Path* (London, 1983).
2   D.R. Schilling, 'Knowledge Doubling Every 12 Months, Soon to be Every 12 Hours', *Industry Tap into News*, 19 April 2013, <https://www.industrytap.com/knowledge-doubling-every-12-months-soon-to-be-every-12-hours/3950>.

incremental improvements. A more structured approach to discovery, and the growth and dissemination of knowledge emerged in classical antiquity, with the embrace of debate, study of logic and philosophy, and progress in mathematics. It was, though, the evolution of more deliberate methods of research by luminaries such as Christopher Wren and Francis Bacon (whose work influenced the Royal Society, established in 1660 to acquire knowledge through 'experimental investigation') and the integration of teaching into a 'research' university by Humboldt in the early nineteenth century which began the exponential growth of knowledge that has led to today's knowledge explosion.

The qualification of Doctor of Philosophy (PhD) has become the gold standard for research training and a benchmark of competence. Its original incarnation in the thirteenth century, at the University of Paris, was most likely awarded on the basis of erudition and mastery of knowledge in a subject.[3] It was not until the German universities in the early nineteenth century developed the seminar to include students' own scholarly work and research, and to require a written transcript that the research PhD emerged.[4] The first recorded PhD in the US was awarded by Yale in 1861 and its enthusiastic embrace by other US universities provided the catalyst for the American economic revolution.

Methods in research extend from the observational to the highly experimental and may be quantitative, analytical or qualitative. The different types or purposes of research are often described using the Frascati definitions, broadly embracing Basic, Applied and Developmental Research.[5] Basic research is undertaken to acquire new knowledge without particular anticipated application. Applied

---

3   D. Bogle, '100 Years of the PhD in the UK', accessed 2023, <www.vitae.ac.uk>.
4   O. Kruse, 'The Origins of Writing in the Disciplines', *Written Communications*, 23/3 (2006), pp. 331–52.
5   OECD, *Frascati Manual 2015: Guidelines for Collecting and Reporting Data on Research and Experimental Development*, The Measurement of Scientific, Technological and Innovation Activities (Paris, 2015), <https://doi.org/10.1787/9789264239012-en>.

research is undertaken to acquire new knowledge with a particular practical outcome in mind. Experimental Development draws on existing knowledge to produce new products or develop new processes. Creating hierarchies of research is unhelpful since each may be equally challenging, and each may require high-quality design and execution and have extraordinary impact. The impact may be to increase our knowledge of and wonderment at the universe in which we live or may have practical or economic benefit to a business or to society more broadly. Willetts makes a strong case for the general usefulness of research, even if it is not always immediately apparent, and that applied research should be considered as worthy as 'blue sky' research.[6] It is anomalous that even he – a strong advocate of good research wherever it is done – suggests that the 'novelty and brilliance' come from the 'leading' research universities, while it is the newer universities which do the more applied, and often locally relevant, research. While there is no doubt some truth in his observation, particularly since many of the younger universities identify themselves as 'business-facing' or entrepreneurial and align their research accordingly, the Research Excellence Framework judges quality and relevance wherever it is found and excellent four-star research from a post-92 is just as 'novel and brilliant' as that from one of the Russell Group universities. While the volume of four-star research may be lower in the newer institutions, it should not be considered inferior. Indeed, even in volume terms some of the post-92 universities, such as Northumbria, are competing well with their older peers. Furthermore, that Willetts himself, as Minister for Higher Education, sought to align the Catapult centres (technology and innovation centres), which he created to replicate the German Fraunhofer institutes (which focus on applied research), with the research-intensive universities and not with the universities characterised by applied or business-engaged research, reflects the perception of which types of university should

---

6  Willetts, *A University Education*.

be supported to deliver research.

Only two government departments in the UK now have substantial research budgets: Health and Defence. Willetts argues that all government departments should have budgets for directed research which is in the public good. The advantage of this would be the facility to fund very specific projects of desired national importance without transgressing the Haldane principle applied to the more general research budget distributed by UKRI.[7] The advantage to the research community of the Haldane principle is that government is unable to use research funding for its own initiatives, nor is it able to direct who receives the money. The allocation of institutional research funding in the UK was carried out by intermediary agency HEFCE until 2018, in order to reduce political interference and retain academic freedom, as recommended by Haldane.[8] While it has largely upheld the Haldane principle, it remains to be seen if UKRI can retain that independence under increasingly directive political pressure.

Research has had an impact on every aspect of life, but it is interesting to consider its contributions to productivity, health, policies, education, culture, global warming and communications in more detail.

## Productivity

It is self-evident that a new or improved product or process will improve the productivity of a business or industry. It will require more than a research discovery to bring a product to market or improve a business process. In order to realise the potential of a new product, substantive infrastructure may be needed, along with a financial investment, a skilled and educated workforce, receptive businesses

---

7 The Haldane principle: detailed decisions on how research money is spent are for the research community to make through the UK research councils without government involvement. This gives researchers the autonomy to bid for research in a broad range of subjects and be to judged on their merits by peer research workers.
8 *Haldane Report.*

and effective supply chains. Nevertheless, businesses or countries that invest more in research are likely to be more productive and ultimately more prosperous.[9] The positive and consistent correlation between R&D spend and prosperity are compelling. It is also likely that more prosperous businesses and nations will have greater resources available to invest in research, and there is no doubt a virtuous cycle between research spend and investment. Switzerland has consistently ranked top of the world innovation index[10], presumably as a consequence of its excellent and highly effective business and educational infrastructure and relatively large spend on research (at 3.15% of GDP it is sixth in the OECD countries). Israel, South Korea and Sweden also spend a large percentage of their GDP on research and rank well for innovation.[11] Countries starting from a more modest base, which invest consistently in innovation, such as Rwanda, have made substantial improvements in prosperity over recent years.

## Health

The impact which research has had on health and more broadly welfare, and therefore on average life expectancy has been profound. Skeleton remains suggest that 10,000 years ago life expectancy was between 25 and 30 years and was certainly impacted by more than currently treatable disease; nutrition, childbirth and trauma events no doubt contributed. Over time, research in agriculture has had an extraordinary impact on nutrient availability and research on environmental hazards has also significantly improved life expectancy. Nevertheless, in more recent history, the impact of largely medical

---

9 World Intellectual Property Organization (WIPO), *Global Innovation Index 2019: Creating Healthy Lives – The Future of Medical Innovation*, 12th edn, eds S. Dutta, B. Lanvin and S. Wunsch-Vincent (Ithaca, NY, 2019).
10 WIPO, *Global Innovation Index 2022, What is the Future of Innovation Driven Growth?*, 15th edn, eds S. Dutta, B. Lanvin, L. Rivera Leon and S. Wunsch-Vincent (Geneva, 2022), <https://doi.org/10.34667/tind.46596>.
11 'Swiss spend almost CHF 23 Billion on Research', SWI Annual Report, 2021, <swissinfo.ch>.

research and discovery on health and longevity has been dramatic. Using census data from England, life expectancy has doubled from approximately 43 years for a woman in 1841 to approximately 86 years in 2011.[12] Furthermore, on a global scale life expectancy rose from approximately 67 years to 73 years between 2000 and 2019.[13] Some of the great early discoveries such as that regarding disinfection in childbirth by Ignaz Semmelweis and regarding the spread of cholera by John Snow (which formed the basis of epidemiology), both in the nineteenth century, and before that the vaccination against smallpox by Edward Jenner in 1796, have formed the basis of disease control through to the present day. The control of Covid-19 involved disinfection, epidemiology and vaccination in greatly more sophisticated ways than those of the early pioneers but built on their work and the extraordinary research progress made in the intervening years. The scale and spread of the research response to the Covid-19 pandemic has been quite spectacular. The first vaccine to be fully authorised for SARS-CoV-2 (the virus which causes Covid-19) was the Pfizer/BioNTech vaccine, barely a year after the discovery of the disease. This compares with four years for mumps in the 1960s which was the previous record holder.[14] This does contrast with a concerning trend in pharmaceutical research, which, if measured by length of time it takes to get a new medicine to market, has slowed in recent years[15] despite global spend on health care substantially exceeding

---

12   Office for National Statistics (ONS), 'How has Life Expectancy Changed Over Time?', Census 2021.
13   World Health Organisation (WHO), 'The Global Health Observatory, GHE: Life Expectancy and Healthy Life Expectancy', 2022, <https://www.who.int>.
14   P. Ball, 'The Lightning-fast Quest for COVID Vaccines – and What it Means for Other Diseases', Nature, 589 (2021), pp. 16–18, <https://doi.org/10.1038/d41586-020-03626-1>.
15   J.W. Scannell, A. Blanckley, H. Boldon and B. Warrington, 'Diagnosing the Decline in Pharmaceutical R&D Efficiency', Nature Reviews Drug Discovery, 11/3 (2012), pp. 191–200; N. Bloom, C.I. Jones, J. Van Reenen and M. Webb, 'Are Ideas Getting Harder to Find', National Bureau of Economic Research (NBER) working paper 23782, September 2017, doi. 10.3386/w23782, <https://www.nber.org/papers/w23782>.

the rate of GDP growth.[16] This is perhaps counterintuitive, given the full sequencing of the human genome, now more than 20 years ago[17] and the more targeted approach to defined molecular sites responsible for clinical disease.[18] It may be that the impact and complexity of post-translational events in the generation of proteins from DNA were underestimated in the immediate heady period following the sequencing of the genome, and that with more sophisticated artificial intelligence and the mapping of sequence and folding of target proteins, the expected bounty in pharmaceutical products will still be realised. It is also likely that stringent safety and environmental regulations with respect to drug and vaccine authorisation (the Covid-19 approvals were made under emergency-use regulations), together with a very high bar for expected return on investment, has meant that only 'blockbuster products' make it to market, such as the rheumatoid drug Humira, which generated sales of $19.8 billion in 2020, or the anti-cancer drug Keytruda, which had sales of $14.4 billion, also in 2020. Nevertheless, the impact of research on health and welfare has been extraordinary. The improved health of a population has the positive knock-on effect of enhancing productivity, and where improvement is made by way of prevention (e.g. through vaccination) also on reduced health costs. This is likely to positively impact countries where sickness blights the working-age population. In more developed countries longevity may add to health costs as people live longer and consequently require more health care.

---

16 'World Industry Outlook: Healthcare and Pharmaceuticals', *Economist Intelligence Unit*, June 2017.

17 International Human Genome Sequencing Consortium, 'Initial Sequencing and Analysis of the Human Genome', *Nature*, 409 (2001), pp. 860–921, <https://doi.org/10.1038/35057062>.

18 C.H. Emmerich, L.M. Gamboa, M.C.J. Hofmann, M. Bonin-Andresen, O. Arbach, P. Schendel, B. Gerlach, K. Hempel, A. Bespalov, U. Dirnagl and M.J. Parnham, 'Improving Target Assessment in Biomedical Research: The GOT-IT Recommendations', *Nature Reviews Drug Discovery*, 20/1 (2021), pp. 64–81, <https://doi.org/10.1038/s41573-020-0087-3>.

## Policy and politics

At a national- and local-government level it is inarguable that policies should be based on evidence and fact. Furthermore, that evidence is best provided by high-quality research. That policies often fail to follow evidence is apparent in everyday life and may be due to the complexity of the issues, competing strands of evidence, self-interest on the part of those making the decisions, or political doctrine. In the UK, at a national level, the evidence relating to housing shortages and the quality of available housing stock is clear, yet political parties come to very different decisions regarding housing policies. Furthermore, at local-government level, housing and planning policies vary dramatically and are radically influenced by the likely voting tendencies of the electorate – 'not in my back yard' – and the self-interest of local politicians. The complexity of the evidence regarding large infrastructure projects makes decisions difficult – balancing the predicted economic benefit of a new high-speed rail link along the west coast of Britain, for instance, against its environmental impact, at a time when working practices and commuting patterns are changing substantially, is highly complex and likely to produce quite different outcomes depending on the perspective of the stakeholder and weighting of the evidence.

Even when the evidence has been reaffirmed by research and by actual practice elsewhere, politicians may be reluctant to change policies. Genetically modified crops have been grown and consumed over large tracts of the planet for years without apparent negative health or environmental impact. Yet a moratorium on their use continues in the EU and UK, suggesting irrationality in our decision-making processes. It is clear also that lobbying by powerful, self-interested factions or industries can sway political will. The US has waxed and waned on its support for the Paris Accord, an agreement signed in 2016 with the aim of limiting global temperature increase to 2°C and reducing emissions to net zero by the middle of the twenty-first century. The US withdrew from the agreement in 2020 and then rejoined in 2021.

Policy changes are influenced by the fossil-fuel industries and swings in political doctrine, not by developments in the available evidence or research findings. Very few politicians have the expertise to effectively interrogate scientific evidence: in the UK only one member of parliament held a PhD in science in 2019, and no hard-science subjects (economics excepted) featured in the top six most common degrees held by UK MPs in 2019.[19] It is true that MPs have civil servants and appoint independent experts who do have the expertise to advise on complex subjects, but when the advice conflicts with political doctrine it is often ignored. Indeed, Michael Gove, the then Lord Chancellor, pronounced that 'the people of this country have had enough of experts', presumably because their expert advice differed from his political agenda.[20]

There is no doubt that the research community could do better in the communication of evidence to both politicians and the general public, but to create policies in the absence of evidence or contrary to the most robust evidence is pure folly, and our system of politics and policy creation must improve to address this.

## Education

Knowledge forms the basis and substance of education, and much knowledge is created through research, the two are therefore inextricably linked. Specific research into education and pedagogy is undertaken to enhance teaching methods and learning outcomes and these were explored in Chapter 4. The relationship between education and research in terms of their independent production and delivery is less clear. The 'research university', as envisioned by Humboldt, supported the philosophy that research was best done in a learning

---

19 'MPs and their Degrees', *Studee*.
20  R. Portes, 'I think the people of this country have had enough of experts', *think at London Business School*, 2017, <london.edu/think/who-needs-experts>.

environment.²¹ There is no doubt that the broader subject expertise which teaching brings to a research academic can enhance their research, by drawing in different perspectives and novel approaches.²² The debate and discussion enjoyed between teaching faculty and undergraduate and postgraduate students is also likely to fertilise ideas and enrich research, the PhD being the linchpin of that philosophy. Humboldt believed that academics should have the freedom of self-determination and should base teaching on evidence and not dogma. The university which he created in Berlin (now the Humboldt University of Berlin) became the model embraced by many of the emerging educational powerhouses of the US, such as Johns Hopkins and Yale. It differed dramatically from the Grandes Écoles of France, where conformity and elitism prevailed.

The evidence that research academics do a better job of teaching than those solely dedicated to teaching is less convincing. It is suggested that high-quality teaching may be as effectively delivered by teaching-only academics as by those who also undertake research.²³ It is not difficult to imagine that those who have chosen to dedicate themselves to teaching only may have self-selected for that route by dint of their own abilities and may dedicate more energy to doing so. Nevertheless, those academics who do research are likely to be able to enliven a topic by lived example, may be closer to the most up-to-date information and may have honed the skills of critical thinking and problem-solving, which are likely to enhance the employability of their students – assuming their teachers have the skills to impart

---

21 K. Mueller-Vollmer and M. Messling, 'Wilhelm von Humboldt', in E.N. Zalta (ed.), *The Stanford Encyclopaedia of Philosophy* (summer 2022 edn).
22 K. Coate, R. Barnet and G. Williams, 'Relationships Between Teaching and Research in Higher Education in England', *Higher Education Quarterly*, 55/2 (2001), pp. 158–74, <https://onlinelibrary.wiley.com/doi/abs/10.1111/1468-2273.00180>.
23 J. Hattie and H. Marsh, 'The Relationship between Research and Teaching: A Meta-Analysis', *Review of Educational Research*, 66/4 (1996), pp. 507–42; M. Tight, 'Examining the Research/Teaching Nexus', *European Journal of Higher Education*, 6/4 (2016), pp. 293–311, <https://doi.org/10.1080/21568235.2016.1224674>.

their knowledge and attributes. It is likely that those who undertake research themselves will enhance the practical elements of laboratory work and encourage and support the final-year research project which is a core element of many UK science bachelors' programmes. Fung suggested that more active connection of the educational curriculum with the research carried out in our universities could have a transformational impact on teaching and learning.[24] Of course, the academic who believes that to teach students simply interferes with their critically important research programme is unlikely to teach well and should not be tolerated where the academic role embraces both teaching and research. Currently in the UK approximately one third of academics are purely teachers, while about a quarter only do research, the remainder do both teaching and research.[25]

While the number (or percentage) of academic staff doing research alone has stayed relatively constant since 2010, the percentage doing both teaching and research has fallen by about 10%, and the number doing teaching only has increased by an equivalent amount (see Table 7.1).[26] In a review of the relationship between teaching and research in UK universities, Dandridge suggested that the various pressures imposed on teaching and research activities could widen the divide further, with the possibility of complete separation not 'entirely fanciful'.[27] She concludes that the growing divide does matter: fewer students will benefit from exposure to research activity and the career progression and academic identity of staff may be negatively impacted. Added to that, less coherent government policies in higher education may emerge, universities may be less able to support national priorities

---

24  D. Fung, *A Connected Curriculum for Higher Education* (London, 2017).
25  Higher Education Statistics Agency (HESA), 'Higher Education Student Statistics: UK, 2020/21', <hesa.ac.uk/news/01-02-2022/sb261-higher-education-staff-statistics>.
26  C. Whitchurch, 'The Changing Profile and Work Experiences of Higher Education Staff in the 21st Century', in Carasso (ed.), *UK Higher Education*.
27  N. Dandridge, 'The Relationship between Teaching and Research in UK Universities – What is it and does it Matter?', HEPI report 162, July 2023.

and industrial strategies, the reputational dynamic of the sector based on an integrated approach to teaching and research could be damaged and, perhaps most importantly, students may be misled. Students, or prospective students, base their choice of university on its reputation, often linked to research intensity, with more research-intensive universities attracting higher-tariff students (that is, students with higher school exam grades). If the education in those universities is not based on an integrated education–research approach, then the choice may be based on inaccurate assumptions.

Table 7.1
Academic staff activity profile.

|  | 2010/11 | | 2021/22 | | % Change |
| --- | --- | --- | --- | --- | --- |
|  | No | % | No | % |  |
| Teaching-only | 45,005 | 24.8 | 81,020 | 34.6 | +9.8 |
| Teaching and Research | 94,760 | 52.3 | 100,160 | 42.8 | -9.5 |
| Research-only | 40,740 | 22.3 | 51,005 | 21.8 | -0.5 |

Source: Data taken from C. Whitchurch, 'The Changing Profile and Work Experiences of Higher Education Staff in the 21st Century', in Carasso (ed.), UK Higher Education.

## Culture

It is undeniable that research into history, music, the arts and philosophy contribute to the culture and indeed civilisation of our societies. Research in the arts and humanities enrich our understanding of historic events and civilisation, and help us wrestle with uncertainties of religion and morality. Research helps us interpret art and literature, and dissects and interrogates the law and justice system. The importance of research into history can be gauged by the popularity of televised history programmes and the cult status of those who present them. Our insatiable appetite for history books and historical fiction confirms the interest which we have in past events, and it is research into these events which allows us to reinterpret them to provide greater clarity and understanding. The joy of cultural experience should not be underestimated within the overall fabric of society and should demand the resource to support it. Enjoyment apart, the impact in economic and employment terms of the arts in film, stage and media substantially justifies the research investments made. The UK film industry in 2010 directly employed 36,000 people and supported 100,100 jobs through supply chains, and in 2009 it contributed £4.5 billion to UK GDP and £1.2 billion to the exchequer by way of taxation.[28] Since then, it has contributed to a growth in the creative industries of four times the rate of the rest of the economy and the creative industries are now estimated to contribute £115.9 billion in Gross Value Added (GVA) to the UK economy.[29] Those with a history degree also contribute to the economy in a substantial way – ranking fourth in the list of degree-holders who lead as CEOs in businesses and institutions in the UK.[30]

## Global warming

Perhaps the most urgent and important research currently being undertaken relates to global warming. It is research that has provided the evidence that the planet is warming more rapidly than might be expected from natural temperature fluctuations and that it is people who are the cause.[31] It is the increased, human-associated, carbon dioxide and other gas production which is trapping more heat in the atmosphere and warming our oceans and lands.[32] Research is also telling us that the impact of global warming will be generally bad for the planet:

---

28 'The Economic Impact of the UK Film Industry', *Oxford Economics*, 2010, <www.oxfordeconomics.com>.
29 UUK, *Our Universities*.
30 A. Fennell, 'Average Graduate Salary UK', 2022, <https://standout-cv.com/average-graduate-salary-uk>.
31 Intergovernmental Panel on Climate Change, *Technical Summary* (Cambridge, 2021), pp. 33–144, <https://doi.org/10.1017/9781009157896.002>.
32 NASA, 'Global Climate Change: Vital Signs of the Planet', NASA's Jet Propulsion Laboratory, California Institute of Technology, 2022, <climate.nasa.gov/evidence/>.

oceans are getting warmer and more acidic, and sea levels are rising. Ice sheets and glaciers are shrinking, and extreme weather events are increasing in frequency. Global temperature rises were first recognised by Guy Callendar in 1938, compiling temperature measurements which he compared with those from historical records. He proposed that the increase could be explained by rising atmospheric carbon dioxide concentrations.[33] A more accurate instrument to measure carbon dioxide was developed by Charles David Keeling and used by him to record atmosphere carbon dioxide concentration 3000 metres above sea level on Mauna Loa in Hawaii. His data showed seasonal variation, but a steady annual increase, subsequently known as the Keeling Curve.[34] Many people have refused to believe the evidence that climate change is happening or have chosen to believe that its impact will be benign. The climate-change deniers are generally those benefitting from processes which produce greenhouse gases, or more generally the population for whom addressing the issues will require uncomfortable behavioural change. It is because of the direct interest of very powerful industries that the evidence for climate change and its likely impacts has had to be compelling. It is also research which provides the only realistic opportunities to arrest global warming. Useful solar cells were first produced by scientists at Bell Laboratories in New Jersey[35], utilising silicone with gallium impurities dipped in lithium. With some refinement, this system was about 6% efficient at converting sunlight into electricity. This has been improved to almost 30% efficiency by Oxford PV, a spin-out company from the University of Oxford. The ability to store electrical energy efficiently has been greatly enhanced

---

33   G.S. Callendar, 'The Artificial Production of Carbon Dioxide and its Influence on Temperature', *Quarterly Journal of the Royal Meteorological Society*, 64 (1938), <https://doi.org/10.1002/qj.49706427503>.
34   C.D. Keeling, 'The Concentration and Isotopic Abundances of Carbon Dioxide in the Atmosphere', *Tellus*, 12/2 (1960), pp. 200–2023.
35   D.M. Chapin, C.S. Fuller and G.L. Pearson, 'A New Silicon p-n Junction Photocell for Converting Solar Radiation into Electrical Power', *Journal of Applied Physics*, 25 (1954), pp. 676–7.

by the development of the rechargeable lithium battery.[36] Battery technology will continue to improve as new anodes, cathodes and electrolytes are utilised, and these will enhance the development of electric cars and other forms of transport, including aviation. Novel LED bulbs, insulation for houses, net-zero livestock production and many other energy-saving (or reduced-gas-emitting) systems have been the product of research, as have more sustainable methods of energy generation from light, wind and nuclear sources. Research will also provide the incentives for behavioural change, encouraging recycling and more efficient work and transport options. It is evident to all that without research the planet has absolutely no chance of supporting a steady-state population (whereby numbers of births and deaths are in balance), predicted to be above 11 billion by about 2100, in a sustainable and harmonious way.

## Communication

Research which has led to increased quantum, speed and complexity of communication has impacted and enhanced almost all other research. The evolution of language was not dependent on research, although the translation and interpretation of contemporary and historic, sometimes forgotten, languages has been, and research into people-movements and fluxes in civilisations has undoubtedly been enriched by the study of the evolution of language. The invention of the (efficient) printing press in about 1440 by Johannes Gutenberg has been credited with democratising knowledge. From that time onwards it became substantially easier to transport knowledge to people rather than necessarily have people travel to knowledge (in universities or libraries). It is also broadly true that since the invention of printing and the efficient replication of the written word, most other forms of communication have simply speeded up and extended transmission

---

36  G. Bruce, 'Rechargeable Lithium Batteries', *Philosophical Transactions of the Royal Society A* (1996), <https://doi.org/10.1098/rsta.1996.0066>.

(telegraph, telephone and radio) rather than increasing the quantum of knowledge, although television has added visual content, and the internet and virtual-conferencing platforms have permitted interaction and extended 'receive only' communication to dialogue and one-to-many engagement. Computer search engines have made the retrieval and interrogation of the majority of the world's knowledge simple and instantaneous. The ability to create and disseminate content is not universally good, since much inaccurate and untrue information is as easily accessed as that which is reliable. Our communication can also be accessed and utilised in more unwelcome ways, thus the receipt of unsolicited adverts on topics likely to spark our interest based on content algorithms from previous innocent communication. Nevertheless, since research is by its nature generally incremental, built on previous research and knowledge, the dissemination of and access to knowledge has quickened the pace of research. It is also likely that the available spectrum of knowledge has enhanced a researcher's ability to make connections, has improved collaborations and broken disciplinary boundaries. The contribution which communication has made to research has been truly profound.

## Unwelcome outcomes of research

Research in each of the areas considered above is undoubtedly a good thing, but research has also been utilised in more sinister ways. Our ability to kill each other by conventional, nuclear, biological and chemical arms has improved spectacularly, indeed to the point that we could undoubtedly destroy our entire planet. Research has enhanced our ability to commit fraud and cyber-attack, and many of the by-products of research are now recognised to cause harm, such as plastics, chemicals and other pollutants. The unintended consequences of social media on individuals' self-esteem and mental health, and the potential for artificial intelligence such as ChatGPT to facilitate cheating and deception are all causes for concern. Nevertheless, it is likely that, for many of these unwanted outcomes, it will be further research which either addresses the problem or allows us to live in greater harmony with it.

## Research facilities

There are, though, perennial questions about the best way to do research. Research is carried out in the public and private sectors. In most countries where universities are considered part of the public sector and receive substantial support from the state, they are often a substantial focus of research activity. Where there are private-sector universities, they may also be able to bid for public-sector research funding. In many countries, public-sector research institutes have evolved independent of universities. The private sector also carries out substantive amounts of research and can do so in-house or may contract or partner with universities or institutes to do the work. There is little objective data to determine whether public-sector research is more effectively done in a university or in a research institute, both types of facility may receive core and competitive funding. Universities have the advantage that they can cross-subsidise from teaching activity to research, and in the UK across the whole higher-education sector that cross-subsidy amounts to about 32% of the total cost. In other words, for competitive funding the funder is on average only paying 68% of the full economic cost.[37] Universities also have the advantage that academics who do both teaching and research may still contribute to the economic viability of the university through their teaching activity during fallow periods of research funding. Those working in research institutes do not have this flexibility and may be required to have a more consistent stream of competitive income to fill any gaps between core income and the full cost of the institution. On the other hand, those working in institutes are able to direct a hundred

---

37   UKRI, 'Costs you can apply for, Principles of full economic costings (fEC)', 17 August 2021, <https://www.ukri.org/councils/epsrc/guidance-for-applicants/costs-you-can-apply-for/>.

percent of their time and energy to research and are not encumbered with the requirement to teach undergraduates. In the UK, research institutes emerged in the first quarter of the twentieth century, mostly to support and enhance the agricultural sector. As such they largely undertook directed applied research with specific targets which in the inter- and post-war eras most often related to increased agricultural productivity. They were notably successful in this, discovering new vaccines for animal health, methods of controlling crop disease and increased meat, milk and crop production. Unfortunately, as post-war agricultural production grew (partly also in response to subsidy) and butter mountains and milk lakes hit the headlines, the political will to support the institutes wilted. Furthermore, research staff were employed on civil-service terms and conditions, which made these workers inflexible to change and the institutional infrastructures were also unsuited to change of purpose. Only those institutes which could fulfil a national requirement, such as disease control, have survived. Some have amalgamated or, more often, been absorbed into universities.

In the UK, the last decade has seen the establishment of a number of highly prestigious research institutes with specific remits. The Francis Crick Institute is a biomedical research institute, supported by Cancer Research, the Medical Research Council and the Wellcome Trust, and by three of London's largest research-intensive universities, Imperial College London, Kings College and University College London. The Alan Turing Institute is also located in London, in the British Library, and is the national institute for data science and artificial intelligence. The Henry Royce Institute, located within the University of Manchester, undertakes advanced materials research and the Rosalind Franklin Institute, situated on the Harwell Science and Innovation Campus in Oxfordshire, undertakes medical research. Other institutes and Public Sector Research Establishments (PSREs) have emerged in the UK in a rather ad hoc fashion and with great diversity of shape and mission. The Medical Research Council's Laboratory of Molecular Biology (LMB), for example, has been notably successful both in nurturing exceptional scientists (twelve Nobel Prize winners) and in collaborations with industry partners, and is one of fifty such institutes throughout the UK. The PSREs are sponsored by government departments and do essential work such as the climate and weather science carried out by the Met Office.[38] Many of the research institutes and PSREs struggle with core funding allocations, often restricted in the competitive funding for which they can apply and burdened by rather inflexible government employment contracts.

The German model of institutes has been much more successful. They undertake a much broader range of research activity and command a much larger core budget. There are 83 Max Planck Institutes which largely undertake basic research into natural, biological and social sciences and the humanities. These are complemented by Fraunhofer Institutes, which undertake applied research and by Leibniz and Helmholtz Institutes, which carry out research on a broad range of topics from the humanities to mathematics. The success of the German institutes no doubt relates to the continued demand for, and interest in, the subjects being investigated and their research culture, but also to the fact that both the Max Planck and Fraunhofer Institutes collectively receive core funding in the region of €2 billion annually. There is a view that the German education system has more technical and applied teaching and training which may account for Germany's good productivity and economy. It should be noted, though, that it also produces more PhDs than the UK (many from its institutes) and they may make as substantial an impact as those with lower-level skills.

It is of interest to note that in the UK some universities have created 'institutes' within their own structures which are dedicated to

---

38  P. Nurse, 'Independent Review of the UK's Research, Development and Innovation Organisational Landscape', March 2023, <https://www.gov.uk/government/publications/research-development-and-innovation-organisational-landscape-an-independent-review>.

specific topical research areas and in which the academic researchers have a light or non-existent teaching load. There is some rationale to this model since it benefits from the operational infrastructure (HR, finance, estate management etc.) and can utilise some of the essential building and facility requirements such as libraries, refectories and sports facilities of the university. These institutes have to be managed carefully to ensure that the associated academics attract sufficient competitive research funding to make them financially sustainable and that the universities' promotion policies do not weight research outputs disproportionately and therefore advantage those who do not contribute to the educational experience.

Research is also undertaken by the private sector, often in excellent facilities, and of course industry and business can often attract excellent researchers with more generous remuneration packages than the public sector. Annually in the UK, businesses spend about £44 billion, whereas universities spend about £13.9 billion and government (mainly in PSRBs) £3.1 billion on research, making the private sector substantially the biggest investor in research.[39] Businesses which invest most in R&D are likely to generate novel products and create new and efficient processes which will make them highly competitive. Government may encourage these R&D investments by offering tax relief for such activity and by offering funding for collaborative research with universities or public-sector institutes. In the UK, government has initiated schemes such as the Catapult scheme in topical areas including biotechnology, energy and agricultural technology, to encourage industry to engage with universities and thus to enhance innovation.

There are some research projects for which the infrastructure costs and uncertainty of outcome are well beyond the resources or likely return on investment of either universities or business. For these, national and even international facilities and programmes

---
39  Ibid.

with massive infrastructure costs have been supported. The Diamond Light Source at the Rutherford Appleton laboratories at Harwell in Oxfordshire is the UK's national particle accelerator. The UK's research in subatomic particles is further supported by access to the Large Hadron Collider, which is a 27-kilometre loop located at CERN (Conseil Européen pour la Recherche Nucléaire) near Geneva in Switzerland and is an international collaborative project to research matter itself. The Square Kilometre Array, which comprises clusters of radio telescopes in Australia and South Africa and, despite its name, has thousands of small antennas spread over several thousand kilometres (the name refers to its total collecting area of approximately one kilometre), has its headquarters at Jodrell Bank in the UK, and will substantially enhance our ability to look into space and understand the universe. It will be fifty times more sensitive than other radio telescopes and will be able to survey space more than ten thousand times further than before.

The discoveries of the Large Hadron Collider at subatomic-particle level and those of the Square Kilometre Array extending to the boundaries of the universe may have profound implications for mankind or may simply enrich our knowledge and understanding for our joy and wonderment.

The different ways of organising research each have advantages and disadvantages, and, like universities themselves, the diversity of the organisations brings value to the whole. The important thing is to ensure that each system operates efficiently and effectively and is appropriately resourced to produce excellent research.

## Measurement of research

Measurement of the amount and quality of research output is somewhat complicated by different subjective views of what comprises quality. For some research, such as that relating to pharmaceutical products to be used in medicines, a guarantee that what is reported is an accurate reflection of what has been done is essential. In order to quality-assure the process, good laboratory or clinical practice (GLP or GCP) should be adhered to and is a general requirement of most drug-regulating authorities.[40] Studies must be carried out to GLP to demonstrate the safety or efficacy of a drug, and while some may be fascinating many are done purely to confirm whether the drug is safe and effective – indeed a negative finding in a safety study is generally a good thing. Studies of this type are unlikely to be highly ranked by those looking for paradigm shifts in understanding and knowledge.

For research academics and students working in a university, citation metrics have become a proxy for quality of output on the basis that if many of your peers are citing your work it is likely that they consider it important. There are now a large number of citation metrics, utilising different publication data sets including Impact Factors produced by Journal Citation Reports (Clarivate Analytics), Source Normalised Impact per Paper (SNIP, from Scopus, Elsevier) and the Hirsch-Index (H-Index, multiple databases) which measures citation and the productivity of a scholar. Citation metrics are now often provided by research academics when applying for research positions and used by the selecting committee. While useful, these metrics need to be contextualised against the size of the pool of researchers working in that particular area of study and therefore the commensurate scale of opportunity to be cited. Where recruitment or promotion decisions are being made, the use of publication metrics and journal titles (by way of prestige) are discouraged and Impact Factors specifically excluded as proxies for quality assessment by the San Francisco Declaration on Research Assessment (DORA).[41] The declaration advocates a basket of indicators as part of a contextual

---

40  OECD, 'Good Laboratory Practice (GLP)', 2022, <https://www.oecd.org/chemicalsafety/testing/good-laboratory-practiceglp.htm>.
41  The San Francisco Declaration on Research Assessment (DORA), 2012, <https://sfdora.org/read/>.

assessment of research quality and has been embraced by 2500 organisations in 158 countries.

At a national level, the UK has led research quality assessments through its Research Excellence Framework (REF, originally called the Research Assessment Exercise [RAE]). This has now been carried out at 5-to-7-year intervals since 1986. Universities submit a package of outputs relating to research and the research environment (usually papers or monographs, plus details of competitive research funding, PhDs completed etc.) and also, in its most recent iterations, the impact of research (usually based on case studies) which is judged by committees of peers in subject-relevant units of assessment. The 2021 REF saw 157 universities submit more than 185,000 research outputs, produced by 76,000 academic staff. Of these, 41% were judged to be world-leading, 43% internationally excellent, with 16% either internationally or nationally 'recognised'. Proponents of the REF can point to the ongoing and improving success of the UK in world rankings of research excellence. The field-weighted citation indices (where 1.0 is the world average) of publications from UK researchers rank highly by international standards (UK 1.44–1.78, US 1.27–1.58). Its critics highlight the expense and bureaucracy of the process and suggest that a purely metric-driven exercise would produce much the same ranking (for discipline areas and for universities overall) at much less cost.

The REF was estimated to have cost £66 million in 2008 and £246 million in 2014 and, although substantial, the 2014 cost reflects less than 1% of the public funding invested in research and compares well with other mechanisms of allocation (research council allocations attract about 13% overhead costs). It is perhaps of interest that few, if any, other countries have replicated the UK and undertaken their own REFs, although with the improving accuracy and wider acceptance of the available metrics, it is possible that these will be utilised for the purpose in the future by the UK and others. Throughout the world, research outputs (if measured by publication) have grown by

178%, from 1.3 million to 3.7 million individual publications between 2002 and 2022, fuelled in particular by a growth in publications from China. The UK's share of world publication outputs between 2002 and 2022 has actually dropped by about 18%, despite a healthy growth in absolute numbers from 97,000 to 219,000, and this can be attributed to the even more spectacular growth elsewhere. Perhaps of greater significance for the UK is that its share of the most highly cited publications (i.e. the top 10%) grew from 15.8% in 2002 to 17.6% in 2022.[42]

## Competition

The REF in the UK is undoubtedly a competition. It ranks subjects and universities by quality and quantity of research and informs the institutional allocation of research funding (QR). The reputational impact of the REF is probably just as important as its financial impact. Research academics seek positions in high-ranking universities and the REF outcomes feed into many of the university league tables (thus perpetuating the high rank of many research-intensive universities). It is of interest that, despite the introduction of the Teaching Excellence Framework (see Chapter 4), those universities which do well in the REF continue to attract the largest number of UK undergraduate student applications. Whether this is associated with league tables or legacy reputation is unclear, but research quality is clearly attractive to prospective students. For younger or early career researchers, the competitive pressures of the REF could cause them to prioritise quantity over quality, scrambling to publish where perhaps greater breadth or depth to a piece of work would enhance its impact and their reputation in the longer term. A change in the number of required outputs in the 2021 iteration of the REF, prioritising quality, may have helped address this concern. Undoubtedly the pressures brought by research competition on institutions drive their recruitment practises, with the REF-ability of potential appointees a highly influential factor.

---

42  Carasso and Plume, 'To Measure is to Know'.

## Research concentration

It has been suggested, by a committee of the Department for Education and by Byrne and Clarke, that, in the UK, research funding should be concentrated on a select number of more research-intensive universities (the top sixty has been proposed) which should be characterised as such, in the belief that research funding might be more productively used by these institutions.[43] Apart from the obvious anti-competitive nature of this approach, there are some compelling arguments against it. Firstly, in the REFs, upon which such judgement would be made, all research is judged in the same way – a piece of research from any university considered world-leading would be so, even if from a university of more modest research scale, and since quality takes primacy over quantity in research currency, that research would justify its contribution. Secondly, over the last three cycles of the REF – i.e. since 2001 – eighteen institutions have moved over the arbitrary boundary proposed, that is, into or out of the top sixty. This very much suggests that the competitive process is working: those acquiring and producing excellence are moving up the league table, and those that are not are falling back. Thirdly, the universities in England (not specialist institutions) which fall below the top sixty and which submitted to the REF 2021, comprise fifty-five universities which received a total of £213 million in QR funding (the quality-related funding distributed as a consequence of the REF outcomes) which is just 1.3 times the QR funding received by Oxford alone. It seems a relatively marginal amount of the overall funding package to retain a competitive system which is fair to all universities. It is debatable whether the £213 million of funding would have greater impact spread over the current 'fat cats' of research intensity or shared between the 'hungry minnows' fighting to improve. Byrne and Clark also make the controversial suggestion that the quality researchers from the

---

43   Education and Skills Committee, *The Future of Higher Education*; Byrne and Clarke, *The University Challenge*.

'non-research-intensive' universities (i.e. those not in the top sixty) are simply transferred into research-intensive institutions, which fails to recognise or reward the support and encouragement required by the originating universities that have nurtured the research success of these academics.[44] Indeed, it does the opposite, penalising those institutions for their efforts. The authors themselves recognise the personal satisfaction and professional pride which academics acquire by their research efforts but fail to realise or acknowledge that they would be denying that opportunity to more than half the academic community by their proposals. In a sector where diversity of mission and institutional character should be celebrated, and where that diversity has been achieved by evolution within a system of equal opportunity, it would be misguided and inequitable to favour institutions with such recommendations, particularly when some of those being favoured have had an 800-year head start in the race. The DfE recommendations resulted in the establishment of a forum[45], chaired by the then Vice-Chancellor of the University of London, Sir Graeme Davies, which in 2004 rejected the recommendations on the basis that research and teaching were 'essential and intertwined' characteristics of a university.[46]

## Research funding

Global spend on research has increased as a percentage of GDP. Spending remained fairly constant at about 2% of GDP from 1996 up until 2012, but since then has increased up to about 2.6% in 2020.[47] This was substantially influenced by a large spend in North America (3.32% 2020) and the EU (2.32% 2020), and for OECD members – 38

---

44  Byrne and Clarke, *The University Challenge*.
45  Education and Skills Committee, *The Future of Higher Education*
46  A. Fazackerley, 'Research Linked to Teaching – Official', *Times Higher Education*, 19 Nov 2004; Dandridge, 'The Relationship between Teaching and Research'.
47  UNESCO Institute for Statistics (UIS) Stat Bulk Download Service, 2022, <apiportal.UIS.UNESCO.org/bolds>.

relatively developed countries which promote economic growth and free markets – was 2.96% (2020). The UK lagged substantially behind with a spend of 1.71% in 2019, but government has since set a target of 2.4% for R&D spend in the UK. While the figures for the UK may be an underestimate associated with the method of calculation, they still leave the UK well behind the leaders in research spend.[48] The GDP spend on R&D includes private-sector spend by business and industry which also lags behind our major competitors. The UK has historically failed to reach R&D spending targets, although this is not a failing peculiar to the UK. Many countries appear to embrace unmet optimism in setting R&D policy targets which are often missed.[49] Although encouraging industry to increase spend on R&D is likely to help progress towards the UK's 2.4% target, it is unlikely that industry-based research will reach that target without the human capital (PhD graduates) required to do the research, which are a major output of university research.[50] It is important to note that the 2.4% target was set when old methodology was used to calculate the quantum. Using newer methodology, the target has already been met, but by way of example the £38.5 billion spending in 2019 using old methods is equivalent to £59.7 billion using new methods.[51] The Labour government, which came to power in the UK in 2024, has had a long-term proposed target of 3% of GDP as spend on research, and has proposed much longer-term funding of up to 10 years for some research institutions. While the detail around these proposals is light, the intention is sound and would address some of the funding issues

---

48 Nurse, 'Independent Review'.
49 A. Carvalho, 'Wishful Thinking about R&D Policy Targets: What Governments Promise and What They Actually Deliver', *Science and Public Policy*, 45/3 (2018), pp. 373–91, <https://doi.org/10.1093/scipol/scx069>.
50 Van de Noort in the foreword to N. Hillman, 'From T to R Revisited: Cross-subsidies from Teaching to Research after Augar and the 2.4% R&D Target', HEPI report 127, 9 March 2020, <https://www.hepi.ac.uk/wp-content/uploads/2020/03/From-T-to-R-revisited.pdf>.
51 A. Panjwani, 'Research and Development Spending', House of Commons Library, 11 Sept 2023, <https://commonslibrary.parliament.uk/research-briefings/sn04223/>.

for institutes outlined previously. Whether it will extend to university funding remains to be seen.

Within universities across the UK the total spend on research amounts to about £12.2 billion (this figure has recently been uplifted to £13.9 billion, following corrections to the methodology and inclusion of increased spend of self-generated income by universities[52]). Of this spend, about £8.5 billion comes from external research-specific funding, of which £1.7 billion is received in the form of QR funding, allocated on a formulaic basis as a result of the REF exercise and not assigned to specific projects. The remainder comes from competitive funding from government (largely allocated by UKRI) and from other national and supranational organisations (e.g. the EU) and from industry-sponsored research. The deficit on research spend (roughly £3.7 billion based on the older calculations of £12.2 billion spend) is a consequence of incomplete cost recovery on research projects, which range from about 15% recovery for institution-funded research to 74% for industry-sponsored research and amounts to about 68% recovery overall (see Figure 7.1).[53] It is likely that these deficits arise for two reasons. Firstly, that universities are prepared to cross-subsidise from other income streams into research in order to boost their reputation, and therefore submit unrealistically low-cost bids in order to win research contracts. Secondly, that the sponsors impose unrealistic ceilings on funding, in the knowledge that universities will accept lower income to undertake research.

Universities with rich endowments may be able to offset some of the deficit with these funds, but the vast majority sustain their research activity by cross-subsidy from teaching.[54] This has become increasingly difficult since universities have received flat funding

---

52  Nurse, 'Independent Review'.
53  Hillman, 'From T to R revisited'; UUK, *Sustainable University Funding: Why it's Important and What is Needed* (London 2023).
54  See OfS, Transparent Approach to Costing (TRAC), published data 2020-21, <officeforstudents.org.uk/data-and-analysis/trac-data/published-data-2020-21/>.

Figure 7.1
Recovery of full economic cost for research by sponsor type, UK higher education institutions (2021–22).

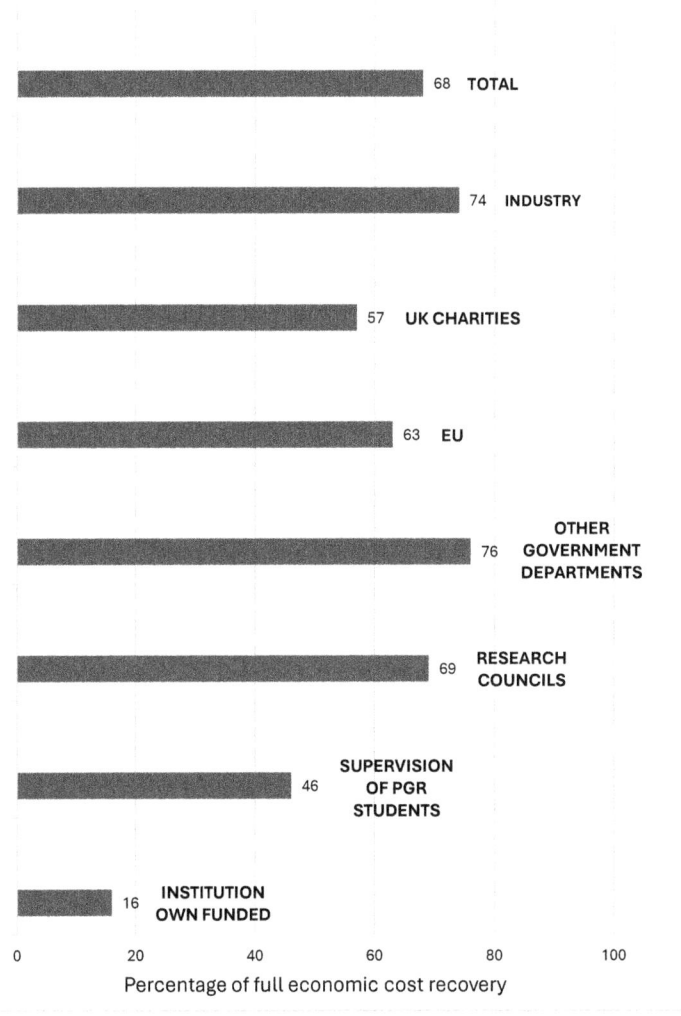

Source: OfS, Transparent Approach to Costing (TRAC), published data 2021–22, <officeforstudents.org.uk/data-and-analysis/trac-data/published-data-2021-22/>.

on UK (and historically EU) tuition fees since 2012 (with one modest uplift of £250 in 2017). The result is that there is also a deficit on the cost it takes to educate UK students estimated to amount to about 1.8% (or £234 million) in 2017/18. In the same year there was a surplus on international student fees of about 28.2% (£1.4 billion of the £4.9 billion received in international student fees[55]). That the majority of cross-subsidy to support research comes from surpluses created on international tuition fees is undeniable, and it is likely that the subsidy has grown since 2017/18 since home student fees have remained static and international student numbers have grown. The cross-subsidy can be justified in three ways: firstly, it is supporting a research base which enhances the reputation – and possibly also the quality of the teaching (see above) in the universities to which the students go.[56] Secondly, it is making a contribution to historic infrastructure costs in universities funded by the UK taxpayer. Finally, it is a free market and international students can choose to go where they anticipate the greatest return (employment or work-based gain) on their investment. By the same token, UK universities can charge what the market will bear. This of course makes the acquisition and treatment of international students vitally important to the UK research base, not to mention the significant contribution that they make to the educational environment, soft power and global human capital outlined in subsequent chapters. Government decisions which have had a negative impact on international student recruitment thus fail to consider their specific and broader contribution.

The evolution of research and the global infrastructure for its conduct mean that it is now electric in pace and unimaginable in breadth and depth. The discoveries made through research have conferred better health and longer lives on human beings. Research has improved living standards and brought joy and wonderment

---
55  Hillman, 'From T to R revisited'.
56  See also Dandridge, 'The Relationship between Teaching and Research'.

through knowledge and understanding. It undoubtedly has brought the potential for planetary destruction, either through terrible weapons or environmental catastrophe. Nevertheless, it is only through research that we have recognised the environmental precipice on which we stand, and only through research that we will develop the products and encourage the behaviours which will avert disaster and allow man and nature to live in harmony.

# CHAPTER 8

# Innovation and Entrepreneurship: Business Engagement

Whether universities should focus their energies on the development of the thinking process, expansion of knowledge and encouragement of criticality in their students and should research into the broad workings of the universe, or whether their teachings and research should confer 'employability', support enterprise and produce useful things, has been hotly debated. Both approaches are beneficial to society and indeed each contributes to the other. Historically the teaching of medicine, law and other vocational courses has had to embrace a more utilitarian approach, and much of early research, or at least discovery, led to useful things: irrigation systems, new plant varieties and so on. Nevertheless, the increasingly focused attention of higher education on enterprise, innovation and entrepreneurship, and the assessment of research impact and business engagement by universities, have become more broadly accepted as core mission, and indeed are now encouraged by government policies in many countries. Government enthusiasm for enterprising and entrepreneurial graduates is no doubt galvanised by the knowledge that graduates are likely to start and enhance businesses which contribute to the economy. The broader support of governments for university-led business engagement and collaboration will be motivated by a vision of enhanced productivity and increased prosperity. Universities benefit by delivering popular courses, sharing equity in start-up companies and receiving financial support from businesses to research new products and improve processes which enhance productivity and profit.

The creation, interrogation and dissemination of knowledge out of sheer intellectual curiosity has inherent value. It provides a deeper understanding of the universe, contributes to human wonderment and forms the basis of civilisation. It was deemed sufficient purpose for education by Aristotle and more recently by John Henry Newman, who promoted reason and reflection as part of a liberal education.[1] The apparent decadence of this approach to education, particularly at the start of the nineteenth century, was soundly criticised by the historian Correlli Barnett, who suggested that it created generations of 'idealistic young men who emerged in a state of permanently arrested development, their minds befuddled by cricket, Christianity, and the classics'.[2] There is a strong argument for education which is useful, which supports graduates getting jobs, enhancing productivity and establishing their own businesses. High-growth businesses have a high proportion of graduate employees and increasing numbers of employees with advanced degrees[3], whilst businesses with fewer graduates tend to have lower productivity.[4] At a national scale, countries

---

1 J.H. Newman, *The Idea of a University*, ed. F. Turner (1852; New Haven, CT, 1996).
2 C. Barnett, *The Audit of War: The Illusion and Reality of Britain as a Great Nation* (London, 1986).
3 C. Volkmann, K.E. Wilson, S. Mariotti, D. Rabuzzi, S. Vyakarnam and A. Sepulveda, 'Educating the Next Wave of Entrepreneurs: Unlocking Entrepreneurial Capabilities to Meet the Global Challenges of the 21st Century', A Report of the Global Education Initiative for the World Economic Forum, Switzerland, April 2009, <https://papers.ssrn.com/sol3/papers.cfm?abstract_id=1396704>.
4 V. Wadhwa, R. Aggarwal, K. Holly and A. Salkever, 'The Anatomy of an Entrepreneur: Making of a Successful Entrepreneur', Kauffman Foundation Small Research Projects research paper 2, 17 November 2009, <http://dx.doi.org/10.2139/ssrn.1507384>.

which invest more in higher education tend to have higher productivity and stronger economies, and although this correlation does not prove cause and effect it is sufficiently consistent to be persuasive (see Chapter 7).

The contribution of their graduates to human capital is almost certainly the largest impact which all universities make to the economy. Over and above this impact in the UK, 90% of the 2.6 million new jobs added to the economy between 2008–18 required university or equivalent education and in 2021/22 graduate vacancies increased by 22%, indicating a growth in the graduate job market.[5] Universities also contribute directly. Research discoveries may bring economic benefit by the creation of new products or processes, and universities are becoming more adept at recognising the potential of research discovery, and at subsequently protecting and exploiting it. Some research which is carried out has a specific product-development objective, but for much it is an unintended, if welcome, outcome. Universities now enter strategic relationships with businesses and receive funding to support their product or process development. Indeed, in the UK the government encourages this through the distribution of Higher Education Innovation Funding (HEIF) and support for Knowledge Exchange Partnerships (KEPs) and Knowledge Transfer Partnerships (KTPs). Academics are also encouraged to undertake and are rewarded for consultancy work, where their knowledge and skill may be of value to a business or industrial client.

## Enterprise and entrepreneurship

Subject competency is clearly an important outcome of a university education, perhaps most obviously in professional and vocational areas such as medicine, law and engineering. It is though not sufficient or each could be delivered by a traditional apprenticeship. In all subject areas a university education should also confer an ability

---

5   UUK, *Our Universities*.

to solve problems, think critically and imagine new ways of doing things. Graduates are between 20% and 40% more productive than those without degree-level education, and a 1% increase in graduate numbers in a business results in about 7.5% increased productivity within three years.[6] It is likely that the broader benefits of a university education contribute to the uplift in human capital, but it is also likely that more specific enterprise and entrepreneurial education can make an additional substantial contribution. Enterprise education will encourage individuals to show initiative, develop novel ideas and be resourceful. It can be, and probably should be, encouraged in almost every university discipline, and is an attribute which every graduate should have acquired. Enterprising individuals no doubt enhance the working environment, whatever that may be, they may also wish to start up their own businesses, although that need not be the prime objective of enterprise education. Fostering an enterprising mindset may be most effectively done through experiential activity, project work or dissertations. Focusing on improvement and innovation is likely to encourage longer-term behavioural or attitudinal changes. A more universal approach to enterprise education may be adopted by universities which include enterprise as a 'behaviour' which they embrace in their desirable graduate attributes.

Entrepreneurial education may encourage enterprise but goes substantially further, teaching specific skills and knowledge which might support and encourage an individual to start up their own business. Within an entrepreneurial programme, an individual might receive education in finance, human resources, leadership, strategy, business law and so on. A programme of entrepreneurial education may be an integrated part of a broader programme, for instance in a

---

6  S. Braguinsky and D.C. Rose, 'Competition, Cooperation, and the Neighbouring Farmer Effect', *Journal of Economic Behaviour and Organization*, 72/1 (2009), pp. 361–76; Ulster University Business Institute, 2019, <https://www.ulster.ac.uk/business/business-institute/services>.

business school, or may be a bolt-on module to other programmes or disciplines. Like enterprise education, it would benefit from experiential learning, but also lends itself to more conventional didactic and blended approaches.

The number of graduates starting their own businesses in the UK has grown substantially from 732 in 2002/03 to 10,956 by 2014/15. Moreover, an increasing number of these businesses are surviving for more than three years (323 in 2002/03 to 4474 by 2014/15). The contribution which these businesses make to the economy is substantial – it is young, growing businesses which generally account for growth in employment and of course which create wealth[7]; graduate entrepreneurs are twice as likely as non-graduates to become the high-value entrepreneurs who make the biggest impact on the economy.[8] For the individual entrepreneurs the benefit is also real: a graduate starting a business was likely to earn (pre-2017 earnings) on average £27,000 six months after graduating as compared to £24,000 for a graduate in employment and the differential persisted throughout at least the first three years after graduation.[9] Many universities now provide incubator facilities for their undergraduate and graduate entrepreneurs, often pump-prime their business with financial support and offer a range of other business-support facilities. This may be given by way of a grant to recipients, or, where a greater investment is made, may be dependent upon the university receiving some form of return, often by way of equity in a startup business.

---

7 B. Gilbert, P. McDougall and D. Audretsch, 'New Venture Growth: A Review and Extension', *Journal of Management*, 32/6 (2006), pp. 926–50, <https://doi.org/10.1177/0149206306293860>.
8 N. Broughton and K. Ussher, *Venturing Forth: Increasing High-value Entrepreneurship* (London, 2014).
9 Centre for Entrepreneurs, 'Putting the Uni in Unicorn: The Role of Universities in Supporting High-growth Graduate Startups', April 2017, <https://centreforentrepreneurs.org/wp-content/uploads/2017/08/CFE-University-Entrepreneurs-Report-WEB.pdf>.

## Business schools

Almost a fifth of all undergraduate students at UK universities study business and management and since the purpose of business schools is to deliver business education, they actively embrace enterprise and entrepreneurial education.[10] The number of business and management students has continued to grow, from 325,000 in 2016 to 530,460 in 2021/22, representing almost a fifth of the total student body, which has also grown.[11] The high-level entrepreneurship and leadership skills taught in business schools are associated with improved growth, turnover and productivity in business.[12] Some business schools have established centres for entrepreneurship which carry out research into entrepreneurship, which they undertake together with their education and business-engagement activity.[13] They may offer mentoring for alumni, together with opportunities for consultancies or work placements, and some have utilised government-funded voucher schemes to offer entrepreneurial teaching.[14] Perhaps unsurprisingly, the degrees which produce the most CEOs in the UK are Business Administration and Management, and while this is no doubt encouraged by the skills and knowledge gained while undertaking their degree in a business school, it is also likely to be influenced by the process of self-selection – those with an appetite or enthusiasm for business leadership select to do those educational programmes.[15] Business leaders and entrepreneurs are not the product of business schools alone, indeed

---

10  Chartered Association of Business Schools, 'Business Schools delivering Value to Local and Regional Economies', September 2016, <https://charteredabs.org/wp-content/uploads/2016/09/Chartered-ABS-Delivering-Value-Report-2.pdf>.
11  HESA, 'What Do HE Students Study?', 31 January 2023, <https://www.hesa.ac.uk/data-and-analysis/students/what-study>.
12  J. Hayton, 'Leadership and Management Skills in SMEs: Measuring Association with Management Practices and Performance', BIS research paper 224, March 2015, <https://assets.publishing.service.gov.uk/government/uploads/system/uploads/attachment_data/file/418404/bis-15-204-leadership-and-management-skills-in-sme.pdf>.
13  Strathclyde Business School, 2019, <https://www.strath.ac.uk/business/>.
14  Ulster University Business Institute, 2019.
15  Fennell, 'Average Graduate Salary UK'.

it is suggested that 59% of FTSE 100 companies and more than half of the UK's leading start-ups are led by graduates with social sciences, humanities or arts degrees and it is likely that the creativity associated with these degree programmes is particularly valuable in the business environment.[16]

## Incubators

Many universities now provide space and support for the start-up businesses of their undergraduate and graduate alumni. The spaces are most often offices, with relevant computer and other communication infrastructure, but can include laboratory space for product development. They often come with a range of support services from finance and human resources to more specific business advice and mentoring. Some fixed-duration support facilities, often with connections to investors, are termed 'accelerators' and the UK can boast about 400 incubators and 300 accelerators, as well as a number of programmes which don't fit comfortably into the precise definitions of either. Between them, these facilities support about 19,600 unique firms, or 5% of all new firms, each year.[17] Graduates tend to be somewhat more effective than undergraduates in starting a business but that is not surprising given that they have completed their undergraduate education and are able to dedicate all of their time and energies to their business, without the additional workload required to get a degree.[18]

In the UK, government funding such as HEIF has been used effectively to establish incubation units. The establishment of new

---

16  The British Academy, 'Shape Skills at Work', November 2022, <https://www.thebritishacademy.ac.uk/documents/4414/BA1096_SHAPE_SkillsAtWork_V8_Digital_Pages.pdf>.
17  Centre for Entrepreneurs, *Incubation Nation: The Acceleration of UK Startup Support* (London, 2022).
18  K. Hermann, 'Developing Entrepreneurial Graduates: Putting Entrepreneurship at the Centre of Higher Education', National Endowment for Science, Technology and the Arts (NESTA), 2008, <https://ncee.org.uk/wp-content/uploads/2018/01/developing_entrepreneurial_graduates.1.pdf>; Centre for Entrepreneurs, 'Putting the Uni in Unicorn'.

businesses in this way supports regional and national economies and, for the hosting university, may allow the acquisition of equity in the new business. It encourages engagement with and connection to the business community and also supports the employability and employment of their graduates. Creating a 'revolving door' between universities and business has supported more effective knowledge exchange.

### Degree apprenticeships

The UK has created a fully integrated business-university education programme by way of higher level (level 4 and above) and degree apprenticeships. The learners are employed as apprentices in a business and attend university or undertake education for at least 20% of their time. In fully integrated degree apprenticeships, the learners complete their end-point assessments and receive their degree award at the same time. These programmes offer the experiential learning which contributes effectively to their employability. They graduate without student loan debt and with a job. Nevertheless, the knowledge, skills and behaviours they are taught are aimed at employment and designed by employers and so may not be best suited to enterprise or entrepreneurship, where establishment of a new business might be the primary objective.

Apprenticeships are seen by many politicians as the answer to the UK's skills gap, and thus to productivity failings in British business. They refer to the German model, where apprenticeships are common and held in high esteem, and wish to replicate it in Britain. There is, no doubt, much we can learn from the German model, and indeed apprenticeships are a good thing. Nevertheless, it is well to consider that in addition to having more apprentices than the UK, Germany also has more PhDs, and the US, which normally ranks at about the top of the productivity rankings, is not renowned for its apprenticeships. The review of the UK's apprenticeship schemes in

2016/17 introduced a levy on large (more than £3 million salary bill) employers to fund the apprenticeships, the standards and assessment of which are designed by employer groups called Trailblazers. As with most workforce-planning schemes (in the broadest sense), apprenticeships did not evolve as government envisaged (with growth of level-3 and technical apprenticeships), and while there has been a decline in lower-level apprenticeships there has been a substantial increase in higher-level (level 4 and above) apprenticeships (a rise of 120% between 2017/18 and 2021/22). Those equivalent to MBAs (at level 7) were withdrawn by the Conservative government in 2021 because the 'wrong' people were doing them, and they were proving a remarkably popular way for businesses to upskill their senior executives. Historically, skills training programmes designed (or at least introduced) by government have had dismal outcomes: Youth Training Schemes (YTS) and the regulatory framework for National Vocational Qualifications (NVQs) have come and gone, despite fanfare and substantial government support in terms of rhetoric and resource. Wolf suggested that their failure owed much to their focus: young people wish to keep their job options open and also appreciate that the technology revolutions of the last four decades mean that training for a specific occupation which may disappear could be career-limiting.[19] Young people now see work in a more fluid way than previous generations, changing jobs in early life more frequently than was historically the case. It may be that programmes, such as those delivered more conventionally in universities, confer a broader, more generic skillset, which will allow movement not only within but between occupations.

It is likely that society will need both the specific skills of the apprentice and the broader attributes of the graduate. Perhaps the integrated apprenticeship end-point assessments with degree attainment provide a happy compromise.

---

19  Wolf, *Does Education Matter?*

## Business engagement

The latter half of the twentieth century saw radical change in higher education. It became much larger, more international and less elite. Funding models have also changed. The US has always had a mix of private and public universities and has had a diverse funding model with tuition fees, philanthropy and business engagement all contributing. Yet even in the US the level of tuition-fee debt as a proportion of overall debt is now eye-watering and amounted to $1.75 trillion by 2021. In the UK, as the number of 18–22-year-olds at university has increased from 5% to approaching 50%, funding from general taxation has had to be largely replaced by tuition-fee income. At the same time universities have more energetically diversified their income sources – seeking philanthropic support, but also engaging much more effectively with business. In 2022/23, there were approximately 77,000 interactions between universities and businesses, this represented a 5% decrease from 2021/22. However, the value per-interaction rose from £4,628 to £5,065 for SMEs, and from £31,496 to £33,580 for large businesses.[20] Other countries have also seen the benefit of effective links between university and business. The universities of Sungkyunkwan and Pohang in South Korea have productive alliances with Samsung in electronics and POSCO in steel respectively (see Table 8.1). Indeed, Pohang has created a specific Graduate Institute of Ferrous Technology.

Built on the back of substantive research investment (4.23% of GDP), South Korea's universities have been a catalyst in the remarkable economic development of that country. Several countries from Northern Europe, including the Scandinavian countries, boast universities which produce a high proportion of their research publications in collaboration with industrial partners (Table 8.1).

In the UK, the responsibility for research and innovation sits within a single organisational structure, UKRI. University research

---

20 National Centre for Universities and Business, 'State of the Relationship 2024', <info@ncub.co.uk>.

Table 8.1
Universities publishing the highest proportion of their research output in collaboration with industry.

| Rank | Institution | Country | Percentage of publications that are industry collaborations |
|---|---|---|---|
| 1 | Pohang University of Science and Technology (POSTECH) | South Korea | 22.98 |
| 2 | National Institute of Applied Sciences of Lyon (INSA Lyon) | France | 18.01 |
| 3 | China University of Petroleum | China | 14.77 |
| 4 | Norwegian University of Science and Technology | Norway | 11.03 |
| 5 | University of East Anglia | UK | 10.23 |
| 6 | Chalmers University of Technology | Sweden | 9.14 |
| 7 | Eindhoven University of Technology | Netherlands | 8.96 |
| 8 | Sungkyunkwan University (SKKU) | South Korea | 8.84 |
| 9 | Institute of Cancer Research | UK | 6.88 |
| 10 | CentraleSupélec | France | 6.18 |

Source: J. Morgan, 'South Korean Universities Lead Way on Industry Collaboration', 9 March 2017, Times Higher Education.

funding is supported by two mechanisms – the dual support system. The first involves roughly quinquennial reviews of university research (the REF), the outcome of which informs formulaic institutional funding, and the second sees UKRI running competitions for different disciplinary and response-mode funding (e.g. doctoral training awards, research programme grants and so on). UKRI also has responsibility for distribution of innovation funding, for instance KTP and HEIF. The UK has tried to replicate America's DARPA (Defense Advanced Research Projects Agency) scheme, by establishing an Advanced Research and Invention Agency (ARIA). The DARPA scheme was a response to Russian success in the space race, and in particular

Sputnik in 1957, which launched the first satellite to successfully orbit Earth. The DARPA programme has claimed notable research success, including the development of the internet, and is a higher-risk research strategy – awarding large funds to proven winners for far-off identifiable goals. The US invests about $4.12 billion (2024) annually in DARPA; the UK government has identified an £800 million fund in the first instance for ARIA. It remains to be seen whether it will have the transformational impact with regard to innovation which is hoped for.

## Spin-outs, start-ups

There are several ways in which academics can engage with business and industry. The most radical is to start up their own business. This is usually built on a product or an idea which has undergone a period of gestation within the research laboratory or classroom. It may then be brought to fruition in the innovation centres (see above) provided in many universities or in the science parks which have sprung up across the world, often in association with universities. Ownership of the intellectual property (IP) associated with the idea or product should be clear from the university's policies and procedures and may be shared between institution and academic.[21] Wrangles over IP ownership are now less common than they were as more robust policies have been put in place. Universities should always bear in mind that it is better to own a small bit of something than a whole lot of nothing (also bearing in mind that it may become a small bit of something very big). That radical start-ups and spin-outs in the UK are not more common is probably down to inherent conservatism and risk-aversion by academics and has been addressed in some universities by holding the budding entrepreneur's staff position open, should the enterprise fail and the academic wish to return. This sort of safety net may be difficult to

---
21  For further discussion of intellectual property rights see p. 162.

offer on a tight budget but would be very attractive to faculty members.

Currently start-ups and spin-outs from UK universities generate £5 billion in turnover each year and are more likely to survive than start-ups not associated with a university.[22]

In 2021 academic spin-outs attracted £2.54 billion in equity investment, however it is sobering to note that 43% of all UK venture capital goes to graduates of just four universities: Oxford, Cambridge, Stanford and Harvard.[23]

## Licences and product transfers

A safer option for an academic and their institution may be to license or even sell the idea or product to an industrial partner, often a preferred option where the development costs and infrastructure are simply beyond a start-up or university's capacity. This sort of arrangement may be an appropriate route to commercialise a pharmaceutical product, for instance. It depends upon the IP being protected, usually by patent, and it is likely to result in a relatively small return – given that the majority of the developmental work (and risk) will be taken by the licensee, although in absolute terms the return may still be substantial and welcome additional income to inventor and university. Given that much of the value may be inside the head of the discovering academic, it requires a trusting relationship to be developed – by both parties.

## Consultancies

A strong relationship may be developed between academic and business by way of consultancy. This usually implies that the academic has a lot of knowledge useful to the industrial partner and is prepared to offer it on a paid-retainer basis. Such relationships can be extraordinarily rich for all parties and may last for whole academic careers. They depend on upfront clarity between academic, university and

---

22  UUK, *Our Universities*.
23  J. Choukeir, T. Kenyon and Z. Meghji, 'Entrepreneurs for Change', *RSA Journal*, 4 (2022), <https://www.thersa.org/comment/2022/11/entrepreneurs-for-change>.

industrial partner about a broad range of relevant issues: how long the academic can spend on 'company business'; the extent to which the work is within or outside of 'university' time and therefore the extent to which the knowledge has been acquired or developed while at the university; how much of the consultancy fee might be retained by the university and how much by the individual; and whether the academic was working for the university during the consultancy period and therefore is indemnity insurance in place? Consultancies may also impart benefit to the consultant, and, by extension, to the university, by way of acquisition of real-world experience which can enliven the consultant's engagement with students and enrich their research.

## Continuing professional development (CPD)

Businesses may also greatly benefit from short-course teaching, by way of CPD for their staff. This can be utilised to very quickly bring cohorts of staff up to speed with technologies or concepts useful to their business. CPD offered by universities can be reassuring to professionals who wish to brush up on contemporary knowledge and skills or upskill in specialist areas. Many professional bodies now demand evidence of this training in order to retain appropriate accreditation. It is likely that lifelong-learning accounts and the evolution of the apprenticeship levy into a growth and skills levy will make CPD courses more viable (see Chapter 12).

## Intellectual property (IP)

The basis of many relationships between universities and businesses is the knowledge, skills and understanding which academics have and which might prove useful to the partnering business. These assets may be 'purchased' from the academic or university by way of CPD or consultancy. Some relationships may depend on exclusivity: consultancies offered by an academic may depend upon them only making their knowledge available to one business partner – for appropriate remuneration. In order to exploit knowledge for financial return, it must often be protected. This can be done in many ways such as by asserting copyright, trademarks or registered designs (plant varieties can also be protected) but for many discoveries made in universities, patents provide the most robust protection. These demand demonstration of the novelty of the idea, which must be described within the patent application. If successfully patented, the product or idea can be exploited for a defined period by the inventor, usually twenty years. However, there may be a tension for the academic between protecting their IP on the one hand and on the other needing to publish their research, since publication is the currency of academic esteem. This may be helpfully considered in the policies of the university. Furthermore, it is often possible, with the permission and support of the commercial partner, to both commercialise and publicise a discovery, since it may be in the interest of the commercial partner to 'market' the product, albeit with a delay. In many countries the protection and commercialisation of IP have been encouraged in their university academics.

In the UK, the impact of research comprises 25% of the formula used to measure research excellence in the REF (2021) and although 'impact' embraces cultural and societal as well as economic impact, there is no doubt that research supporting commercial outputs is highly valued. There are more patent filings made by commercial companies than by universities – presumably reflecting the more 'urgent' need to protect and commercialise as a result of industry research than university research. In the US, in the twenty years up to 2015, businesses accounted for a total of 2.25 million patents, whereas universities accounted for 1.1 million and there has been a global increase in patents during that period from 718,000 to 1.98 million annually, with the biggest increase in China.[24]

---

24 PatSeer, 'Worldwide Innovation Filing Trends 1995–2015', <http://www.slideshare.net/gridlogics/patseer-worldwide-filing-trend-report>.

Despite the encouragement to commercialise discovery in the UK, it has been apparently less successful than elsewhere. The discovery of graphene at the University of Manchester had generated some 26,000 patents by 2015, with China (47%), the US (18%) and South Korea (15%) all above the UK in the Relative Specialisation Index (RSI) for graphene, which compares the research profile for a subject within a country with the total world publications on a subject.[25] In 2015 the ratio of patent filings between business and universities was 22:1 in the UK, whereas in the US it was 2:1, suggesting that universities in the US are more effective at recognising and protecting their intellectual property – accepting of course that the patented ideas have some useful purpose.[26]

## Research contracts

Many universities now encourage academics to accept specific contract work from business or industrial partners. This is in effect similar to an academic accepting a competitive grant from a research council or similar public body but is likely to be more directed in its desired outcome (a product or improved process) and is likely to have more strings attached – confidentiality, conduct within GLP or GCP guidelines, reporting timelines and agreed publication (or not). This may sit uncomfortably with an academic used to the freedom afforded by public accountability, where the expectation is publication. Nevertheless, research contracts can provide a rich vein of funding for academics with particular skills and, with patience, can also support publication. There is of course substantial benefit delivered to the industrial partner in these relationships. It has been estimated that

---

25   Intellectual Property Office (IPO), 'Graphene: The Worldwide Patent Landscape in 2015', UK Intellectual Property Office Informatics Team, March 2015, <www.ipo.gov.uk/informatics>.

26   Q. McKellar, 'Business Engagement is no longer an Optional Extra for Universities', in A. Badran, E. Baydoun and J.R. Hillman (eds), *Universities in Arab Countries: An Urgent Need for Change* (Cham, 2018), pp. 123-41, <https://doi.org/10.1007/978-3-319-73111-7_6>.

businesses working with universities might expect up to 40% improvement in product and process innovation, and up to 72% improvement in novel product sales. Furthermore, they are substantially more likely to reinvest in R&D.[27]

It is perhaps not surprising that universities which do best in the assessment of their research quality also rank highly in the amount of contract research that they carry out (Table 8.2).

Table 8.2
Relationship (ranking) between universities undertaking quality research (QS) and those doing industrial or contract research.

| University | QS Ranking | Industrial Funding for STEM Research | Contract Research |
|---|---|---|---|
| Cambridge | 1 | 3 | 11 |
| UCL | 2 | 4 | 3 |
| Oxford | 3 | 1 | 1 |
| Imperial | 4 | 2 | 2 |
| Manchester | 5 | 5 | 4 |

Sources: QS: Quacquarelli Symonds Limited <https://www.topuniversities.com/subject-rankings>; A. Witty, 'Encouraging a British Invention Revolution: Sir Andrew Witty's Review of Universities and Growth', BIS/13/1241, 2013, <www.gov.uk/bis>.

It is also unsurprising that universities undertaking high-quality research, as assessed by the quality of their research outputs, also do well in the ranking of their research impact. In the 2021 REF in the UK, seven of the ten most highly ranked universities by research quality were also in the top ten for research impact (Table 8.3).

It is apparent that those countries with policies and schemes which incentivise university–industry linkages do better in the number of collaborations which develop between universities and industry. The UK has offered KTPs, HEIF and Catalyst funding for such schemes and rose from twelfth (2007/8) to second (2011/12) in the world

---

27  M. King and E. Woolley, 'Estimating the Effect of UK Direct Public Support for Innovation', BIS analysis paper 4, BIS/14/1168, November 2014, <www.gov.uk/bis>.

ranking of university–industry collaboration.[28] It has seen growth in income for collaborative research with industrial partners rise from 3.2% per annum between 2008 and 2012 to 15.5% between 2012 and 2014, as percentages of the total knowledge exchange income.[29] The value of contract research undertaken by UK universities for small and medium-sized enterprises (SMEs) has grown from £48 million in 2014/15 to more than £72 million in 2020/21.[30]

Table 8.3
The top ten universities as assessed by research quality and research impact in the UK's 2021 REF.

| Ranking | Quality Grade Point Average | Impact |
|---|---|---|
| 1 | Imperial | London School of Hygiene & Tropical Medicine |
| 2 | Institute of Cancer Research | Liverpool School of Tropical Medicine |
| 3 | Cambridge = London School of Economics | Imperial |
| 4 |  | Institute of Cancer Research |
| 5 | Bristol | UCL |
| 6 | UCL | Kings |
| 7 | Oxford | Southampton |
| 8 | Manchester | Oxford |
| 9 | Kings | Manchester |
| 10 | York = London School of Hygiene & Tropical Medicine | St Georges |

## Science parks

Science parks and innovation hubs have sprung up spontaneously or been encouraged strategically around universities and research institutes. Universities, local authorities and even private investors have provided land and often supported building for innovative and

---

28  UUK, *The Funding Environment for Universities 2015: The Economic Role of UK Universities* (London, 2015).
29  T.C. Ulrichsen, 'Assessing the Economic Impacts of the Higher Education Innovation Fund: A Mixed Method Quantitative Assessment', HEFCE, Bristol, UK, 2015.
30  UUK, *Our Universities*.

emerging business. The initial intent may be to encourage the universities' own start-ups and spin-outs to grow their businesses in these parks, but they are usually supplemented by other emerging innovative businesses which see the benefit of a close relationship with a university. In some locations, clusters have emerged as businesses seek proximity to other like-minded businesses and to the intellectual resource produced by the associated universities. Boston, San Francisco, London and Cambridge all have maturing and expanding business clusters around their related world-class universities. Innovation hubs have also grown up around universities in Malmö (Sweden), Oregon (US), Dresden (Germany) and elsewhere, and in the UK universities have contributed to the 'cluster' effect by establishing science parks such as the one at the University of Surrey, or by engaging effectively with regional authorities and businesses as at the universities of Teesside and Lincoln. In the UK there are now more than 118 science parks, employing more than 80,000 people directly and 120,000 in associated businesses on science park locations.[31] The impact of one or more universities on a local economy may take time and require investment. It is interesting to note that the clusters in Boston and San Francisco benefited from substantial post-war investment in research by President Truman which they have paid back many times over in the course of the intervening years.

Throughout their history universities have been a remarkable source of ideas which contribute to progress. They have more recently embraced an increasingly directed approach to the encouragement of these ideas for purpose. They now exploit the new ways of doing things, and the new products which emerge from their ideas, for commercial benefit and encourage their use in society. While this may conflict with the purist's idea of a university, it has brought extraordinary benefits to both universities and society more widely.

---

31 UK Science Parks Association (UKSPA), accessed December 2022, <http://www.ukspa.org.uk>.

# CHAPTER 9
# A World of Learning: Internationalisation

The world has become more connected, and international and transnational education more available and more popular. International studies provide opportunities for home-based students to study curricula which enhance understanding of different cultures, economies and geographies. The opportunities to study abroad, or to study programmes delivered by universities from other countries, have grown enormously, as travel, technologies and trading regulations have evolved. There are now almost six million internationally mobile students in the world and these numbers are likely to grow as the cohorts of 'university age' people increase with changing demographics.

Scholarship is by its nature international. The creation, assimilation, interrogation and dissemination of knowledge depend upon an external horizon, whereby scholars look beyond the parochial environment. Medieval scholars were remarkably mobile, often spending periods of study in foreign and distant universities, facilitated in doing so by Latin, the common language of scholarship at the time. Prior to the invention of the printing press and consequent mass transmission of knowledge in text, it was necessary to move between centres of learning to disseminate and accumulate knowledge. With print, ideas could be transmitted and disseminated much more widely, and without the need for human migration. The idea of distance learning and cross-border institutions substantially evolved in the mid-nineteenth century with the University of London's distance-learning programmes. Encouraged by Royal Charter in 1858, these were probably limited to examination boards in their original incarnation, but rapidly became instructional, with printed material widely disseminated across the globe, now in English and no doubt facilitated by the large tracts of imperial territories where English became the dominant or at least a pervasive language. Charles Dickens is thought to have coined the term 'The People's University' for the University of London, most likely as a consequence of the democratising impact of its distance-learning programmes. The University of London distance-learning programmes currently attract 50,000 students worldwide, many of whom still access printed material for their learning.

Internationalisation in higher education has developed in context, size and complexity. This has been facilitated by globalisation itself, by the greater interconnectivity of people across the globe thanks to rapid and relatively cheap transportation and instantaneous communication. Just as containerisation enhanced the trade and commodification of goods and materials, so have aviation, telecommunication and computerisation commodified education on a global scale.

## Rationale

There are many good reasons to encourage internationalisation. It supports the dissemination of knowledge and enhances understanding of different cultures and perspectives, just as it did in medieval times. From an entirely altruistic perspective, it may offer opportunities to those who would not otherwise receive quality higher education, and thereby develops their human capital and life chances. Exchange programmes bring cultural capital to participants, broadening their horizons. Academic exchanges support the development and enhance the subject knowledge and understanding of both the visiting and host academics; they may also encourage research collaborations and new ways of doing things, as well as fresh insights into teaching and learning. The social and cultural enhancement brought by the mobility of staff and students is patently substantive: partners learn and appreciate differences in ethnicity, religion, politics, behaviour and culture, which may strengthen their own beliefs or open their minds to the beliefs of others. This contributes to what has been termed 'soft political power', whereby societal leaders who have experienced education elsewhere are more likely to be receptive to the ideals of the country that hosted them, are likely to encourage trade and other exchanges, and are less likely to consider military aggression or conflict, or economic barriers such as trading tariffs. In 2018 there were 57 prime ministers, presidents or monarchs of countries throughout the world who were educated in the UK and although some have become authoritarian and dictatorial, it is fair to imagine that the British values of democracy, rule of law, respect for others and individual liberties may influence positively the thinking and actions of the majority.[1] Soft power has been characterised as the attractiveness and magnetism which inspires imitation and supports persuasion, and is enhanced by the exchange of ideas and people and the longer-term partnerships which take place in our universities.[2]

Professional bodies, such as the Association of Chartered Certified Accountants (ACCA), offer qualifications accredited by Oxford Brookes University and the University of London, to around 542,000

---

1 N. Hillman, 'UK slips behind the US, which takes the number one slot, for educating the world's leaders', *HEPI blog*, 14 August 2018, <https://www.hepi.ac.uk/2018/08/14/uk-slips-behind-us-takes-number-one-slot-educating-worlds-leaders/>.
2 UK Soft Power Group (UKSPG), 'The Future of UK Soft Power: Building a Strategic Framework', 2023, <https://www.ed.ac.uk/sites/default/files/atoms/files/the_future_of_uk_soft_power_-_building_a_strategic_framework.pdf>.

students in 178 countries. Many international standards and regulations originate in the UK as a consequence of our soft power, and international science-and-technology clusters are supported by our strong and outward-looking scientific and research activity, which in turn support inward investment in British science exploration.[3]

International collaborations enhance research outputs, with papers produced by collaborators from different countries being highly cited.[4] This is probably the result of experts with synergistic knowledge, skills and abilities engaging with each other and producing outputs which are more than simply additive in impact. This has been encouraged by national policies – perhaps most effectively in the Horizon programmes of the EU, where funding is made available for joint research between partners from more than one EU country. With a budget in 2023 of €95.5 billion, Horizon Europe is the largest single research programme worldwide.[5] Some infrastructure programmes also lend themselves to international collaboration, either because of their size and complexity or because there is a shared objective. The Large Hadron Collider is the world's largest and most powerful particle accelerator. It is part of the CERN complex and is run by 23 member states with several other associate and observer states. It has made major progress in understanding matter, including discovery of the Higgs boson in 2012 (see Chapter 7). The proportion of publications globally which are the outcome of international collaborations has grown substantially from 12.1% in 2002 to 22.2% in 2022, and by

---

[3] Department for International Trade (DIT), 'Inward Investment Report', August 2021, <https://www.gov.uk/government/statistics/department-for-international-trade-inward-investment-results-2020-to-2021>.
[4] S. Goldfinch, T. Dale and K. DeRouen Jr., 'Science from the Periphery: Collaboration, Networks and "Periphery Effects" in the Citation of New Zealand Crown Research Institutes Articles, 1995-2000', *Scientometrics*, 57/3 (2003), pp. 321–37, <https://doi.org/10.1023/A:1025048516769>; R. Sooryamoorthy, 'Do Types of Collaboration Change Citation? Collaboration and Citation Patterns of South African Science Publications', *Scientometrics*, 81/1 (2009), pp. 177–93, <https://doi.org/10.1007/s11192-009-2126-z>.
[5] E. Hazelkorn, 'The Geopolitics of Rankings: The Positioning of UK Higher Education and Research', in Carasso (ed.), *UK Higher Education*.

an even larger margin in the UK (from 29.8% to 63%[6]), demonstrating the interconnectivity of the global research community and presumably the ease with which communications make collaboration possible.

There is also an economic incentive to international education. At a national level, economic prosperity is enhanced by having a well-educated population. For those countries with relatively less-developed higher education systems it may be highly beneficial to allow or even encourage citizens to travel to high-quality international universities – or to receive high-quality education delivered in country by distance or franchise arrangements. This of course depends on those receiving that education returning to or remaining in the country where their enhanced human capital can make a difference. Where those receiving international education do not contribute to their home nation, they comprise a 'brain drain' and conversely the recipient countries achieve the economic benefit of brain gain. For countries encouraging balanced exchange programmes, or where their student exports are balanced by imports, there is likely an economic benefit which enhanced human capital will deliver. There is also a positive economic benefit to the university, institution or business delivering the education to the international student, either in person on a home campus or through distance, franchise or branch-campus delivery.

In many countries where universities have successful international recruitment programmes, the recipient universities generate substantial income from international students. This may even exceed that of home students, for whom their government often impose a tuition-fee cap or fund at a fixed rate from tax revenue. In the UK, the fees that universities can charge international students are unregulated, and thus prices are set by individual universities. There is perhaps no need to justify the cost of tuition fees for international students. They are 'customers' and fees will settle at a level which the customer can afford and is willing to pay – more for the most expensive subjects and at

---

6   Carasso and Plume, 'To Measure is to Know'.

universities with a high reputation (both of which may contribute to better job prospects and are likely to be repaid by graduate-earnings premia). If justification is needed, it can be made on the basis that international students should pay a premium since they have not contributed over the years to the infrastructure costs of universities, which have been largely paid for by the receiving nation's taxpayers or tuition-fee or capital-grant income. Universities may engage in international collaborations to enhance their reputation – and this is most likely to be successful when they 'trade up', collaborating with institutions higher up the international league tables. They may also attract high-quality students demonstrating either academic or sporting excellence to enhance their own academic or sporting reputation, often by offering scholarships and other inducements and are repaid by the reflected glory of the achievements of their students and graduate alumni.

It is clear that there are many strategic reasons to encourage internationalism within a university. However, often, the early shoots of international engagement spring from the motivation of academics – who simply love to travel. This is not of itself a bad thing: they develop research collaborations, start international teaching programmes and encourage staff and student exchange and international recruitment to enrich their working lives, and in doing so, their university's research and reputation. Nevertheless, as internationalisation has become more competitive, and approaches to it more professional, careful management of international activities is essential to ensure they are all broadly contributing to the university's strategic direction.

## Curriculum

Internationalisation has affected the curriculum in many ways. Specific courses on internationalisation have been developed and delivered both on campus and at distance. These courses embrace subjects such as politics and history and may be specific to a country or region of interest or choice. Issues around conflict, trade, cooperation and cross-border relationships may be considered and truly global issues such as the environment, where borders are in some ways meaningless, may be taught. The curriculum is also likely to be impacted by exchange programmes or international recruitment. In exchange programmes for professional subjects there has to be sufficient commonality and structure to ensure the broad professional competence of the exchangees. It would be concerning if a medical or veterinary student graduated without knowledge of the kidney because it was studied in the third year of the host university but the fourth year of the home university (assuming the exchange happened in the fourth year).

The funding mechanisms for exchange programmes are important to their success. The Erasmus programme was established in a way so that the receiving institution carried the cost, thus net-importing countries like the UK (when it was in the EU) had to accept that the more general benefits of the scheme outweighed the overall cost to the country. International exchange programmes, such as the Erasmus programme in Europe and now the Turin programme in the UK, are extraordinarily beneficial to the students who engage in them: they embrace the culture and learn the language of the host country, and immerse themselves in a different learning environment. Their success in cultural integration can be measured by the number of babies born to students who met their partner on an exchange programme. Almost half of Erasmus students meet their current partner while on the programme and 23% meet their life partner while on exchange, and at least 16% have Erasmus babies.[7]

In Europe, the Bologna protocol enhanced the flexibility in exchanges by broadly describing quanta of education required for

---

7   EU, European Commission, Directorate-General for Education, Youth, Sport and Culture, 'Erasmus + Higher Education Impact Study', Final Report, 2019, <https://data.europa.eu/doi/10.2766/162060>.

bachelor's, master's and doctoral degrees. For international students at a receiving university there may be ways in which the curricula can be enhanced. Although most receiving universities (and immigration authorities issuing visas) will require accredited competence in the language of delivery, international students often benefit from further language support which may be offered as part of the course or as a bolt-on by the host institution. Curricula can also be helpfully adjusted to enhance the learning of international students (and often, by extension and exposure, home students) by embracing a more international and inclusive approach to the material being delivered. Adjustments may also need to be made to allow transition from different learning methods – perhaps rote-learning, memorisation and/or receive-only, to more engaged, questioning, interactive and discussive approaches. The adjustments made to the curriculum may be beneficial to home-based students by giving them a more international outlook and, when sharing the classroom, a lived experience of students with different cultural, political and social outlooks.

## Mobility

Student mobility has grown substantially over the last twenty years, from 2 million students in 1999 to 5.6 million in 2018.[8] This will have been enhanced by the general increase in globalisation outlined above, but also by demographic and economic changes whereby there are more 18–23-year-olds with the economic wherewithal to travel and support themselves during an international education programme. For students moving to study in another country there are several factors which influence their country of choice. Major destinations are English-speaking countries, including the US, UK, Australia and

---

8   United Nations Educational, Scientific and Cultural Organization (UNESCO), 'Inbound Internationally Mobile Students by Country of Origin', September 2021, <data.uis.unesco.org>.

Canada.[9] English is still the world's most widely spoken language, with 1.5 billion speakers worldwide, of whom only 400 million consider it their first or native language. It is also increasing in popularity, the number of those speaking English having increased from 1 billion in 2006. The second most widely spoken language is Chinese Mandarin with 1.1 billion speakers. There are other student 'flows', apparently influenced by political, cultural, linguistic and historical proximity, such as movement from the Balkans and the Middle East to Turkey, which is now one of the most popular destinations worldwide[10], and from Latin American countries to Mexico.[11]

In the UK, inward flows of international students increased up until 2010/11, plateaued until 2016/17 and have increased again since that time. The plateau in student inflows was probably the result of a change in the visa regulations for students introduced by Theresa May, the Home Secretary, in 2012, whereby only students who had a firm job offer at the time of graduation could acquire a post-study work-route visa. This condition was reversed from July 2021, and all international students successfully graduating from their degree courses are currently (2024) eligible for an automatic two-year post-study graduate visa in the UK. The ebbs and flows of international students are greatly influenced by the visa requirements, and in particular by the flexibility for post-study work in the hosting nation; changes in the visa requirements in Australia, the US, Canada and the UK have substantially affected the flows to these countries. The US has consistently been the recipient of the largest numbers of international

---

9   OECD, 'Education at a Glance 2009: OECD Indicators', <https://www.oecd.org/edu/eag 2009>; UNESCO Institute for Statistics, 'Global Education Digest 2010: Comparing Education Statistics Across the World', <http//www.uis.unesco.org/>.

10   Y. Kondakci, 'Student Mobility Reviewed: Attraction and Satisfaction of International Students in Turkey', *Higher Education*, 62/5 (2011), pp. 573–92, <https://doi.org/10.1007/s10734-011-9406-2>.

11   B. Cantwell, S.G. Luca and J.J. Lee, 'Exploring the Orientations of International Students in Mexico: Differences by Region of Origin', *Higher Education*, 57/3 (2009), pp. 335–54, <https://doi.org/10.1007/s10734-008-9149-x>.

students (950,000 in 2022) and saw particularly substantial growth between 2011 and 2015 of 28%, as a consequence of President Obama's open-door policy. This contrasts with the UK's 2.6% growth over the same period under Prime Minister May's less liberal regimen.[12] The UK attracted approximately 273,000 first-year-entry international students in 2018/19[13], comprising 65,000 EU and 208,000 non-EU students. Of these students, about 93% were full-time, 52% postgraduate (taught) and 6% postgraduate (research). China was the largest sending nation (87,000 students), with India (18,000) and the US (12,000) next largest.[14] By 2020/21 there were 2.5 million students studying in the UK, of which 557,000 were non-UK, which includes returning international students as well as first-year-entry students. Those from the EU numbered 148,000 and those from outside the EU and UK 409,000.[15] The number of first year students coming to the UK from the EU halved, from 64,120 in 2020/21 to 31,400 in 2021/22[16], most likely because tuition fees, which were capped at £9250 while we were in the EU, became unregulated and rose substantially as a consequence of Brexit. This had differential effects across the devolved nations of the UK, since each of the devolved countries had to treat EU students the same as their own home-based students when the UK was a member state. The increase from capped home-nation tuition fee to unregulated international tuition fee has been larger in Scotland and Northern Ireland than in England or Wales because home-based tuition fees are set at a significantly lower rate in those two home

---

12  S. Marginson, 'The UK in the Global Student Market: Second Place for How Much Longer?', Centre for Global Higher Education research finding, HEFCE, 2018, <www.researchcghe.org>.
13  London Economics, 'The Costs and Benefits of International Higher Education Students to the UK Economy', 2021, <www.london.co.uk>.
14  Ibid.
15  HESA, 'Non-UK HE Students by the Provider and Country of Domicile', 2022.
16  HESA, 'Higher Education Student Statistics: UK, 2021/22 – Where Students come from and go to Study', 2023, <https://www.hesa.ac.uk/news/19-01-2023/sb265-higher-education-student-statistics/location>.

nations.[17] There has also been a change in flows – for instance students from the Republic of Ireland who traditionally travelled to Scotland, where they were charged Scottish tuition fees, are now more likely to travel to Northen Ireland or England/Wales where the international fees are likely to be more competitive.

During 2024, the Conservative government of the UK stopped international students bringing dependants with them when they came to study in the UK unless they were undertaking a PhD, other doctoral qualification or a research-based higher degree. They also instructed the Migration Advisory Committee (MAC)[18] to undertake a review of the graduate-route visa, by which international students are automatically entitled to a two-year post-study work visa on graduation from a university in the UK. The MAC did not find evidence of any widespread abuse of the graduate route. They found that those accessing the graduate route were earning similar income to domestic graduates fifteen months after graduation, and that those who moved on to the skilled-worker-route visas had similar earnings to domestic UK graduates. They concluded that the graduate route was not undermining the integrity and quality of the UK higher-education system and recommended retaining the graduate route in its current form.[19] Also in 2024, the QAA undertook a review of international pathway programmes, which are Foundation or Year 1 programmes undertaken by international students as a prelude to full recruitment onto a UK university degree programme. The QAA found that in the vast majority of cases, the standards of entry and progression from these programmes were in line with expectations and were broadly

---

17  UK home-nation fees: Scotland: £1820; Northern Ireland: £4630; England: £9250; Wales: £9000.
18  MAC is an independent, non-statutory, non-time limited, non-departmental public body that advises the government on migration issues.
19  MAC, 'Rapid Review of the Graduate Route', May 2024, <https://assets.publishing.service.gov.uk/media/6641e1fbbd01f5ed32793992/MAC+Rapid+Review+of+Graduate+Route.pdf>.

equivalent to entry requirements for domestic students. The outcome of the MAC and QAA reviews was greatly reassuring and supports the continued attraction of international students to the UK, although the prohibition of these students to bring dependants has had a negative impact on the numbers applying to UK universities.[20] The Labour government elected in July 2024 has introduced a much more positive tone towards international students, with the Secretary of State for Education, Bridget Phillipson, announcing that we should 'Be in no doubt: international students are welcome in the UK. This new government values their contribution to our universities, to our communities, to our country' and that government would 'offer the opportunity to remain in the UK on a graduate visa for two years after their studies'.[21]

## Collaborative provision

Many universities have developed partnerships with universities or colleges in other countries – sometimes called transnational education. These take many forms depending upon the desired model of the franchising institutions and the higher-education regulations of the franchisee and franchiser countries. They commonly involve the franchiser offering a curriculum, teaching support and assessment accreditation to the franchisee. The teaching support may be delivered entirely by in-country academics, partially online or may be provided by 'fly-in' faculty or fully placed sabbatical or 'placement' staff. From validation and full franchise (where the host delivers the curriculum almost in its entirety) to supported distance learning (where the host provides limited in-country support), the range of models available

---

20 HEPI, 'UK student recruitment numbers down, but is that the whole story?', May 2024, <https://www.hepi.ac.uk/2024/05/30/uk-student-recruitment-numbers-down-but-is-that-the-whole-story/>.
21 Bridget Phillipson's speech at the Embassy Education Conference, 23 July 2024, <https://www.gov.uk/government/speeches/bridget-phillipsons-speech-at-the-embassy-education-conference>.

are driven by the requirements of the regulators in each country. In 2018/19 there were approximately 667,000 students undertaking transnational education with UK providers and of those 52% were registered at the partner organisation.[22] Transnational education was primarily delivered by UK providers in Asia (50.2%), Africa (20.3%), the EU (12.4%) and the Middle East (9.2%).

Such arrangements can be greatly beneficial to both parties and may become long-standing, with successive generations of graduates completing from trusted partners. Nevertheless, it is well to prepare for termination of an arrangement in good time. It may take longer than imagined as successive years must be taught out, and cognisance taken that failures and resit or retake years may mean that substantial resource is required to allow small numbers of students to complete.

## Articulation agreements

This term may be used to describe several models of collaboration but is used here to describe programmes where one or a number of years are completed at the partner university, then one or a number at the home (UK) provider. In articulation agreements the receiving UK provider may guarantee a place on a programme when the student has successfully completed a level of award at the international partner institution. Collaborative provision may involve two- or three-years' study at the international partner then two or one year/s at the UK provider or different combinations or extensions of these models. In some arrangements where the programme has been designed and delivered collaboratively by two institutions and appropriate quality-assurance processes put in place, dual, joint or double degrees may be offered.

---

22  Universities UK International (UUKi), 'The Scale of UK Higher Education Transnational Education 2018/19', October 2020, <https://www.universitiesuk.ac.uk/sites/default/files/field/downloads/2021-08/the-scale-of-UK-HE-TNE-2018-19.pdf>.

## International branch campuses

International branch campuses (IBCs) are not a new thing. The American University in Beirut was established in 1866 (as the Syrian Protestant College, renamed in 1920) and as its original name suggests, was established by protestant philanthropists from New York. It has a particularly distinguished history, tempered in more recent times by the darker days of the Lebanese revolution. International branch campuses have grown in number since the early 1990s with 282 sites worldwide by 2015.[23] This growth has been encouraged by the globalisation and internationalisation of higher education and facilitated to an extent by World Trade Organisation rulings on trade in services. The altruistic purposes of education and of knowledge creation and dissemination no doubt underpin many international campus ambitions, but so too does a profit motive often unobtainable in the parent institutions' country of origin. Since by definition an IBC embraces at least partial ownership or investment, creating one carries risk. Nevertheless, notable success and long-term resilience has been seen in some campus developments – Heriot-Watt Dubai, Nottingham Ningbo, Curtin University Malaysia, Georgia Tech-Lorraine (now Georgia Tech-Europe) and RMIT Vietnam (a branch of Royal Melbourne Institute of Technology), for example. There have also been specific initiatives to attract high-quality international partners to some countries. Qatar has developed 'Education City', a complex of nine prestigious institutions including Texas A&M, Hautes Etudes Commerciales de Paris, University College London and Hamad Bin Khalifa University, housed in signature designed facilities and funded by the Royal Family's Qatar Foundation. Several IBCs

---

23 Cross-Border Education Research Team (C-BERT), 'Branch Campus Listing', 2015, <http://www.globalhighered.org/branchcampuses.phd>; M. Lanford and W.G. Tierney, 'The International Branch Campus: Cloistered Community or Agent of Social Change?', in C.S. Collins, M.N.N. Lee, J.N. Hawkins and D.E. Neubauer (eds), *The Palgrave Handbook of Asia Pacific Higher Education* (New York, 2016), pp. 157–72, <https://doi.org/10.1057/978-1-137-48739-1_11>.

have also clustered in some areas, no doubt encouraged by liberal local planning and educational regulation. The EduCity in Iskander in Malaysia has branch campuses from some nine institutions from the UK, Netherlands, Singapore, US and Malaysia and comprises schools as well as university branch campuses. The economic uncertainty around IBCs is best illustrated by the fact that, of the more than 280 established, at least 30 have closed. For some, stringent or changing local educational regulation will have made operating an IBC difficult, but most of the failures have been associated with unanticipated set-up costs and unrealised student numbers and tuition fees.[24]

## International distance learning

Overall, the numbers of people engaging with distance learning, together with those engaging with programmes delivered by institutions from outside their country of residence, are undoubtedly growing. Determining the exact numbers of those undertaking international distance learning is difficult, since many universities and other providers deliver distance-learning programmes, but don't differentiate their markets by country of access. Nevertheless, it is clear that the market is large and growing, boosted by the large amount of material made available online as a result of Covid lockdowns, but likely to have been inexorable despite Covid. The online learning platform Coursera showed in-year growth in number of enrolments between 2019 and 2020 equivalent to growth in the previous three years, 2016 to 2019, before Covid struck.[25] It has been estimated that in 2023 there were about 682 million users of online learning platforms worldwide, but of these only around 27

---

24  D.C. Kent, 'Challenges in a Disrupted World: Branch Campuses from the United States', *International Higher Education*, 104 (2020), pp. 14–15, <https://ejournals.bc.edu/index.php/ihe/article/view/14343>.
25  World Economic Forum, 'These 3 Charts Show the Global Growth in Online Learning', 27 January 2022, <https://www.weforum.org/agenda/2022/01/online-learning-courses-reskill-skills-gap/>.

Figure 9.1
Global growth of online education.

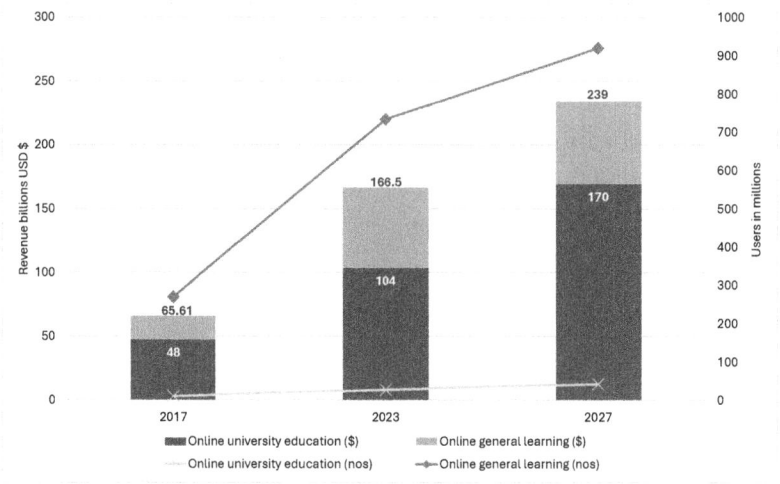

*Source*: Statista, 'Online Education – Worldwide, Statista Market Forecast', 2023, <https://www.statista.com/outlook/dmo/eservices/online-education/worlwide#key-players>.

million were accessing them for university education or professional accreditation.[26] This does not tell the whole story, since many of those accessing distance-learning programmes do so within their home country. The largest university in the world, Indira Gandhi National Open University, based in New Delhi, India, has more than 4 million enrolled students and delivers both in-person and distance programmes. In the US, in 2021, there were 9.4 million students (61% of the total undergraduates) enrolled in at least one distance-learning course. Of these, 4.4 million (28% of the overall total) were undertaking solely distance-learning courses (up from 15% in 2019), and, of these, 3.2 million were studying with institutions in the same state in which they resided (i.e., 74% of them). In the US, of those studying exclusively on distance-learning courses,

---

26   Statista, 'Online Education – Worldwide, Statista Market Forecast', 2023, <https://www.statista.com/outlook/dmo/eservices/online-education/worlwide#key-players>.

58% were doing so with private for-profit institutions, 28% in public institutions, and 21% in private non-profit institutions.[27] The revenue from global online education shows a different pattern to the participants' data (see Figure 9.1), with total revenue of about USD$167 billion in 2023, but almost $104 billion of that associated with online university education; it's forecast that the total market will grow to about $239 billion by 2027, of which about $170 billion may be attributed to university education.[28] This suggests that people value the courses and credentials they acquire from accredited university distance-learning programmes, which enhance their employability, and for which they are prepared to pay.

Of the corporate providers of distance learning in 2021, the two largest by revenue were in China and the next three based in the US (Table 9.1). Much of the material delivered by the Chinese providers is for tuition of school students towards their university entrance exams.

Table 9.1
Online corporate providers 2021.

| Provider | Location | Revenue (Billion USD) |
| --- | --- | --- |
| Tal Education | China | $4.39 |
| New Oriental Ed | China | $3.11 |
| 2U | USA | $0.95 |
| UDEMY Inc | USA | $0.52 |
| Coursera Inc | USA | $0.42 |

Source: Numbers taken from Statista, 'Online Education – Worldwide, Statista Market Forecast', 2023, <https://www.statista.com/outlook/dmo/eservices/online-education/worlwide#key-players>.

---

27  NCES, 'Undergraduate Enrolment'.
28  Statista, 'Online Education'.

In the UK, the Open University and the University of London are the largest providers of transnational education, accounting for 46,000 and 37,000 students respectively, the majority of whom access distance-learning courses.[29] Distance learning is often enhanced by the support delivered by individual or partner institutional tutors, who are able to respond when students are struggling with material, and to encourage them to continue with what could otherwise be a lonely learning experience. Supported distance learning (SDL) is now a widely practised part of transnational provision.

International learning and mobility has grown and is likely to continue to grow as enabling technology becomes more pervasive and international travel and global interconnectivity improve. The university-age demographic in China, India and Africa is growing substantially, and hopefully the prosperity of that demographic will allow them to engage in higher education. Furthermore, provision of distance learning, franchise campus collaborations and IBCs will mature and improve, bringing opportunity to many throughout the world who would not otherwise have had access to university education.

---

29   OfS, 'Transnational Education: Protecting the Interests of Students Taught Abroad', 2023, <https://www.officeforstudents.org.uk/publications/transnational-education-protecting-the-interests-of-students-taught-abroad/>.

# CHAPTER 10
## How to Pay For it All: Funding

Universities are expensive to run. By far the largest cost relates to the academic and professional support staff required to deliver the education and research activities. However, the infrastructure, campus buildings and information technology for campus and distance-learning providers, as well as the myriad facilities which support the overall student experience, also cost a lot. Different societies have evolved different models to pay for universities, from the extremes where the taxpayer carries the total burden, to that where the consumer or student carries the full cost, and almost every conceivable combination between these poles. Even within the UK, there has been substantial divergence in mechanisms of paying for universities, from the highly state-subsidised system in Scotland, to the tuition fee and loan schemes in England and Wales. No doubt the costs and funding of universities will continue to evolve, and will be influenced by the societal and political will to have populations educated to provide the requisite workforce for the next century, but also those educated to live in technologically and sociologically complex environments, and those who simply derive happiness and satisfaction from their educational attainment.

## Financial sustainability

According to their 2022 annual accounts, universities cost a lot of money to run, even those which provide online or distance delivery only. The Open University in the UK had expenditure of about £596 million (after stripping out pension adjustments), almost all of which was attributed to staff costs to support 152,000 students. Campus-based universities are inevitably more expensive (on a per-student basis) because of the costs associated with their infrastructure, and those which do research as well as education carry the additional costs of the required facilities, consumables and staff time. In the UK, University College London (UCL) is one of the largest in terms of student numbers, with about 47,000 students (2022) and total expenditure of about £1.7 billion, substantially the largest part of which (£939 million) is attributed to staff costs. UCL attracts around £795 million in tuition fees, but also around £525 million in research grants. Nottingham Trent is one of the largest post-92 universities in the UK and undertakes less research than UCL. It teaches around 41,000 students, has total expenditure of £396 million, of which about £255 million is spent on staff. Nottingham Trent attracts about £344 million in tuition fees and £9 million in research grants. The difference in ratio between student numbers and tuition-fee income in UCL and Nottingham Trent presumably reflects higher numbers of international students paying higher unregulated fees at UCL. The Higher Education Statistics Agency (HESA) data on international students indicate that in 2021/22 UCL had 24,200 international students and Nottingham Trent 6600. Their websites indicate that in 2024 UCL tuition fees for international students are more than £24,000, whereas for Nottingham Trent they are less than £17,900. Cambridge University has a smaller number of students (about 23,000) but much larger expenditure than either UCL or Nottingham Trent, at about £2.3 billion, reflecting, in part, the 'tutorial system' where students receive almost individual engagement with academics, but also the necessary cross-subsidy into research, required to maintain its stellar position in research league tables. It attracts roughly the same income for research (£552 million) as UCL, but also attracts substantial income through Cambridge University Press and its assessment functions (£860 million), and much larger donations (£53 million) and investment income (£181 million) than UCL (which attracted £22.5 million in donations and £7 million in investment income). Even the totals for UCL and Cambridge appear modest compared to Harvard in the US, which has total expenditure in 2022 of $5.4 billion (£4.29 billion). Although staff are also the biggest expenditure, at around 52% of the total, the income has a very different profile, with only 21% and 17% attracted in tuition fees and research funding respectively, but a whopping 45% attracted under the heading philanthropy (presumably donations and investments).

Looking across the whole of the UK, there have been many changes in the nature of tuition-fee income and funding-body grants over the last 23 years (Figure 10.1).

While there has been overall growth in income to the sector in each of the home nations of the UK, reflecting growth in student numbers and increased research activity, the most striking feature is the change in ratio of tuition fees and funding-body grants in England and Wales, where tuition fees rose 8-fold and 7-fold respectively between 2001/02 and 2021/22. During the same period, funding-body grants fell (England) or remained roughly the same (Wales). In Scotland and Northern Ireland, while tuition fees have increased by 6- and 4.5-fold respectively, funding-body grants have also increased by 1.7 and 1.4 times respectively. These shifts reflect changes in tuition-fee charges against home students and increased numbers of international (or out-of-devolved-nation) students, paying unregulated fees, together with the political will to support home-nation students through funding-body grants in Scotland and Northern Ireland. Changes to the percentage of income received by UK higher education institutes from

## Figure 10.1
Funding levels and sources in the UK's home nations (note different scales on the y-axis).

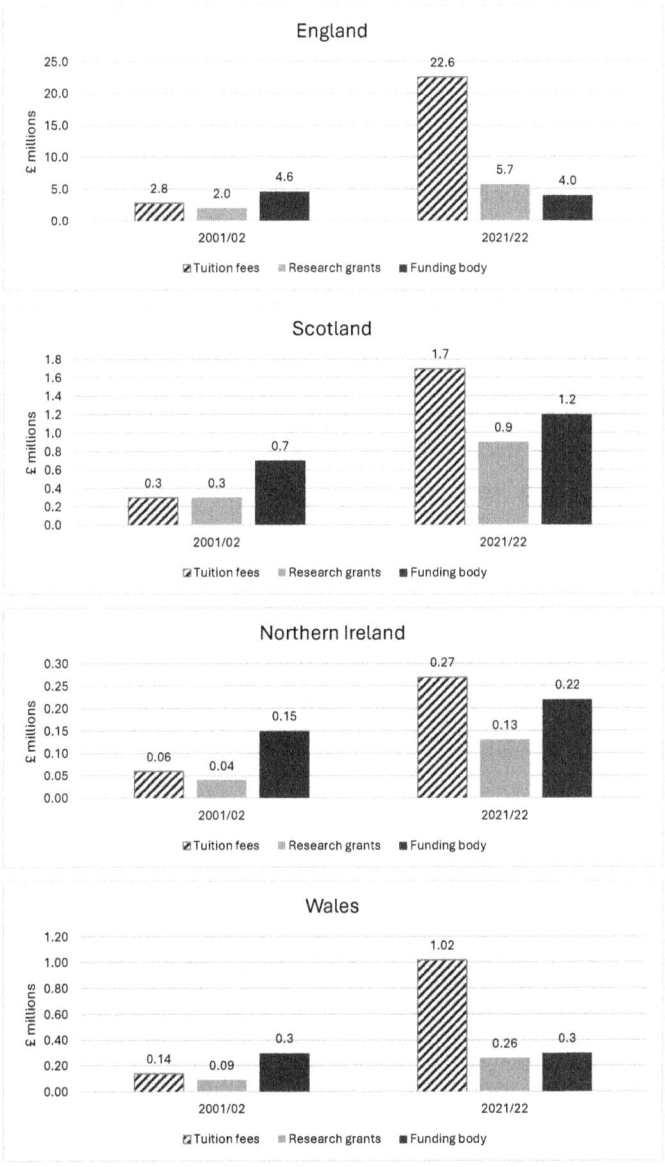

*Source*: H. Carasso and A. Plume, 'To Measure is to Know: Two Decades of Change in UK Higher Education through the Lens of the Sector's own Statistics', in H. Carasso (ed.), *UK Higher Education – Policy, Practice and Debate during HEPI's First 20 Years*, Higher Education Policy Institute (HEPI) report 161 (Oxford, 2023).

different sources are shown in Figure 10.2. The changes in 2020/21 are particularly stark. These changes and the deficits now associated with both publicly funded teaching and research can be seen in Figure 10.3.[1]

The 2023 OfS financial sustainability update for education providers in England indicated that the total income for English providers in year-end 2022 was £40.8 billion, which is an increase of about £3.7 billion from 2021.[2] They made a surplus of £2.4 billion and had a cash flow of £4.8 billion. Borrowing fell from £14.1 billion in 2021 to £13.6 billion (33.3% of income) in 2022, and net liquidity rose from 166 to 168 days. These relatively positive aggregate figures cover a broad range of performance across the sector, with 78 providers (31% of the sector) reporting deficits, and about 35 of these forecasting that they will have three-year consecutive deficits, and 31 providers reporting liquidity of less than 30 days, calling into question their longer-term sustainability. An updated OfS report on financial sustainability produced in 2024 for the 2022/23 accounting year showed a decline in financial operating performance with surplus levels, operating cashflow and net liquidity all falling compared to 2021/22. The OfS also undertook some scenario-planning which suggested that, without cost-reduction measures, by 2026/27 there could be a £4.54 billion reduction in net income (against optimistic sector forecasts) by which

---

1  The data in Figure 10.3 is derived from OfS Transparent Approach to Costing (TRAC) information. It differs from the OfS annual accounts derived data given below, in that it includes a sustainability adjustment of £4.2 billion, calculated from Earnings Before Interest, Tax, Depreciation, and Amortisation (EBITDA) for Margin for Sustainability and Investment (MSI), and is for all UK higher education institutions and not only those in England. The MSI is calculated on the average cash generated in the current and previous two years, together with forecast required cash generation for the next three years. This six-year average is taken as a proportion of current total income (excluding capital grants and permanent endowments). The TRAC figures (approximately 9.8% in 2016/17) are not greatly different from the sustainability estimates (EBITDA margin) of 10.6% (2017) used by Australian universities and are lower than those used by many capital-intensive industries.
2  OfS, 'Financial Sustainability of Higher Education Providers in England: 2023 Update', OfS 2023.20, updated 23 June 2023, <https://www.officeforstudents.org.uk/media/0b7d9daa-d6c7-477e-a0b2-b90985d0f935/financial-sustainability-report-2023-updated-june-2023.pdf>.

Figure 10.2
Percentage changes to total income from different sources for UK higher education institutions.

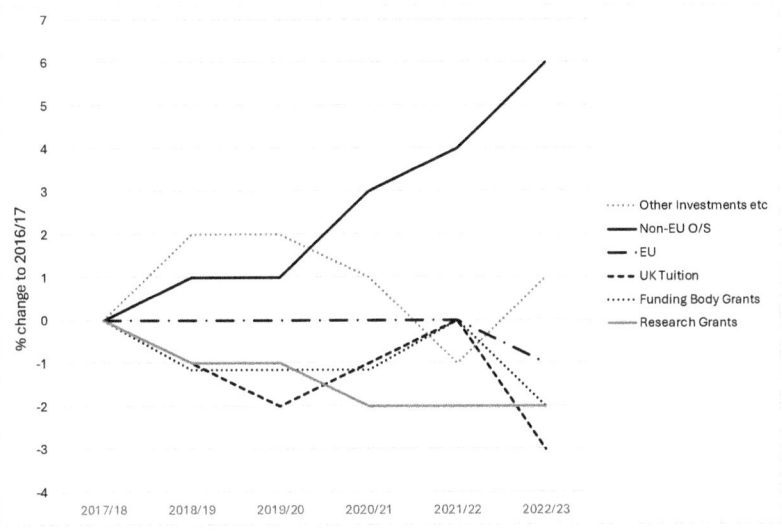

Source: From HESA finance records in UUK, *Sustainable University Funding: Why it's Important and What is Needed* (London 2023).

Figure 10.3
In-year (2021/22) surplus/deficit associated with different activities.

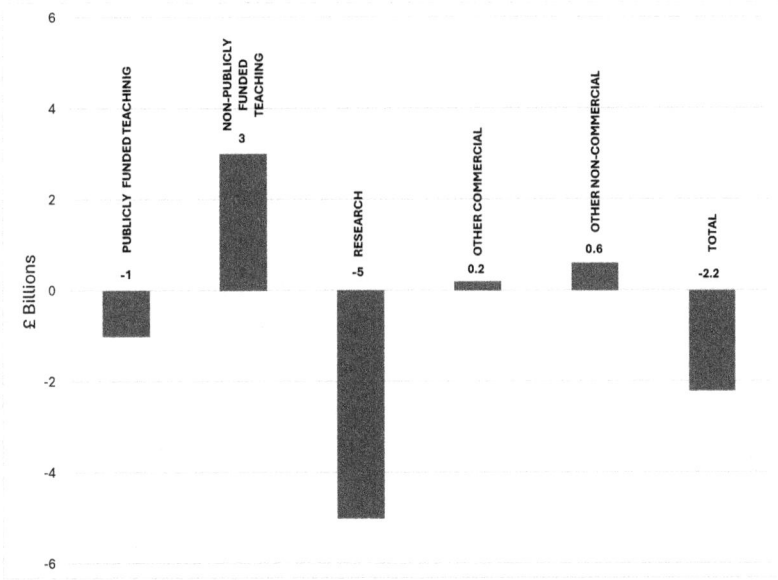

Sources: OfS, Transparent Approach to Costing (TRAC), published data 2021–22, <officeforstudents.org.uk/data-and-analysis/trac-data/published-data-2021-22/>; UUK, *Sustainable University Funding: Why it's Important and What is Needed* (London 2023).

time 202 (75%) providers could be reporting deficits, with 135 (50%) of providers having low year-end liquidity.[3] The OfS reports suggest that the major risks facing providers include inflation, reliance on international student recruitment (especially single-country source), affordability of pension schemes and required investment in facilities (especially to achieve net-zero carbon emissions). There may also be a mismatch between the actual growth in UK undergraduate student numbers and those predicted by the sector. Recruitment fell by 2.4% between 2021 and 2022, and although the Office for National Statistics projects an increase of almost 13% in the UK 18-year-old population (up to 2026), the sector is predicting a 19% growth in recruitment. A drop in UK undergraduate recruitment would have a major impact on the sustainability of UK universities without increases in international recruitment or increases in postgraduate entrants to compensate. International recruitment was buoyant in the UK until 2023 and has contributed enormously to the positive aggregate financial position of the sector, although political uncertainty around the graduate-route visa and ability to bring dependants on student visas caused a decline in international recruitment in semester B (January '24 recruitment). It has been suggested that international students are now displacing potential UK undergraduate students, and that this might be a deliberate policy to swap students whose fees are capped with those whose fees are unregulated and consequently higher. This charge has been particularly levelled at Russell Group universities, which are selecting rather than recruiting their undergraduate students (they have more applicants with requisite qualifications than places on courses). No doubt, in a capacity-limited system, this would be true, but in England the only capacity issues relate to infrastructure space

---

3 OfS, 'Financial Sustainability of Higher Education Providers in England 2024', OfS 2024.21, 16 May 2024, <www.nationalarchives.gove.uk/doc/open-government-licence/version/3/>.

and people to teach – neither of which have reached saturation.[4] In Russell Group universities, the number of UK undergraduate students rose from 121,000 in 2020/21 to 129,000 in 2021/22, and although the total number (undergraduate and postgraduate) of international students in all UK universities rose from 139,000 to 143,000 in the same period, the total number of UK students also rose from 196,000 to 199,000.[5] It is clear that the near flat funding in tuition fees (£9000, with an uplift to £9250 in 2017) since 2012, has put considerable financial pressure on universities. Efficiency savings (reduced capital expenditure and increased student-to-staff ratios) have been made, but many universities are now registering deficits and weak liquidity. The Labour government elected in 2024 acknowledged this as one of its many thorny problems and has agreed a single annual increase in tuition fees equivalent to Retail Price Index excluding mortgage interest (RPIX) (3.1%), which may be imposed across all years of undergraduate students in England (new entry and returning students) for September 2025. Similar percentage uplifts may be applied to part-time and accelerated undergraduates. It seems unlikely that funding for universities in the UK will reach a sustainable level without some form of annualised inflation-linked uplift. It remains to be seen in 2024 if there is sufficient political backbone to make this happen.

## Funding models

That universities are expensive is undeniable. However, their continued (and globally increasing) popularity suggests that societies are prepared to pay for them. Indeed, the increasing number of international students (see Chapter 9) who generally pay the full cost of their education directly, suggests that to the individual consumer they offer value for money and adequate return on investment, ensuring their

---

4  M. Corver, 'The Perennial Challenge of Funding Undergraduate Higher Education', in Carasso (ed.), *UK Higher Education*.
5  HESA, 'Higher Education Student Statistics: UK, 2021/22'.

Table 10.1 Funding models in selected OECD countries.

| | Australia | Canada | Finland | Japan | Korea | New Zealand | USA | UK |
|---|---|---|---|---|---|---|---|---|
| Participation in HE (% of 25–34-year-olds with bachelors or equivalent) | 33% | 30% | 26% | 47% | 45% | 35% | 29% | 34% |
| Spend as a proportion of GDP (2019) | 1.9% | 2.2% | 1.5% | 1.4% | 1.5% | 1.6% | 2.5% | 2% |
| Average debt on graduation USD (2018) | 19,819 | 17,874 | 16,884 | CAT 1 loan 23,105; CAT 2 loan 32,884 | N/A | 26,232 | 26,500 | 58,571 |
| Annual average gross amount borrowed per student USD | 3,925 | 5,397 | 6,563 | 7,336 | 5,153 | 8,340 | 4,600 | 18,169 |
| When after graduation students start paying back loans | When salary exceeds $35,335 ($23,628 USD) | 6 months | 1.5–2.0 years | 7 months | When salary exceeds variable minimum, subject to the type of loan | When salary exceeds $25,312 ($15,788 USD) | 6 months | When salary exceeds £27,300 ($34,700 USD) up to 2022 £25,000 ($31,700 USD) from 2022 |
| Repayment rate on loan | Tapering 1–10% of salary | Fixed | Fixed bank rate 5–15yrs | Income contingent 15yrs or 20yrs | Fixed or variable (choice) 9yrs | Income contingent to 12% | Income contingent with 8 repayment plans of up to 25yrs with standard 10yrs | Income contingent 9% of salary above threshold |
| Interest on loan | Inflation | 0% (since 2021) | Below commercial (Government guarantee) | Means tested 0% CAT 1 3% CAT 2 | 2.2% | 0% while resident in NZ | Fixed for federal loans | 3%+RPI (to 2023) RPI (from 2023) |
| Write off of outstanding loan | No | 15yrs | No, it is a bank loan, but there is a loan guarantee for 30 years from Government | No | No | No (written off on death) | 20yrs or 25yrs | 30yrs (to 2023) 40yrs (from 2023) |
| Loan forgiveness | Teachers in remote areas | Healthcare workers in remote areas | 33% of graduates | 0.3% of graduates | No-interest loans for Rural Students | No | Teaching and healthcare in rural areas. Lawyers in low paid fields | No |

*Note:* All currency converted to USD (January 2024). *Sources:* Data collected by the University Alliance in 2023, see also OECD, 'Education at a Glance 2023'; <https://doi.org/10.1787/e13bef63-en>.

popularity. For those countries with the economic wherewithal, and the political/societal belief in educational investment, the question then arises how to do it and, beyond that, to what extent to incentivise it. Different systems have developed across the world (Table 10.1). Some countries perceive university education purely as a public good and are prepared to fund it entirely through the taxpayer. The other extreme imposes the full cost of tuition on the recipient, and, of the developed countries, England and Wales have most closely followed this model, although even in England and Wales, with considerable tuition-fee burdens, students are subsidised through a benign (or at least forgiving) loan system in which those on lower salaries are unlikely ever to fully repay their loans.

Historically, in the UK, universities were seen as a public good and were funded by the taxpayer through grants from the treasury (although fees had been charged to students on a means-tested basis up to 1975). The scale of such funding from taxation when 4% of the 18–20-year-old population went to university was manageable – it was a whole other question when more than 25% (1990), and now approaching 50%, began to go. More critical analysis of the benefits of university were also being undertaken. It was clear that there were three major beneficiaries: 1) the graduates themselves, whose lifetime earnings were shown to be substantially greater than those of non-graduates – many of whom, as taxpayers, were also contributing to the costs; 2) the state, which was a major beneficiary, not only in its required human capital – doctors, engineers and so on – but also in tax returns, the higher earners paid more tax; and 3) business and industry, as the recipients of a highly educated workforce – although they claimed, with some justification, that they actually paid for this through various corporation and other industry-levied taxes. The introduction of a levy on businesses paying more than £3 million in salary costs to fund apprenticeships has not been universally popular or effective, many businesses choosing to take on relatively highly paid management apprentices, contrary to the government-inferred intention that it would support level-2 and -3 apprentice jobs. In Washington State in the US, businesses embraced a self-imposed tax to support less advantaged students to attend university and thus address the chronic skills and workforce shortages which they faced. Businesses supporting education is not a new thing: in the early twentieth century the Ottomans imposed a levy on animals slaughtered in a Damascan abattoir in order to fund a medical college.[6]

In the UK several options were available to government beyond general taxation. The most appealing (depending on individual perspective) were a graduate tax or a direct tuition-fee charge on the students (either could be modified by direct government support to acknowledge the broader benefits to taxpayers). While a graduate tax might have been the simplest and most obvious solution, vice-chancellors were deeply sceptical that all the graduate tax receipts would end up back in universities. The government was equally wary of a hypothecated tax, which it wouldn't be able to plunder as more pressing calls on funding arose. A graduate tax also has the disadvantage that it will not bring in sufficient revenue to pay for universities until well after the first cohort of graduates have developed their careers and begun to pay higher-rate taxes. It also has the disadvantage that linking the tax payments to the university from which the worker graduated would be difficult and without such a linkage there would be no incentive for universities to produce high-earning graduates. Contrarily if there was a link between the tax returns of the graduates and the income to the university, it could create the perverse incentive to only produce high-earning graduates – doctors rather than nurses or economists rather than teachers. Direct tuition fees had the attraction to vice-chancellors that universities would get the money – and that it would follow the student, thus encouraging

---

6   A.-K. Rafiq, *Tarikh al-Jami'ah al-Suriyyah: al-bidayah wa' l-numuww, 1901-1946* (Damascus, 2004); S. Moubayed, 'The Founding of Damascus University 1903–1936: An Essay in Praise of the Pioneers', *Journal of Arabic and Islamic Studies*, 18 (2018), pp. 179–200.

further growth in the sector. Tuition fees would though put off students without wealthy parents or beneficiaries unless some form of loans were introduced simultaneously.

Although it was the Dearing Committee (National Committee of Inquiry into Higher Education), which was established in 1996/97 by Gillian Shephard, the Secretary of State for Education, in a Conservative government, which made the recommendation regarding tuition fees,[7] they were first introduced in 1998 by the Labour government of Tony Blair at £1000 per year. The Labour government also recognised the legacy of underfunding in higher education, manifest as high student-to-staff ratios and a decaying estate, and sought to rectify it by increasing the overall unit of resource (tuition fee plus government grant per student) and by offering substantial capital grants on the unwritten but implied understanding that universities would have to create a sustainable funding model within which they would be largely responsible for operational *and* capital costs. The relatively generous contribution from the taxpayer meant that the treasury had to control its overall spend on universities and did so through the intermediary of HEFCE. HEFCE imposed number caps on universities and had responsibilities to ensure the quality of education being delivered, which it did through the QAA. HEFCE also had responsibility for ensuring that universities were being efficiently and effectively run through the accountable officer (vice-chancellor) and by encouraging the Committee of University Chairs (CUC) to create guidelines on good governance.[8]

## Tuition fees

A more radical approach to growth and funding was established in 2012, when tuition fees in England and Wales were increased to up to

---

7  *Dearing Report.*
8  Committee of University Chairs (CUC), 'Guide for Members of Higher Education Governing Bodies in the UK', November 2004, <dera.ioe.ac.uk>.

## Table 10.2
### Changes to the university funding schemes in the UK and Northern Ireland since 1998.

| England | 1998 | 2006 | 2012 | 2017 | 2018 | 2022 | 2023 |
|---|---|---|---|---|---|---|---|
| Tuition fees non-means tested | £1000 (means tested) | £3000 | £9000 | £9250 | | | |
| Income-contingent loans | | £3000 | £9000 | £9250 | | | |
| Repayment threshold | | £15,000 | £21,000 | | £25,000 | £27,295 | £25,000 |
| Time until write-off | | 25yrs | 30yrs | | | | 40yrs |
| Interest | | RPI | RPI+3% | 6.1% | | | RPI (capped at 6.3%) |
| Maintenance | Yes | Means tested grant £2765 (abolished in 2016) | | | | | Loan £4221–£13,022 |

| Scotland (numbers capped) | 1998 | 2001 | 2012 | 2023 |
|---|---|---|---|---|
| Tuition fees | £1000 (means tested). Abolished in 2000 | | Non-EU/Scotland £9000 | £1820 Paid by Student Awards Agency for Scotland for Scottish domiciled students |
| Maintenance loans means tested | Yes | Yes | | £6000–£8000 |
| Grants means tested | | £2000 | | £2000 |
| Graduate endowment (repaid post-graduation) | | £2000 (abolished in 2007) | | |

| Northern Ireland | 1998 | 2006 | 2012 | 2023 |
|---|---|---|---|---|
| Tuition fees | £1000 | £3000 | £3465 (£9000 ex NI UK) | £4710 |
| Income-contingent loan | | £3000 | | |
| Maintenance | Loan | Grant £2765 | | Grant £3475 |
| | | | | Loan £6766 |

| Wales | 1998 | 2007 | 2010 | 2012 | 2023 |
|---|---|---|---|---|---|
| Tuition fees | £1000 | £3000 | | £9000 | |
| | | | | £3465 (Welsh resident) | |
| Income-contingent loan | | £3000 | | £9000 | |
| | | | | £3465 | |
| Fee grant non-means tested | | £1845 | Abolished | £5535 (studying in England) | Loan and grant |
| Maintenance | Loan | | Grant means tested £5000 | | Loan £9950 |

*Note*: Students from Northern Ireland, Scotland and Wales receive support equivalent to the cost of their tuition fees when studying in the UK outside their home nation.

*Source*: C. Callender, 'Policy Divergence: Changes in Student Funding Systems across the UK since 2002/03', in H. Carasso (ed.), *UK Higher Education – Policy, Practice and Debate during HEPI's first 20 years*, HEPI report 161 July 2023, <https://www.hepi.ac.uk/wp-content/uploads/2023/07/UK-higher-education-Policy-practice-and-debate-during-HEPIs-first-20-years.pdf>.

£9000 on the recommendation of the Browne Review.[9] The increase in tuition-fee ceiling was introduced by a coalition Conservative/Liberal government, against the manifesto intention of the Liberals, which was to abolish tuition fees. It is thought that this had a catastrophic long-term effect on the popularity of the Liberal Party in the UK, particularly among younger voters. In the first instance fees could be charged *up to* £9000, but it very quickly became apparent that there was little price sensitivity by applicants (given a reasonably generous loan and repayment scheme) and all universities moved to the maximum fee. The consequent substantial reduction in direct government contribution towards higher education meant that the numbers caps could be lifted, and a relatively free market established, encouraging further growth in student numbers. There was an indirect cost to the taxpayer beyond the small grant contribution which universities still received. This was termed the Resource Accounting and Budgeting (RAB) charge and was the projected shortfall in repayment of the tuition-fee loans which was predicted as a consequence of the repayment schedule. In the first iteration this required graduates who earned more than £21,000 to repay 9% of the difference between £21,000 and their salary per annum. Any remaining debt would be written off after 30 years. Clearly some students would never earn enough in their lifetime to make the full repayment, and this comprised the RAB charge. The interest charged on the student loan has varied from zero (2004), Retail Price Index (RPI) (2011), RPI+3% (2012), 6.1% (2017) and back to RPI (2023) but capped at 6.3% as RPI rose above this level. There have also been several iterations to the total tuition fee (now £9250) and the salary above which repayment commences, and the time beyond which the loan will be written off. From 2023 repayment will start when grad-

---

9  *Browne Report*, 'Securing a Sustainable Future for Higher Education: An Independent Review of Higher Education Funding and Student Finance', BIS/10/1208, 12 October 2010, <https://www.gov.uk/government/publications/the-browne-report-higher-education-funding-and-student-finance>.

uates earn more than £25,000, will be levied at 9% of the difference between £25,000 and their salary and will not be written off for 40 years. A more appropriate interest rate of the equivalent of RPI will be applied to the loan, which means that graduates will not repay more than they borrow in real terms (see Table 10.2).

In England, the extraordinary rise (up to 2022) in the number of 18–22-year-olds going to university has continued despite the substantial tuition fees and consequent associated debt for graduates. Perhaps surprisingly, the introduction of tuition fees and increases to them have not had a negative impact on those from poorer backgrounds seeking a university education. The gap in access to university by those from the most disadvantaged backgrounds (POLAR1) and the least disadvantaged (POLAR5) has fallen in relative and absolute terms although it is still significant. Although the overall gap has reduced, those from the most disadvantaged backgrounds are less successful at accessing places in the most prestigious universities.[10] The reason for the increase in students from more disadvantaged backgrounds, which was greater in England than Scotland (Table 10.3) where tuition fees were lower, may be attributed to the relatively generous maintenance loans for living costs made available to eligible students in England (eligibility is by household income). In 2024/25 they stand at up to £8610 for students living with their parents and up to £13,348 for students living away from their parents (with the maximum loan applied to those in London).

Table 10.3
Participation (%) of university-age students from the lowest-income quintile of the population going to university.

|  | *2011* | *2015* |
|---|---|---|
| England | 13.8 | 17.0 |
| Scotland | 7.3 | 9.7 |

---

10  UCAS, 'End of Year Cycle Data Resources 2021'; P. Bolton, 'Higher Education Student Numbers', House of Commons Library research briefing 7857, 2 January 2024, <https://commonslibrary.parliament.uk/research-briefings/cbp-7857/>.

The degree programmes and funding schemes for universities in the devolved nations of the UK differ from those in England. Wales (£9000 per annum rising to £9250 from September 2024) and Northern Ireland (£4630) each run three-year undergraduate programmes for the most part and supplement the tuition fees to differing degrees from devolved administration budgets. Scotland has retained a four-year undergraduate degree as its core offer and fees are currently (2022) charged at £1820 per annum (paid by Student Awards Agency for Scottish domiciled students). Furthermore, the Scottish government subsidises the interest payable on loans taken out by Scottish students, who only have to pay interest of 1.5% per year on their loans. When the UK was part of the EU, the Scots imposed differential tuition fees for those students coming from England in contrast to those from Scotland and the rest of the EU (for whom European law prevented discrimination). English students effectively paid the same for a Scottish four-year degree as they would have paid for a three-year English degree – both of which were substantially more than other EU citizens had to pay. Entry to Scottish universities, for Scottish school-leavers, is generally based on acquisition of 'higher' qualifications in a broader range of subjects than the conventional English A-levels, with the goal of greater specialisation as students progress through the four-year university programme.

There remains an issue of inequity throughout the UK in the tuition-fee system – all students within each devolved nation pay the same, yet it costs less to teach a law or business student in a classroom (or digital) environment than it does to teach a creative arts, engineering or biology student, and in particular a medical, veterinary or dentistry student. Students studying medicine or related subjects require studios, laboratories, practicals, clinics and placements, all of which add cost both by way of facilities and because of the necessarily higher teacher-to-student ratio. The fact that cross-subsidy from one student to another occurs is undeniable – the extent is more contentious and will depend on class size and course content, and may differ for the same course in different universities. Creating a system of exact charging is likely to prove impossible, but in some countries, such as Australia, differential fees are charged, and this is done by banding subjects according to different criteria: Band 1 A$3300 for arts, humanities and nursing; Band 2 A$4700 for computer sciences, engineering, business and economics; and Band 3 A$5500 for medicine, dentistry, veterinary medicine and law. The banding takes into account likely graduate earnings as well as costs (a lawyer is likely to earn more than a nurse, but the course is likely to cost less) and demonstrates that differentiation can be done and does seem fairer. Some vice-chancellors argue for undifferentiated fees on the grounds that all students receive other things like gyms and counselling, but of course all students (including the high-cost ones) have access to these on an equal basis.

A series of essays published by the Higher Education Policy Institute explore several different funding options for universities and provide analysis by London Economics of the likely costs of each option compared to a baseline of the current (2024) funding system. Models include a purely public-funded option, having a system where incremental funding is linked to performance (measured by the Teaching Excellence Framework), a stepped system where higher-earning graduates repay with a higher rate of interest and a model based on an employer levy.[11]

All systems of higher education are expensive. Mass distance or electronic delivery may reduce costs, but must be updated and refreshed to retain credibility, and must be accredited and assessed in order to confer credit on the participant, all of which costs money. Heavily research-intensive universities, or, perhaps even more so, small specialist institutions carry a heavy cost in terms of facilities

---

11  R. Stephenson (ed.), 'How Should Undergraduate Degrees be Funded? A Collection of Essays', HEPI Report 173, April 2024, <www.hepi.ac.uk>.

and infrastructure. How these are paid for depends on the wealth and philosophies of the societies in which they exist, and of course the policies of the governing political parties. Consequently, funding models have become as diverse as the institutions themselves, and even within a sovereign state such as the UK, with four devolved country authorities, the funding schemes have diverged dramatically. In most societies, as more people have entered higher education, the individual participants have had to pick up more of the cost. It remains to be seen whether there will in time be a coalescence towards a model of shared cost, which recognises the contribution higher education makes to the individual, to the business community and to society, and how that might be embraced in different political doctrines.

# CHAPTER 11
## Decree or Support: Governance

The 'governance' of a university encompasses its stewardship, the policies and regulations it creates to govern itself, and the oversight of its operational activities, which are carried out by its executive. In an age of accountability, this may threaten the autonomy of the institution, where the government or its regulator impose governance requirements, such as governors rather than academics having ultimate responsibility for academic quality. Many universities are a great age, and many are now very substantial businesses, and their governance mechanisms have evolved to suit their size and complexity. That so few have ever gone out of business, and that so rarely are there governance concerns, suggests a sector with good practices and effective processes. Nevertheless, more intrusive regulation, more intense competition and a tougher financial environment mean that governance will have to continue to evolve to ensure the vitality of the sector.[1]

The governance of an organisation or institution encompasses the way in which it conducts its affairs and agrees its policies. The

---

1   OfS, 'Financial Sustainability of Higher Education Providers in England: November 2024 Update', <https://officeforstudents.org.uk/publications/financial-sustainability-of-higher-education-providers-in-england-november-2024-update/>.

financial aspects of corporate governance were first considered in the Cadbury report in 1992.[2] More broadly, the outcomes of good governance should include an ethical culture, good performance, effective controls, and sound legitimacy according to Mervyn King, former judge of the Supreme Court of South Africa (who carried out a review of corporate governance for the government of South Africa).[3] Those responsible for governance should conform to the Nolan principles of selflessness, integrity, objectivity, accountability, openness, honesty and leadership, and although this is critical principally to public-sector institutions, it is also appropriate in the private sector, accepting that self-interest may help drive performance and that accountability may be to shareholders.[4] The government of a country constitutes its governing body, and its laws and regulations are equivalent to the policies of a company or university. Governments themselves often stray beyond the desired outcomes suggested by King and politicians often fall at the first Nolan hurdle (selflessness), not to mention some of the others. Nevertheless, governments have responded to corporate governance failures by imposing standards which must be met within their jurisdictions, for example the Sarbanes–Oxley Act, which mandates certain financial reporting and record keeping for corporations in the US (see below).

## Historical failures

There is a chequered history of governance failure in state-supported corporations, oil companies, banks, accountancy firms and universities. The British East India Company, which controlled half of all the world's trade, had to be bailed out by the British government and

---

2  *Cadbury Report*, Report of the Committee on the Financial Aspects of Corporate Governance (1992, London).
3  Institute of Directors in Southern Africa, 'King IV: Report on Corporate Governance for South Africa 2016', <https://www.adams.africa/wp-content/uploads/2016/11/King-IV-Report.pdf>.
4  *Nolan Report*, First Report of the Committee on Standards in Public Life, cm 2850-I, May 1995, London: HMSO.

was eventually dissolved in 1874, and by today's standards would have failed on each of the King outcomes. It has been suggested that the concessions negotiated by the Anglo-Persian Oil company (later Anglo-Iranian and then British Petroleum) with the Persian leaders, after oil was discovered in 1908, failed the tests on ethical culture and legitimacy, casting a shadow over the UK's relationship with Iran for decades. Arthur Andersen, one of the world's largest accounting firms, was effectively made bankrupt in 2002 after apparently misstating the returns of the giant energy company Enron. It demonstrated poor controls, unethical behaviour and lack of legitimacy. It was the failure of Arthur Andersen in the US which catalysed a US Senator and a US House Representative to sponsor a bill, in 2002, introducing responsibilities for Boards of Directors regarding corporate compliance and criminal penalties for misconduct. The Sarbanes–Oxley Act has been credited with improved corporate governance in the US and by other countries which have imposed similar laws.[5] Lehman Brothers bank in the US and the Royal Bank of Scotland (RBS) in the UK both demonstrated poor controls, and certainly in the case of Lehman's, ethical failings associated with the subprime mortgage market, which led, in 2008, to the bankruptcy of Lehman's and the bail-out of RBS, and are credited, if that word can be used, with the 2008 global recession.[6]

## Universities

Although the financial implications of governance failures in universities are unlikely to be on the same scale as failure in a multinational corporation or a bank, to the individual university they can be catastrophic.

---

5 The Sarbanes–Oxley Act – named after its sponsors, Paul Sarbanes, US Senator Maryland, Democrat, and Michael Oxley, US Representative Ohio, Republican.

6 Further details on governance failures in these corporations can be found in Q. McKellar, 'Friend or Foe? Governors and Governance in Higher Education', in A. Badran, E. Baydoun and J.R. Hillman (eds), *Higher Education in the Arab World, Government and Governance* (Cham, 2020), pp. 81–95, <https://doi.org/10.1007/978-3-030-58153-4_2>.

In 2009, HEFCE clawed back £36.5 million from London Metropolitan University, against claims which had been made for non-completing students between 2005/06 and 2007/08.[7] Furthermore, an audit carried out by the UK Border Agency in 2012 found that almost 25% of its international students had no leave to remain in the UK,[8] causing it to lose its authority to take students from outside the EU. At that time, £30 million of London Metropolitan revenue was associated with its international students' tuition fees. Remaining international students had to transfer to similar courses at other (mostly local) universities to complete their studies. The specific failures at London Metropolitan were associated with lack of controls and poor performance but may also call into question the ethical culture which existed, and issues of openness, accountability and objectivity with regard to the governing body. The chair and members of the governing body resigned, and a new vice-chancellor was appointed. It was considered to be an unprecedented failure of management and governance in the UK's higher education sector and its implications for the size, vibrancy and reputation of London Metropolitan University have lasted for over a decade. The failures at London Metropolitan were those of operational control, and have been attributed to the managers and executive of the organisation. The governance failures were manifested in a lack of sufficient oversight and detailed knowledge of the operations, and thus either ignorance of the poor operational practices or ineffective attempts to improve them. This gets to the heart of 'good governance' since it should be about higher-level oversight rather than operational activity: the 'art' of governance is to acquire and retain sufficient knowledge of the operation without descending into managerial activity, and yet be able to challenge managerial malfeasance when it is suspected.

---

7 'Funder's errors do not excuse London Met, audit finds', *THE*, 13 August 2009, <https://www.timeshighereducation.com/news/funders-errors-do-not-excuse-london-met-audit-finds/407756.article>.
8 J. Meikle and S. Malik, 'London Met Crisis will Damage UK's Brand, says Vice-Chancellor', 30 August 2012, *The Guardian*.

## Governors and managers

The relationship between governors and managers is therefore critical. The governors need to have sufficient confidence and trust to allow the executive and management to get on with running the business, but sufficient and sufficiently authoritative sceptical enquiry to ensure that the operations are indeed efficient and effective. Breakdown in trust and confidence between governors and managers forms another reason for governance failure in universities. This most often manifests as a breakdown in relations between chair and chief executive or vice-chancellor. It is not surprising that tensions may develop in this relationship. Vice-chancellors are chosen for their leadership skills, authoritative articulation and strategic thinking, which are likely to come across as assertiveness if not arrogance. Chairs are selected on the basis of success – often in industry positions which demand the same skill set and self-belief as the vice-chancellor. It is perhaps surprising that clashes do not occur more often. When they do it is greatly helpful to have an intermediary with highly honed diplomatic skills to adjudicate and resolve. In differing universities this may take the shape of the secretary/registrar, often the most senior non-academic in the institution and often with responsibility for governance issues. Some governance boards also appoint a senior independent governor to embrace the responsibilities of arbitration should difference arise. In the UK there have been several instances where a breakdown between vice-chancellor and governors has led to a crisis in governance. Perhaps the most widely reported such event happened at the University of Plymouth in 2014. The exact reasons and circumstances were never made fully public, however an enquiry into the failures of governance at Plymouth made fifteen recommendations, suggesting that 'no one individual is greater than the institution they serve' and that staff should be treated 'fairly and with dignity' and that individuals should instinctively 'do the proper thing'.[9] It also highlighted the breakdown in trust and confidence between the chair of the board of governors and the vice-chancellor and recommended the appointment of an academic registrar as the conscience of governance.

For obvious reputational reasons universities do not advertise when there are governance breakdowns like the one described at Plymouth; that they do happen is undeniable and may perhaps be inferred by the exit of a vice-chancellor in undue haste, often followed by a set of statutory accounts with a note under vice-chancellor's emoluments or compensation for loss of position. It is perhaps a sign that the sector is relatively well-governed that so few such incidences occur and that, after a period during which vice-chancellors' average length of tenure had been decreasing, in the year 2021/22 it increased. From the late 1970s until 2011 average tenure for vice-chancellors declined from 6.4 years to 4.1 years (a decline of 36%) but since then it has increased by 15% to almost 5 years and the number of those serving for more than 10 years has increased from 2% in 2010 to 16% in 2021.[10] The more difficult financial environment experienced since 2021 may cause this trend to reverse.

## Regulation

In the UK, regulation of higher education is devolved to each of the home nations and is under the authority of the OfS in England, the Scottish Funding Council in Scotland, the Commission for Tertiary Education and Research, which replaced HEFCW, for Wales and the Higher Education Division of the Department for the Economy in Northern Ireland. The most radical change occurred in England in 2017/18, with the move by government to replace the relatively

---

9  Good Governance Institute, Review of Governance for Plymouth University, March 2015, <https://www.plymouth.ac.uk/students-and-family/governance/review>.
10  HEPI, 'Digging in? The Changing Tenure of UK Vice-chancellors', HEPI policy note 34, May 2022, <https://www.hepi.ac.uk/2022/05/26/digging-in-the-changing-tenure-of-uk-vice-chancellors/>.

benign 'critical friend' that was the arm's-length intermediary agency between government and the sector, HEFCE, whose authority was bestowed by virtue of its funding function, and which acted on behalf of state and sector in equal measure, with the Office for Students. The OfS acts only on behalf of students, although often it seems to act on behalf of what government thinks or wants students to wish for rather than what students actually ask for. More robust regulatory environments tend to lead to a tension between university autonomy and state accountability, and this is common to governance models of higher education throughout the world.[11] By requiring accountability for all aspects of university operation, from financial security to academic delivery, university autonomy is constrained. Indeed, in some ways government intervention is absolute, for instance in imposing a hard maximum on home tuition-fee charges and that 'British Values' are taught in degree apprenticeship courses. In others, it restricts decision making, for example, in demanding action on perceived grade inflation, or suggesting that universities should adopt the International Holocaust Remembrance Alliance. The OfS has bombarded the university sector with consultations on everything from quality and standards to funding and the TEF. These consultations have been entered into by the sector in a spirit of cooperation, with much time and effort spent on the institutional responses, not always rewarded with changes to regulation which reflect the sector view. Consultation on the National Student Survey (NSS – an independent survey of final-year students in the UK) resulted in some 90% of respondents wishing to retain the summative question 'Overall I am satisfied with the quality of the course'. The OfS has progressed with its original stated intention to remove the question. The overall satisfaction question has consistently produced results above 75% and

---

11   J. Waterbury, 'Governance of Arab Universities: Why does it Matter?', in E. Baydoun and J.R. Hillman (eds), *Universities in Arab Countries: An Urgent Need for Change* (Cham, 2018), pp. 55–70, <https://doi.org/10.1007/978-3-319-73111-7_2>.

frequently above 80%, it is difficult to find fault in a sector with such outstanding satisfaction (for comparison, satisfaction surveys of the UK government generally result in approval ratings of less than 40% and often closer to 20%[12]).

The burden associated with OfS regulation in English universities is substantial. In 2023, UUK commissioned consultants Moorhouse to undertake a review of the burden of regulation on the English higher education sector (116 universities). Moorhouse estimated that across English universities, 128 full-time equivalent (FTE) Executive-, 638 FTE Manager/Director- and 1289 FTE Officer/Co-ordinator-level jobs were dedicated solely to regulatory compliance.[13] A report by the House of Lords suggested that the relationships between the OfS and its key stakeholders were unsatisfactory, that its approach to regulation was arbitrary, overly controlling and unnecessarily combative, and that it acted like an instrument of government policy rather than an independent regulator.[14] The report made 80 conclusions and recommendations, suggesting that a reset in the relationship between regulator and sector was called for. A subsequent independent review of the OfS was carried out by Sir David Behan.[15] The review recommended that the OfS reduces the number of strategic objectives it has, and focuses on monitoring financial sustainability, ensuring quality, protecting public money and regulating in the interests of students. It also recommended that the OfS be given consumer enforcement

---

12  YouGov, 'Government Approval', 2022, <https://yougov.co.uk/topics/politics/trackers/government-approval>.
13  J. McGarry, 'Understanding the Burden of Regulation', Moorhouse Consulting, 2023, <https://www.universitiesuk.ac.uk/sites/default/files/uploads/Reports/Moorhouse-regulatory-burden-report.pdf>.
14  'Must Do Better: The Office for Students and the Looming Crisis facing Higher Education', Industry and Regulators Committee, 2nd Report of Session 2022–23, HL Paper 246, 13 September 2023.
15  Independent Review of the Office for Students – Fit for the Future: Higher Education Regulation towards 2035, July 2024, <assets.publishing.service.gov.uk/media/66a261fda3c2a28abb50d758/Indpendent_review_of_the_office_for_students.pdf.pdf>.

powers and that students have a role in the governance and regulatory activity of the OfS itself. It recommended that the OfS take on the role of the designated quality body, and that it reconsider the non-interventionist position of government (and by extension the regulator) with regard to market exit (that is, the possible financial unsustainability of a provider).

## Quality assurance

The second significant change to affect UK university governance cascades from the first. Direct accountability of the university governing body for academic quality was made a condition of registration by the OfS. This has impacted a long cherished binary divide in UK universities whereby the academic content, culture and structure of the institution was determined by the academic community through a senate or academic board. The more utilitarian financial management was under the control of the executive, with direct oversight by the governing body. This divide had inherent merits: the academic 'texture' was designed by those with the knowledge to do so and by those who were going to have to deliver it. A broader range of managerial and financial expertise was engaged to run the 'business' of the university. The responsibility of the governing body has been clearly articulated by the CUC which states that governing bodies 'must actively seek and receive assurance that academic governance is robust and effective' and by the OfS that academic quality oversight by the governing body must be 'adequate and effective'.[16] University governing bodies have sought to reassure themselves of the academic quality of their institutions and the governance thereof in a number of ways, receiving annual (or more frequent) reports on the business of the academic

---

16  CUC, 'The Higher Education Code of Governance', 2020, <https://www.universitychairs.ac.uk/wp-content/uploads/2020/09/CUC-HE-Code-of-Governance-publication-final.pdf>; OfS, 'Public Interest Governance Principles', 2017, accessed January 2024, <https://www.officeforstudents.org.uk/advice-and-guidance/regulation/registration-with-the-ofs-a-guide/public-interest-governance-principles/>

board, with relevant metrics such as continuation rates, completion rates, grade outcomes and performance in student surveys such as the NSS. Some boards have appointed independent members to lead on academic quality, other universities have encouraged governors to attend their academic boards. Some university audit committees now receive reports from their academic quality committee.[17]

Historically, universities in the UK (and elsewhere) self-regulated their educational quality and standards, as autonomous institutions designated by charter or legislation, with individual degree-awarding power. This is unlike schools and colleges, where the exam boards, not the individual institutions, award qualifications.[18] 'Quality' refers to the learning opportunities and teaching activity, that is to say, the process of education. 'Standards' set out the level of achievement required, in other words the outputs of the educational programmes. In the self-regulated environment, quality was assured by a sectoral understanding of the educational requirements and thresholds for achievement. This was built on an established set of frameworks for higher-education qualifications and subject benchmark statements, together with an external-examiner system whereby consistency was achieved between institutions and minimum quality and standards subjected to 'independent' oversight. This was further 'enhanced' in the case of professional subjects such as medicine and engineering, by the professional and statutory regulatory bodies, which often imposed conservative and sometimes draconian regulatory requirements for course content and assessment processes.

Following the post-Dearing expansion of universities in 1992, it was considered that self-regulation provided insufficient reassurance to students and the taxpaying public that quality processes within

---
17  A. Bols, 'Why it is time for University Governors to do more on Academic Quality', HEPI policy note 36, July 2022, <https://www.hepi.ac.uk/wp-content/uploads/2022/07/Why-it-is-time-for-university-governors-to-do-more-on-academic-quality.pdf>.
18  D. Watson, 'Quality, Standards and Institutional Reciprocity', in J. Brennan, P. de. Vries and R. Williams (eds), *Standards and Quality in Higher Education* (London, 1997).

universities were robust. The Quality Assurance Agency (QAA) was established in 1997 to promote continuous improvement in quality and standards of universities, and sought to do so by undertaking periodic reviews of the systems and processes of universities and publishing the results of these audits. At roughly the same time a process of subject review was introduced, considering curriculum design; teaching, learning and assessment; progression and achievement; support and guidance; learning resources; and quality assurance management and enhancement. Each area received a numerical score out of 4, giving a possible total of 24, which immediately created a league table of 'teaching quality' by subject. Providers 'wailed' at the bureaucratic burden and, no doubt, the negative perception of those subjects performing poorly. The system was dropped in 2003 in favour of internal institutional subject-level reviews, informing a more external periodic institutional review by the QAA.[19] The quality assurance systems overseen by the QAA offered significant reassurance and encouraged continual improvement of quality and assurance of standards.

Nevertheless, there have been ongoing concerns about quality in relation to grade inflation, contact hours, external examining, equality of standards between institutions, plagiarism, and quality of international provision.[20] To address some of these issues and to create a system which would objectively allow the government/regulator to differentiate fees (uplifts in line with inflation would only be conferred on institutions doing sufficiently well in terms of teaching excellence), a system of assessment of teaching excellence, the Teaching Excellence Framework (TEF), was introduced in the UK in 2017, and

---

19  S. Jackson and J. Bohrer, 'Quality Assurance in Higher Education: Recent Developments in the United Kingdom', *Research in Comparative and International Education*, 5/1 (2010), pp. 77–87, <https://doi.org/10.2304/rcie.2010.5.1.77>.

20  R. Fisher, 'Grade Inflation: What can Universities do about It?', UUK, 3 August 2022, <https://www.universitiesuk.ac.uk/latest/insights-and-analysis/grade-inflation-what-can-universities-do>.

significantly reviewed and relaunched following extensive consultation for 2022. The current assessment is largely metric-driven, using the NSS results relating to teaching, assessment and academic support to measure student experience; and university performance in the OfS's B3 condition of registration which benchmarks continuation, completion and progression to measure student outcomes (see below for details). Progression data was in the first instance derived from the Destination of Leavers from Higher Education (DLHE) survey, which was a survey carried out under strict guidelines by each university of its own graduates. The DLHE survey has since been replaced by an independent survey of graduate employment, the Graduate Outcomes Survey, which surveys graduates fifteen months after completion of their course and reports through HESA.

In its original form, the TEF was a voluntary exercise, and the results were translated into Gold-, Silver- and Bronze-level awards, but in 2022, all institutions with over 500 students studying at undergraduate level were required to enter the TEF, providing a 15-page narrative, to contextualise the metrics, and in the latest round a short student-led submission was expected. In this second round, a further category of 'Requires Improvement' was introduced. A significant number of institutions received either Gold or Silver awards during the initial iterations of the TEF and, furthermore, the Bronze awardees did not fit comfortably into the perception of which universities delivered high teaching quality, with many post-92 universities rated more highly than Russell Group institutions. The changes in the second round have shifted the balance, although there were still some interesting outcomes.

Needless to say, the promised uplifts to tuition fees for the Gold/Silver awardees never materialised, and further consultations were undertaken on subject-level TEF and more broadly on quality. Since 2023, quality in English universities has been judged broadly on outputs relating to student continuation, student completion and graduate progression. 'Student continuation' broadly refers to progression from year 1 to year 2 of the degree programme and for full-time first-degree students the numerical threshold considered acceptable is 80% continuation. 'Completion' refers to the successful completion of the degree programme and the acceptable threshold is at least 75%. Graduate progression refers to a move into full-time employment or further education and should meet or exceed 60%. Universities may be subject to an intervention by the OfS if they fail to meet thresholds. It is anticipated that these metrics will be applied at a granular level to individual courses within a university and are likely to prove most challenging for those courses where employment outcomes are least certain, such as the humanities. Where courses have poor employability outcomes, universities may choose to stop teaching those subjects altogether, and while this could catalyse an intellectual exodus of students from these subjects, that was unlikely to worry the Conservative government which introduced them and was determined to minimise the loss on tuition-fee repayments – those graduates with poorest employability are also those least likely to fully repay their tuition-fee-loan debt. Continuation and completion metrics in the UK have been generally good by international standards. The percentage of those completing a degree programme in the US may be as low as 60%.[21] This may not be entirely a quality issue. In the US most universities provide a continual assessment or grade point average for their students and this may allow students to step off their educational programme with a recognised assessment of their academic ability, which may be used by employers in recruitment. Students at US higher education institutions are also more likely to move to continue or complete their degree programme at

---

21  ThinkImpact, 'College Dropout Rates', 2021, <https://www.thinkimpact.com/college-dropout-rates/>; I. Bouchrika, 'College Dropout Rates: 2023 Statistics by Race, Gender & Income, Universities & Colleges', 26 September 2022, <https://research.com/universities-colleges/college-dropout-rates>.

a different institution than the one they commenced at. In the UK, most universities require completion of the whole programme before a degree is awarded, thereby offering little in the way of credential before full completion.

It is of concern in England that the QAA has recently rescinded its support of the OfS with regards to UK university quality assurance, on the grounds that the proposed new quality criteria sit outside internationally recognised systems of quality assurance. The European Quality Assurance Register for Higher Education requires student participation in assessment panels and requires publication of review reports. The evolution of quality assurance in England is moving somewhat against the global trend, which is towards strengthening national capacity and convergence, cross-border recognition, multi-accreditation and international quality assurance schemes.[22] The Bologna protocols within the EU strengthened quality processes and recognition throughout the Union and have led to flexibility in the labour market for degree-level recruits. While the outcomes-based approach to quality assurance, together with the other oversight measures of quality in the 'B conditions', embraced by the OfS, have the benefit of simplicity and objectivity, they lack the stimulus for evolutionary enhancement brought by the QAA. It may be that other countries will follow our lead in quality assurance, but if not we may find ourselves isolated, and our reputation for high-quality education threatened.

## Governance models

The growth and evolution of universities, together with the changing complexion and requirements for governance have led to a range of governance models in our universities.

---

22 D. Van Damme, 'Trends and Models in International Quality Assurance and Accreditation in Higher Education in Relation to Trade in Education Services OECD/US Forum on Trade in Educational Services', 23–24 May 2002, <https://www.oecd.org/education/skills-beyond-school/2088479.pdf>.

The governing bodies of most UK universities comprise between fifteen and thirty-five members (the 1997 Dearing report recommended twenty-four), of which the majority are 'independent' or external to the university. Most have student and staff members and, in the case of Scottish universities, union members. This raises a question about governor responsibilities, which should be in the best interests of the institution, not just in the interests of a stakeholder group such as the staff, who union members are likely to represent. There has been an evolution towards smaller (and hopefully more efficient) governing bodies, typically with fewer than twenty members. They are less representative (Scotland's unions excepted) and are now more often selected following recruitment processes designed to fulfil skills requirements. The governing bodies of our two most ancient and exclusive universities are quite different. Cambridge hosts the 'Regent House' comprising around 5500 university academics and senior officers or college members. It has a subordinate council which acts as the principle executive body and, unlike other UK universities, has only four external members but nineteen elected members from the university community. Oxford has a 'congregation' with more than 5000 members and also has a council of twenty-eight, with four externals. The Oxbridge models have developed over 800 years to suit the complexities of their college systems and their academic ethos. That the two universities continue to consistently rank in the top ten in the world suggests that their governance is effective. It is also undeniably a conservative system, designed to perpetuate and self-replicate the established model. In Scotland, the ancient universities have courts, chaired by a rector who is elected by their student body. The Oxbridge and Scottish models hark back to the communities of academics which comprised the medieval university and which embraced the ideals of autonomy and self-direction. It remains to be seen whether these systems will stand up to the rigour of greater external accountability, imposed in England and Wales by the regulator and in Scotland (and

Northern Ireland) by the devolved administrations. Most university governing bodies appoint subsidiary committees to consider finance, audit and remuneration and may delegate some of their decision-making powers to those committees. For obvious reasons it is important to have governors with expertise and experience in finance, audit and human resources issues. It is also important, for the sake of transparency and accountability, that the vice-chancellor is not a member of either the audit or remuneration committee which sets his/her salary.

Since the CUC's Code of Governance indicates that the governing body is unambiguously and collectively accountable for all matters relating to the university, and that the staff and student members of the governing body carry the same responsibility as independent members, they should not be routinely excluded from discussions. There may be rare circumstances when there is a conflict between the member's job and governance role and, in these circumstances, they may be recused. The growth and consumerisation encouraged by government has undeniably resulted in a higher-education market, where the 'customer' pays (even if supported by government loans) and universities compete for market share and reputation. Shattock suggests that this has 'encouraged' universities to appoint board members with financial, legal or business backgrounds, with more direct experience of commercial markets, and that governing bodies have become like company boards and vice-chancellors more akin to CEOs.[23] The governing bodies now monitor institutional performance – a role greatly encouraged by the OfS, which demands from them financial statements, annual sustainability assessment, Transparent Approach to Costing report, annual five-year forecasts and QAA Statements.[24] The vice-chancellor's executive is seen to report directly to the governors, while academics see their role in university

---

23  M. Shattock, 'University Governance Reformed: The Transformation of a "Self-governed" to a "Regulated" University System', in Carasso (ed.), *UK Higher Education*.
24  Ibid.

governance much diluted, if not entirely emasculated. The strengthened managerial structures now in place are not welcomed by many academics, who look back at the halcyon days of virtually complete autonomy and minimal accountability. The growth and complexity of universities, and in the UK the direct link through tuition fees to the student, make these wistful dreams impossible. More directed management and sound governance are simply the realities of the modern university.

## Resolving ethical dilemmas

The vice-chancellor may have to carefully balance the reputation of their institution against a potential large donation. The London School of Economics and Political Science (LSE) accepted a donation from the Gaddafi Foundation in 2010 of £1.5 million, two years after awarding Saif al-Islam Gaddafi, the son of the Libyan leader, a PhD degree. The then Director of LSE, Howard Davies, resigned stating that he had made two errors of judgement, firstly that the donation from the Gaddafi Foundation was accepted and secondly that he had acted as a financial advisor to the Libyan government. It is important to undertake robust due diligence when donations are received, but also to have a collective governance view on the acceptable reputational risk associated with any substantial donation.

Universities face dilemmas of conscience when engaging with countries which are known to infringe human rights or where conflicts exist. Following the Russian invasion of Ukraine, the University of Hertfordshire chose to close a programme which it had been running with a reputable institution in Moscow for almost twenty years. It did so in a way which protected the interests of students currently being taught, who could complete the current semester or transfer to a UK-based course run by the university. It was a disappointing outcome to a valued relationship, and one in which neither party had any influence over the political currents and practical hurdles which caused the almost inevitable closure. Other relationships are less clear cut; many universities have teaching and research collaborations in China, indeed the University of Nottingham has a campus there. Human rights issues and accusations of patent and other intellectual property infringement and even overt spying have been levelled at Chinese students by the popular press. Universities rightly suggest that engaging with states like China, Saudi Arabia and Qatar is more likely to have a positive impact on their human rights attitudes than disengaging, and that engagement promotes the liberal values on which British democracy is founded.

Universities have also been faced with dilemmas regarding their endowments and investments. Should they convert to renewables (and how quickly)? Should they invest their endowment funds in tobacco, armaments or oil companies? If they are not prepared to invest in companies providing arms, should their researchers work with British defence companies? Even with the best efforts and intentions, investment may end up in unintended businesses as a consequence of the opacity of business linkages. Likewise, discoveries made with peaceful intent are also often useful in conflict.

Freedom of speech has been considered in more detail in Chapter 5. Suffice to say that, within the law, universities should encourage and ensure the freedoms of their academics and students to express and debate controversial and difficult issues. Indeed, this may be the single most important thing they do. That the last Conservative government considered it necessary to create a specific Higher Education Freedom of Speech Bill is a sad reflection on a sector which should be leading government in this regard, and on a government which did not trust us to do so. The Labour government elected in 2024 has reconsidered the Freedom of Speech Act in light of the attendant bureaucracy, and is likely to scrap some of its most burdensome provisions.

## Subsidiary companies

Universities may wish to establish subsidiary companies, where a commercial model may be deemed more appropriate than the quasi-public-sector model. This may also confer tax, employment, pensions and liability benefits. Coventry University (CU) has perhaps the most sophisticated model, with some twenty-three subsidiary companies comprising commercial, service and academic units, several of which offer a different course complexion than the main CU offering. For instance, CU London and CU Scarborough offer more vocationally based courses with flexible-learning options. Universities with international campuses have the added governance requirements of compliance with local laws and regulations, including what can often be complex educational regulations. They must also be assured of the financial sustainability of the international entity.

## Appointment periods

There is no set rule for the period of appointment of members or the chair of a governing body. Nevertheless, the most common models comprise two three-year or two four-year periods of office, with the second in each instance dependent upon satisfactory performance in the first. The periods of tenure may exceptionally be extended where, for instance, a member is appointed chair or very exceptionally if a skills-matrix determines that someone has a rare skill-profile which would be difficult to replace.

## Board effectiveness reviews

Board effectiveness reviews are now expected on a cycle of less than four years. Finding individuals or agencies competent to do a good review may be difficult, since with most consultants a report may emerge which recommends further use of consultants. To some extent the effectiveness will be self-evident: performance in the league tables, the REF and TEF; generating surplus, having sufficient reserves and appropriate borrowing demonstrated in annual accounts. Over and above these basics, effectiveness reviews may consider the relationship between governors and executive, the mechanism for assurance on quality and standards in education and the university's principles of autonomy, academic freedom and the best interests of its students.

University governance is by many measures excellent. Very few have ever gone out of business, most make remarkable contributions to their local communities and may make substantial contributions well beyond their immediate location. Governance models differ, sometimes dramatically, within nations and even more profoundly between nations, yet many countries have universities which are substantially older than any other business or agency, often outliving political regimes or government structures. Nevertheless, it seems likely that the regulatory environment for universities will become more stringent, since governments will want to ensure that fee-paying students and the taxpayer are achieving good value for money. This may create tension between the autonomy of the institution and its accountability to government and the public. It may result in universities becoming more bureaucratic and less agile, and they are also likely to become more risk-averse.

# CHAPTER 12

# After and Beyond: Employability, Alumni and Community

Knowledge and work are growing and changing at an electric pace, perhaps more profoundly than at any time in history, including the industrial revolution. Universities will have to balance the encouragement of knowledge, skills and behaviours, when each is in demand, to produce graduates for today and for tomorrow. Employability is demanded by government and employers and professional bodies, and will be enhanced by placements and apprenticeships. However, employability is also enhanced by critical thinking and problem-solving and universities will have to ensure that their educational programmes enhance these attributes as well as imparting knowledge and skills. Possibly the most significant change in our universities will be the response they make to requirements for upskilling and reskilling. This is one of the greatest challenges and substantial opportunities they face for the coming decades.

As discussed previously, the total of all human knowledge was estimated to double every 100 years up until 1900, by 1945 the doubling time had reduced to 25 years and by 2000 to 1 year.[1] It is now doubling every day, according to various estimates, and that time will soon be down to 12 hours according to IBM (see p. 118). This has at least two clear implications for university education: the first is that in all disciplines it is now impossible to know all there is to know. Indeed, knowing factual information is less important than being able to access it, filter it, and understand it when you do. The second implication is that the nature of work has changed and will continue to change both in the way we access knowledge for the jobs we do, but also in terms of the jobs themselves. Automation is likely to result in a change to about 30% of jobs by the mid-2030s, boosting the global economy by about $15 trillion, but making 44% of workers with low education at risk of job loss or change.[2] There are various estimates on the net change to employment, some quite pessimistic, but the World Economic Forum estimated that, by 2025, technology would have created at least 12 million more jobs than it destroyed.[3] There is also an increasing trend to have several jobs in a lifetime. In the US, the Bureau of Labor Statistics estimates that this might amount to, on average, 10 jobs before the age of 40 and 12 over a lifetime. Furthermore, the higher an individual's education, the lower the number of their unemployment stints and the longer they will remain with each employer.[4] There has also been a rise in the number of people accessing work in the 'gig economy' (doing 'gigs' or temporary flexible jobs). While a freelance employment economy may enhance flexible lifestyles, it also erodes the relationships between employers and their workers, and reduces the liabilities employers have for employee benefits like sickness and holiday pay, redundancy

---

1 Buckminster Fuller, *Critical Path*.
2 PWC, 'Will Robots really Steal our Jobs?', 2018, <https://www.pwc.co.uk/economic-services/assets/international-impact-of-automation-feb-2018.pdf>.
3 See A. Nunes, 'Automation Doesn't Just Create or Destroy Jobs – It Transforms Them', *Harvard Business Review*, 2 November 2021.
4 US Bureau of Labor Statistics, 2021, <www.bls.gov/nls>.

pay and pension contributions. The gig economy largely impacts low-skilled jobs but has also had a direct effect on university workers, with many visiting or part-time academics hired on this precarious basis. The Covid pandemic has further accelerated a growing trend for more flexible work locations. For many jobs this only requires access to a computer and competence to use it. The relatively modest level of digital competence required to hold a meeting and communicate electronically became apparent during the pandemic, when up to half of the population of the planet (3.9 billion people) were in lockdowns.[5]

The implications of the changes in work, as a result of growth of knowledge, automation, career changes, the gig economy and home or flexible working, for universities are profound. It is clear that current education practices will have to change to create graduates able to negotiate the new realities of work and we will have to provide a means to upskill and reskill those in and between jobs.

## Skills, knowledge and behaviours

In 2023, the Conservative government in the UK tied its flag to the mast of skills. It encouraged an education system which measures quality by the number of graduates getting highly paid jobs. They quoted employers who want 'oven-ready' graduates, able to 'hit the ground running' and decried the then current crop for not being as good as they used to be. As Eric Thomas, a former UUK President said, this is a criticism of every generation back to Nestor in *The Iliad* who preached that the young soldiers were not as good as they used to be. It is of course nonsense, and graduates of today are every bit as good, if not better, than those of yesteryear. They have generally had to accept debt, work part-time in order to live, and embrace the digital technologies essential to their learning. They drink less

---

5   A. Sandford, 'Coronavirus: Half of Humanity now on Lockdown as 90 Countries Call for Confinement', *euronews*, 2 April 2020, <https://www.euronews.com/2020/04/02/coronavirus-in-europe-spain-s-death-toll-hits-10-000-after-record-950-new-deaths-in-24-hou>.

and work harder than the baby-boomer generation and yet retain an optimism and enthusiasm for a better future. They are also somewhat brighter if the Flynn effect of rising IQ is to be believed (see Chapter 3).[6] Nevertheless, challenges remain in ensuring that graduates have the knowledge, skills and behaviours essential to make good workers. Universities bear the responsibility in deciding how much disciplinary knowledge is essential and that we create the critical thinking, problem-solving capabilities and enterprising behaviours that our graduates will need. Graduates should have all the skills necessary to undertake a new job, and to know how to build on these when they enter work.

It has been suggested that it takes 10,000 hours at a complex task to gain expertise and so it seems unlikely that universities could, and inappropriate that they might try to, produce the finished article.[7] As with most things, a good education requires compromise. Universities, through their curricula, should ensure that their graduates have sufficient disciplinary knowledge and the ability to access and utilise more to give them early career competence. They should have the breadth of rudimentary skills which, with practice and perseverance, will make them expert and they should have the 'attributes and behaviours' appropriate to their work environment and to the broader role which they should embrace as active citizens in our societies.

## Employability

Universities (and the individuals or societies that fund them) should of course ensure that their graduates are able to get decent jobs. As well as the subject-related knowledge, skills and behaviours mentioned above, it is fair to expect that graduates might be articulate and that they might have an idea of what to expect in a job interview. They might also have been given support and advice in the creation of

---

6   Flynn, 'The Mean IQ of Americans'.
7   M. Gladwell, *Outliers: The Story of Success* (London, 2009).

a curriculum vitae and a job-application letter. They may be given advice regarding dress codes and behaviours which will make them attractive as employees. Some will consider this patronising and for them I recommend reading Hashi Mohamed's book *People Like Us* in which he clearly demonstrates why it is important to understand the expectations of potential employers and to present yourself in the most advantageous way during the recruitment process.[8] University careers offices are now providing this sort of support. It is also of interest to ask large employers of graduates what they want and what they ask of prospective employees in the recruitment process. Some large tech companies now expect subject-level competence as a given and focus their selection processes on attributes such as communication skills and teamworking ability. They rightly anticipate that employees with excellent communication and teamworking attributes will very quickly acquire any subject-level competencies which they lack at the time of recruitment. Enthusiasm for the role, interpersonal and communication skills, and some work or project experience are all highly valued by employers during the recruitment process.[9]

## Placements

Beyond immediate pre- or post-graduation support, many universities provide and encourage opportunities for placement periods within the undergraduate (or postgraduate) curriculum. Most extracurricular work contributes positively to the work-related behaviours which make prospective employees attractive – provided of course that students don't spend too much time working and not enough time on their studies. Most universities recommend a maximum number of hours per week: from zero at Oxbridge to about 20 hours for most others. It is self-evident that it will be helpful to a student to find work

---

8   H. Mohamed, *People Like Us: What it Takes to Make it in Modern Britain* (London, 2020).
9   CBI Economics, 'To what Degree? Understanding what UK Businesses look for in Graduates', 2024, <cbi.org.uk/cbi-economics>.

while at university closely aligned to their desired post-graduation job, thus providing enhanced and more targeted skills and behaviours. This idea generally forms the basis of the placement or internship schemes offered by many universities – some, such as Aston and Bath, to remarkable recruitment success. Placements are often highly beneficial to both the student and the employer. The student gains the skills and behaviours essential to their future employment, further consolidates their attraction (or otherwise) to their chosen career, perhaps gets a 'foot in the door' with a future employer, adds a string to the bow of their CV and often improves their chance of acquiring a good degree. Students who do placements do better on average than those who don't, with regard to their academic achievement.[10] This could be directly associated with the behaviours picked up in the workplace (for instance, they work harder) or it could be that more able and energetic students are the ones that choose to do a placement.

For the employer there is a range of benefits: they get an enthusiastic (hopefully), energetic and eager employee, and they may assess the placement student as a future full-time employee – it can be a very fruitful and extended job interview. They also pick up the latest teachings from the university and may consequently introduce new products or practices. They can use the placement as a way of engaging with the university and vice versa. It should not be seen as cheap employment, but, given the career stage of the placement student, is likely to require only modest investment. It should also be embraced by the employer as an opportunity to help the learning process, and universities should work with employers to give placement students a very positive learning experience. It is obvious that an employer will have to make some early investment in the process – induction and health-and-safety training being essential. In this regard, longer placements (six months to a year) are often more helpful to the employer who then has time for some return on their investment, and these

---

10  Brooks and Youngson, 'Undergraduate Work Placements'.

resemble older sandwich-type courses. Shorter-term placements are still useful to the student; veterinary students for example may spend time during their early vacations on sheep farms, in dairies, stables, kennels or piggeries, or in abattoirs, picking up the basics of husbandry and animal welfare, and in some relatively lower-skilled tasks which may still be extremely useful to their future career and give them some credibility when they first go into practice.

## Apprenticeships

As discussed in Chapter 8, apprenticeships represent the ultimate work-based educational experience, but rather than a work experience while in education it becomes an education experience while in work. The system of apprenticeships in England was reviewed and refreshed in 2017, with a more structured opportunity for higher-level (level-4 and above and degree) apprenticeships. In integrated degree apprenticeships the learner can do their endpoint assessment together with their degree assessment in an integrated way, thus completing their apprenticeship and acquiring a degree at the same time. The revised apprenticeship model required employers with a salary bill of more than £3 million to contribute to a levy of 0.5% of their salary bill. For universities, this provided the opportunity to become providers of apprenticeship education, employers of apprentices and funders of the scheme, and also to make a contribution to the creation of apprenticeship standards, although these were primarily created by employer groups relevant to each discipline area.

For learners, apprenticeships offer the opportunity to have a job and thus earn money while studying for a degree, without the burden of tuition fees. This no doubt contributes to the popularity of apprenticeship programmes at level 6 and above, which increased by 21.2% in 2021/22.[11] Learners have to devote 20% of their time to 'off the job' studying. Although they are not guaranteed a job at the

---
11  UUK, *Our Universities*.

end of the apprenticeship, they are often ultimately employed by the same business which provided the apprenticeship, and which has made such a large investment in them. While those doing higher and degree apprenticeships in universities will have the same access to all the university's clubs, sports and support, the nature of their jobs may restrict their ability to fully participate and therefore they might not get the full traditional campus-based university experience. For those who desire this type of education, apprenticeships provide a wonderful opportunity. The benefits to the individual – no student debt and earn while you learn – are substantial, and arguably unfairly greater than the benefits to the conventional graduate who has to fund their education through the loan scheme and often has to take up part-time work to cover living expenses. For apprentices, even the time 'off the job' dedicated to learning is done during work time, thus impacting the employer's efficiency. There is a strong case that some of the learning should be done in the learner's personal time, thus more equitably balancing contributions from business, state and individual.

For universities offering apprenticeships there is an additional element of risk (if quality assurance is seen as a risk) since apprenticeships fall under the remit of the quality-regulator Ofsted (Office for Standards in Education) and not, as until recently (in England), under that of the QAA as the designated quality body for the OfS, or directly under the quality scrutiny of the OfS itself. Universities experiencing an Ofsted inspection for the first time may be unprepared for the intensity of the process and the detailed requirements on safeguarding or British values. It is also challenging that the Ofsted process encourages the separation of apprenticeship learners, at least from an operational perspective, from the general student population. More integrated systems, where apprentices and conventional undergraduates are taught together, are undoubtedly more difficult to quality assure, given the different regulatory authorities with responsibility, but do have the advantage of more rapidly and effectively embracing good practice across the learner and student populations. A further limitation of Ofsted is that its processes have evolved to inspect institutions (schools and colleges) which largely teach students who are eighteen years old or younger. Many university apprentices are twenty-five years old or more and, when asked about their evening participation in co-curricular societies, are likely to respond that they need to get home to look after their families. Ofsted encourage co-curricular activities as part of the learning experience.

While apprenticeships are undoubtedly valuable, they are often advocated by politicians and others as preferred alternatives to conventional degree programmes for unjustified reasons. Having individuals with the knowledge, skills and behaviours essential to a job is likely to enhance their productivity in employment and should be encouraged – what it will not do is create or encourage the mindset necessary to establish a new business. While some former apprentices may ultimately establish their own businesses, graduates who have been exposed to enterprise and entrepreneurship education are more likely to do so (see Chapter 8). Since new businesses tend to have greater impacts on employment and economic development than older, established businesses, it is important that we continue to encourage these traits in our university graduates and support the more conventional degree programmes in which they are fostered.

## Professional bodies

Many, particularly vocational, courses taught within universities require accreditation by the relevant Professional, Statutory and Regulatory Bodies (PSRBs) in order for the graduate to practise their profession subsequently. While the PSRBs undoubtedly maintain and protect the standards required of professional practitioners, they can be perceived to be at odds with best educational practice. They may for instance demand particular staff-to-student ratios, curricular content and university infrastructure without evidence that these are necessary to educate competent practitioners. Furthermore, the inspectors generally comprise those who have succeeded within their professions, not necessarily those who have studied or considered excellent pedagogy. Most PSRBs now justifiably require continuing professional development (CPD) of their practising members. The requirement for CPD is likely to grow further and become more structured and quality-assured, as the general public become more litigious. This provides an opportunity for universities to enhance their CPD provision and create more opportunities for lifelong learning.

## Lifelong learning

The growth in knowledge as well as the evolution of work make lifelong learning essential. Many universities offer short CPD courses to upskill individuals whilst longer courses, to degree and master's level, exist for reskilling. The uptake of longer courses, and in particular longer 'part-time' and 'from-the-workplace' courses declined in the UK when funding for equivalent or lower-level qualifications (ELQs) or second first degrees was withdrawn in 2008. It seems quite justifiable if funding is tight and provided by the state, to preferentially fund those who have not yet undertaken a degree programme, rather than those who already have a degree. Nevertheless, for all the reasons stated above in relation to future work and given that the emphasis in the UK at least has changed from state funding to loan funding, this needs to be revisited. The UK government introduced a Lifelong Learning Bill, which received royal assent in 2023, with a view to going live in 2026. While the details need to be clarified, it is likely that everyone will be entitled to about four years (480 credits) of post-school education, which can be taken at any time throughout an individual's working life, with a maximum of 180 credits taken in any 12-month period. People will probably be able to take packages of 30 or more credits (one credit represents 10 hours of learning) and may be able to transfer these between universities. It is also likely that loans will be available to those who have already completed educational programmes at the same or even at a higher level, thereby removing the ELQ restrictions and thus basing study on entitlement rather than qualification.[12] This proposal is to be greatly welcomed, indeed our future as an enterprising, energetic and economically vibrant society depends on it.

For universities to deliver in such a flexible way will demand substantial change. Flexibility of curriculum, timetable, start and finish dates, type of delivery (e.g., a blended approach) and facilities (classrooms as well as laboratories – if they exist as we know them, since online teaching and simulated laboratories may well be utilised) will be essential. It is likely that employers will also have to change – learning opportunities can only be offered if they are financially viable to the academic provider, this requires minimum cohort sizes (even for effective online delivery). Employers may need to start thinking about block release and partnering with other businesses with similar skills shortages, and universities must consider weekend, evening and traditional vacation courses. Employees will also have to change: lifelong learning will require investment of time and energy in their learning activities. People will have to devote time and effort to upskilling and more frequently to complete reskilling, perhaps within their own vocation or beyond.

## Expectation inflation

As knowledge grows and more countries wish to benefit from the knowledge economy which depends on quantity, quality, accessibility and interpretation of knowledge and information, it is clear that those embracing it require higher-level skills. Jobs which previously required bachelor's-level education now require master's level, and the

---

12 'Lifelong Learning Entitlement Overview', <https://www.gov.uk/government/publications/lifelong-learning-entitlement-lle-overview/lifelong-learning-entitlement-overview>.

research skills developed during a PhD are more sought after then ever before. Between 2014 and 2018 the number of students graduating with a bachelor's degree in the UK increased by 6.8%, those graduating with a taught master's increased by 18.3% and those graduating with a PhD by 10.4%.[13] In the US, a survey suggests that 37% of employers are hiring graduates with bachelors' degrees for positions which would have historically gone to those with high-school-level diplomas and 27% of employers are hiring master's graduates for positions which would previously have gone to bachelor's-level graduates.[14]

There is an unhelpful narrative advanced by some of our politicians and commentariat that too many people go to university and that they end up doing jobs which could as easily be done by those without degrees. Recommendations regarding the optimal proportions of the 18–23-year-old population who ought to go to university are open to subjective judgement, but the contribution of graduates to the economy is considered in Chapter 6 and broadly supports the contention that more is better. It is certainly incorrect that we are producing too many graduates for the job market. There are (as of 2022) one million more professional jobs than workers with degrees to fill them, and double the number of UK employees are under-qualified than over-qualified.[15] This is despite a rise in UK workers in professional jobs from 11.1 million in 2004 to 15.9 million in 2022.[16]

## Ageing population

The global median age is getting older; it was 21.5 years in 1970 and

---

13  HESA, 'Higher Education Student Statistics: UK 2018/19 – Qualifications Achieved', 16 January 2020, <hesa.ac.uk>.
14  L. Nikravan, 'More than 1 in 4 Employers are Hiring Employees with Master's Degrees for Positions that had been primarily held by those with Four-Year Degrees in the Past', *PR Newswire*, 17 March 2016, <prnnewswire.com/news-release/more-than-1-in-4-employers-are-hiring-employees-with-masters-degrees>.
15  UUK, *Busting Graduate Job Myths* (London, 2022).
16  ONS, Employment by Occupation, 2021, <https://www.ons.gov.uk/employmentandlabourmarket/peopleinwork/employmentandemployeetypes/datasets/employmentbyindustryemp13>.

was over 30 years by 2019.[17] However, this hides very great variation in median age by country. In 2015 Japan had the highest median age (46.3 years) while Niger had the lowest (14.9 years). Higher-income countries tend to have higher median ages.[18] In the UK the median age was 34.9 in 1950 and 40.8 in 2020 and that upward trend is likely to continue, although it is somewhat tempered by the lower median age of those from mixed ethnic and Asian groups.[19] Although people in the UK are likely to have to work longer, as pension funds strain under the ageing demographic, increasing lifespan means it is also likely that there will be a larger population of retirees experiencing relatively long periods of potentially healthy free time. This could provide an opportunity for recreational learning and could offer universities the opportunity to utilise facilities outside normal working or learning hours. It could also helpfully utilise libraries, learning resource centres and sports facilities as well as filling cafes and refectories.

## Alumni and community

The relationship between universities and their alumni is perhaps stronger in US universities and some of the ancient universities in the UK than with the more recently established universities. In the US this is largely cultural: alumni who succeed – even when they have paid for their education – are often enthusiastic to support their alma mater financially. In 2023, the largest endowments in US universities were eyewatering, with Harvard ($40.9 billion), University of Texas ($30.8 billion) and Princeton ($25.9 billion) leading the list. There is also developed a bond of allegiance with the university sports teams and particularly the football team (not to be confused with soccer).

---

17  H. Ritchie and M. Roser, 'Age Structure Our World in Data', 2019, <https://ourworldindata.org/age-structure>.
18  United Nations Population Division (Median Age), 2017, <https://ourworldindata.org/age-structure>
19  ONS, 'Ethnic Group differences in Health, Employment, Education and Housing shown in England and Wales', Census 2021, 15 March 2023.

In US universities and colleges football is enormously popular – in some areas even more popular than its professional equivalent – and followed on television, social media, as well as live, where more than 100,000 fans may turn up for a single game – the Michigan Wolverines (University of Michigan) averaged over 112,000 fans each game during 2021.

The relationship with alumni in the UK is developing, but simply by dint of longevity (more graduates and older graduates) it is likely to be stronger in the older universities. The opportunity for substantial fundraising through alumni is also enhanced where the alumni are more successful and have greater disposable wealth – also often a feature of older universities with a high reputation. Universities, and more broadly higher education institutions, have of course a long history of fundraising from their alumni and communities for their own charitable purposes, and often by way of 'Rag weeks' for more general charitable causes. The Royal Veterinary College undertook a particularly imaginative fundraising appeal in the 1930s: using a specially constructed horse 'nosebag' (claimed to be the 'World's Largest') into which the coins were thrown, they collected almost 130 million farthings, which contributed to the rebuilding of an animal hospital in Camden in London. The changing world of work offers further opportunities to engage alumni beyond simply fundraising. If a university has done a good job first time round it is likely that alumni will look favourably when selecting options for CPD or upskilling, or indeed when advising their own offspring on their choice of university. It is also possible that when and if lifelong learning entitlements are introduced, people may find a university which suits them and dip in and out of education in that institution throughout their lives. Universities may well find it sensible to offer discounts or incentives to keep loyal customers.

Universities are themselves communities, often large communities, of academics, professional and support staff, as well as more transient communities of students. They are also anchored in place, sometimes so integrated that their names (Cambridge or Cranfield for example) are synonymous with their towns or cities. They engage with their local communities in many ways: education, research, business, housing, transport and leisure. Local Enterprise Partnerships, Chambers of Commerce, housing associations and schools' governing bodies are often populated with university employees. Students volunteer in their communities and work part-time in local shops and businesses. Universities also contribute to the cultural and sporting facilities which local communities enjoy. University galleries in the UK attracted almost 6 million visitors in 2019/20 and more than a million people attended free drama, music and dance events. Furthermore, public lectures which contribute to the town-and-gown experience of most university towns attracted 2.3 million people.[20] In total, attendance and engagement figures increased from 528 million to 544 million between 2021/22 and 2022/23.[21]

The world of work is changing, and the role of a university to deliver opportunities for education after and beyond the 18–22-year-old window is growing. This will be greatly enhanced if and when a lifelong learning scheme is introduced in the UK. It is likely that the growth of knowledge and the evolution of work will require this globally and those universities which are able to respond with flexible offerings will be most successful.

---

20  UUK, *Our Universities*.
21  UUK, 'New Data shows Universities Open their Doors to Local Communities', 2024, <https://www.universitiesuk.ac.uk/latest/insights-and-analysis/new-data-shows-universities-open-their>.

# CHAPTER 13
# Splendid Institutions: Evolving and Improving

There are many books written about universities, often suggesting apparently radical ways in which university education might be revolutionised, universities restructured, or indeed even replaced. This is not one of them. Rather it celebrates the excellent contribution which universities make in the UK and elsewhere to enlightenment and prosperity. Most of the radical improvements suggested by others, and the revolutionary redesign of our universities, are already happening. Universities are remarkably plastic organisations, adapting and transforming all the time. That the 'modern' university has evolved, survived and flourished over a millennium is testament to that. It is much more likely that the digital revolution and artificial intelligence will be embraced, and will enhance the existing, ever-evolving model, rather than replace or consign universities to history.

There are, though, a number of suggestions made throughout this book which would, if adopted in the UK, improve what is an already excellent university sector. These are the author's own proposals for the further evolution of the university sector.

## Access
In relation to access, in England we have a fixation on A-levels for

entry. This narrows outlook too early in the educational journey, and the recommendation by the then Prime Minister Rishi Sunak to introduce an 'Advanced British Standard', embracing both technical and academic education, is to be welcomed. Whether the Advanced British Standard will confer on English 18-year-olds sufficient prior learning to adequately prepare them for a three-year bachelor's degree programme remains to be seen. The breadth of Scottish Highers is a prelude to a four-year undergraduate degree programme, as are SATs in the US. The English three-year bachelor's degree is built on the back of a school's A-level programme, which focuses on depth of learning at the sacrifice of breadth. The Labour government elected in 2024 may wish to revisit the Advanced British Standard proposal and if it does so, it should seek to give greater breadth and broader horizons to students prior to university, accepting that they must be sufficiently prepared for a three-year degree programme.

The mechanics of the entry process in British universities could also be improved. A post-qualifications admissions process based on actual rather than predicted grades, and contextualised for previous educational disadvantage (measured by the Index of Multiple Deprivation), should be uniformly embraced. The details are expanded in Chapter 3, but this could and should be adopted and does not require any changes to the timetable for publication of school or college exam results, or the start dates of university semesters in September. Nor would it require legislative changes by government, simply a consensus move by all higher education institutions and administrative adjustments by the UCAS, together with collective adjustments by schools with regard to timing of careers advice and guidance. Changes to candidate personal statements, towards more structured short-response questions designed to demonstrate motivation and preparedness, are already being implemented and should be encouraged. It should also be possible to have more harmonised interview processes where these are an absolute requirement, for instance for health-related courses where professional bodies demand them. A single interview, with the outcome accepted by several universities to which the candidate has applied, would be less burdensome to candidates and universities alike.

Universities should use real retrospective data to advertise minimum-entry requirements for courses, rather than fabricated (elevated) entry requirements designed to enhance brand image. UCAS is already making this data available, and it should be utilised in university marketing material. This could be more robustly regulated if the OfS were to mandate real retrospective data for marketing purposes in university conditions of registration.

## Education

It is unnecessary to make specific recommendations regarding the embrace of new and improved pedagogy, such as flexible blended approaches to learning, or about the way that artificial intelligence and data analytics might be used, since universities are already embracing these technologies and will quickly adapt to use the most successful methods. It is important, though, that they resist the utilitarian approach encouraged by some politicians toward skills-based programmes with employability targets, at the expense of critical thinking and problem-solving. Society and employers need to accept that graduates are produced who understand the basic concepts of their discipline and have the fundamental knowledge, skills and behaviour from which full competence and expertise can be developed in the workplace. Of course, this can be substantially enhanced by placements and internships, which should be encouraged in our students and supported by employers. Skills are enormously important for our future prosperity, and universities have a duty to confer appropriate basic skills, but an appropriate level of skills competence can only be gained by experience and practice, and for that the workplace is essential. Degree apprenticeships, sandwich courses and placements are excellent for skills training, but even in these programmes skills should not be prioritised over critical thinking and problem-solving.

## The experience

Universities must uphold freedom of speech and academic freedoms, unconstrained by political doctrine. The legislation which safeguards free speech (if it survives its passage through parliament) should be seen as a low tide only, and the crashing waves of debate and discourse encouraged across all the difficult and contentious subjects faced by society. There is no place for no-platforms in our universities, and while trigger warnings may help prepare a student for disturbing material, students should not absent themselves, nor should they be exempted from material critical to their discipline – the study of which may confer essential competencies. Inclusive curricula which relate to diverse cultures should be encouraged, but there should be no attempt to blank out parts of history, however controversial or disturbing they may be.

## Research

Research should remain an integral part of university purpose, and should be funded on merit, whichever type or size of university undertakes it. Any attempts to create closed shops or favour a particular group of universities – even those with historically excellent reputations for research – should be resisted, and research funded purely on fair competition. There is much to be said for the proposals made by David Willetts that all government departments should have budgets for directed research.[1] Of course, these should not come at the expense of funding for the quality-related or response-mode research carried out by our universities. Furthermore, the Haldane principle (arm's length from government), regarding the appropriate areas eligible for research funding and the methods of distribution, should prevail.

---

1   Willetts, *A University Education*.

Although it is controversial to suggest it, there is much merit in the idea of REFs being carried out largely on metrics. This would not allow the narratives which in the current REF submission colour the research environment or the impact case studies, and which, together with the research outputs, make up the measures used. Metrics are justifiably criticised because weightings given to particular topics or journals, by dint of the numbers of academics researching these areas, bias the results. The most prestigious journals also gain excessive power by their attractiveness to researchers, and would do so even more overtly if metrics were used. However, with more sophisticated data analytics, carefully balanced metrics are likely to give a very similar outcome to the current panel-based methodology, at much less cost. A metrics-based methodology also runs contrary to the embrace of the San Francisco Declaration on Research Assessment (DORA), which suggests that metrics should only be used when appropriately contextualised. Nevertheless, it would dramatically reduce the cost (£471m in 2021) of the REF and would reduce the time and effort required by universities to make their submissions. There remains an intransigent problem of research funding – its competitive nature encourages universities to undertake research at less than full economic cost and to cross-subsidise (now largely from international student tuition-fee income) to make up the difference. If research is ever to become fully sustainable, it needs all universities to reset the quantum that can be carried out for the investment made, and it needs the funders (government, industry and charities) to fund adequately for the research they commission. This is unlikely to happen unless legislation dictates that only funding allocated for the purpose could be spent by universities on research. Even then, it would be difficult to accurately allocate teaching and research time to the academic doing both activities (the Humboldtian model), and it would erode the autonomy of the university to be so directive. Nevertheless, without a collective move to more efficient cost and accurate spend on research activity, universities will continue to cross-subsidise, and funders will be getting their research 'on the cheap' and at the expense of student education.

## Funding

Perhaps the most difficult and most important problem universities face is that of sustainable funding for teaching as well as research. Unlike research, where universities could simply do less of it to make it more cost effective, doing less teaching does not solve the problem, since each home-based UK student delivers what is now a fixed unit of resource, and that unit does not cover the cost of teaching in many subject areas. Indeed, doing more, where efficiencies of scale may bring down the unit of cost has merit, but only marginally, and no matter how big the class, it still carries a cost to deliver. In times of financial constraint, universities can stop capital construction and can increase student-to-staff ratios, but both strategies impact quality and of course can only offer temporary relief – eventually the buildings become uninhabitable and the student-to-teacher ratios unmanageable. Sustainable funding therefore is ultimately dependent on a system which provides increases in income in line with inflation (or close to that, assuming some efficiency savings). The current system could easily provide sustainability if the student tuition fees were index-linked to inflation, or if the government was prepared to supplement tuition fees with inflation-linked teaching grants. Index-linking tuition fees should not impact student loans in real terms, the current £9250 tuition fees are worth £6500 at 2012 costs, and graduates are now borrowing relatively less in real terms than they did in 2012. Indexing appropriately should ensure that future generations make the same contributions in real terms to the students of today. The problem is patently political and not structural. Government is also concerned about the level of repayment it receives on the tuition-fee loans it offers, there being a net loss in the current system associated with students who are unable to fully repay over a lifetime of earnings. Again, this could be largely solved by simply tweaking the current system rather than radically changing it. Decreasing the point at which students repay from a £25,000 salary to a £20,000 salary for instance, increasing the amount repayable from 9% of salary to 10–11%, and not writing the loan off (although the 40-year repayment period now in place has effectively done that). It could also be made more progressive by increasing the percentage repayable for higher paid graduates, although this would simply result in them paying off their loans earlier and would not result in larger overall government receipts, unless there was an expectation (adjustment) which made higher paid graduates repay more than they borrowed. There is a compelling argument that all student loans should only carry interest at the rate at which government can borrow money (or say RPI for simplicity) and not at some of the rates which have been imposed up to the present time (see Chapter 10).

The large number of participants in higher education, and therefore its very large cost, make funding from general taxation unattractive. It would also be unpalatable to those who do not go to university and therefore do not directly benefit. A more targeted graduate tax would have the disadvantages that if only those graduates following the introduction of the graduate tax were affected, it would attract insufficient income to pay for the system – at least in the first instance, and that it would require some sophisticated bureaucracy to ensure that the funding was distributed to universities according to the number of students that they teach, or number caps and restricted intake would have to be imposed. It has been suggested that an all-age graduate tax could be imposed[2] and that this would have the advantages of intergenerational equality, would fully fund the system if

---

2  A. Green and G. Mason, 'The Case for an All-Age Graduate Tax in England', London Centre for Learning and Life Chances in Knowledge Economies and Societies LLAKES Research Papers 61, 2017, pp. 1–37.

levied at the appropriate percentage of tax payable, and would require a lower rate of repayment/taxation than that imposed by the current loan repayment scheme of 9% (of salary above £25,000). Sperlinger and colleagues[3] propose a modified version which they call a 'participatory education tax', which would require all graduates (apart from those who had already repaid loans in the current schemes, or those who had partially repaid who could transfer into the tax scheme) to contribute. In this scheme there would be a differential rate of tax, dependent upon how many credits had been accumulated at university and on whether individuals were basic or higher-rate taxpayers. It would be a full lifetime tax, continuing into retirement, and they estimate that imposing a participatory education tax of between 0.5% and 2.0% on those who received subsidised education could generate £2.6 billion in annual revenue. This would still leave a large hole in the overall funding required for universities, which could of course be filled by levying a higher percentage tax, but it would also come as a nasty shock to those who went to university on the understanding of the funding models which existed at the time. Considering all the options for funding, the loan scheme, with modifications to make funding sustainable for universities and to reduce the loan-scheme deficit, is the most appropriate and equitable way of funding universities and should be maintained.

One further inequity in funding needs to be addressed. As outlined in Chapter 10, classroom-based subjects are generally less costly to teach than laboratory or clinical subjects, and the graduates of some subjects, medicine and economics for example, earn much more than those of nursing and teaching. The tuition-fee rates in universities should be adjusted accordingly. This has been achieved in Australia, by banding tuition fees according to cost of delivery, likely future salary benefits and the needs of society (nurses are expensive to teach

---

3   T. Sperlinger, J. McLellan and R. Pettigrew, *Who are Universities For? Re-making Higher Education* (Bristol, 2018).

and are unlikely to have high salaries, but we certainly need them). A banding system of this type should be introduced in England and should be embraced within the modified loan scheme proposed above.

A contribution to tertiary education should be made by business. Currently, businesses with a salary bill of more than £3 million pay 0.5% of their salary bill into an apprenticeship levy (which will become a skills levy), primarily to pay for apprentices in their own businesses in England, but into a communal pot for apprenticeship-funding in Scotland. Most businesses, large and small, benefit from access to graduate employees, and the benefits extend to those graduates who undertook conventional degree programmes as well as graduate apprenticeships. Furthermore, the access to employees with relevant knowledge, behaviour and skills is supported by both further and higher education. There is a very persuasive argument that all businesses should contribute to a tertiary-education levy, indeed, that it might be more than 0.5% of salary bill. UK businesses spend about half that of their European competitors on employee training, and this has fallen by 28% since 2005.[4] While this generally comprises post-college or -university training, overall underinvestment in education and training no doubt accounts for much of the overall poor productivity of British business and industry. A larger business levy for tertiary education may prove unpopular in the short term, but could greatly support improved productivity and benefit businesses in the long term. Graduate apprenticeships are undoubtedly a very good option: the apprentices have a job and get paid while doing their apprenticeship, they graduate without student-loan debt, and they get time off their work to study. Compare this to the conventional undergraduate-degree student, who has to take out a loan to pay for

---

4 Learning and Work Institute, 'Employer investment in training plummets 28% since 2005, putting the Government's ambition of a high skill, high wage economy at risk, report warns', April 2022, <https://learningandwork.org.uk/news-and-policy/employer-investment-in-training-plummets-28-since-2005-putting-the-governments-ambition-of-a-high-skill-high-wage-economy-at-risk-report-warns/>.

their fees, may take out a loan to support their maintenance, and, since the maintenance loans have not been inflated, is likely to have to work part-time to survive. They will graduate with a substantial loan burden and will not have had the engagement with a business which supports the apprentice getting a permanent job. There is a strong case that apprentices receive a disproportionate amount of support, and that the 20% off the job during which they engage with education should be undertaken in their own time. This would give their sponsoring employer 20% more return on their investment and would make the programme more akin to a conventional degree programme. It would likely require universities to provide evening or weekend education for degree apprentices, which might also prove attractive to other learners.

## Business engagement

A notable success of universities over the last twenty-five years has been their increased engagement with business and industry. This is manifest in the degree apprenticeships described above, in the impact of their research as highlighted in the REF, in the number of patents they produce and processes they enhance, and in the spin-out and start-up businesses emerging from universities. All of this has been greatly enhanced by the various funding streams, including HEIF KTP and KEP funding, which have been made available to universities. These schemes should continue to be encouraged and receive uplifts in line with inflation. The discovery of new products and processes in universities, with their subsequent protection and exploitation, are greatly beneficial to the economy and, by the return of royalty or other payments, to the discovering university. Academics should be incentivised to exploit their ideas by direct support from universities, through patent or protection offices, provision of spin-out facilities and even start-up funding. It has been suggested that university equity in spin-out businesses should be restricted to between 10% and 25%

for life science spin-outs[5] and the restricted ownership by the parent university should help incentivise the discovering academic to take the commitment to spin-out, with the prospect of greater ownership and profit. Universities should also consider safety-net policies, whereby an academic stepping out to start up a business may have a guaranteed (funding permitted) return to an academic post should the start-up fail. This could overcome the fear of failure and reluctance to take risk. Government should also consider increasing and simplifying the process by which businesses receive tax relief on funding invested in collaborative or sponsored research in universities.

One further recommendation which might support business and the economy is to make enterprise modules part of all undergraduate degree programmes. Many disciplinary leaders will suggest that there is not enough space in the curriculum for an enterprise module. However, I believe that a reduction in disciplinary content in any course to make space for education in enterprise would be worth it. Even in those courses where graduates are unlikely to want to start or enter a business, an enterprising mindset would challenge the status quo of their discipline with positive effects.

## Internationalisation

One of the greatest achievements of British universities over the last twenty-five years has been their internationalisation. In particular, the contribution that international students coming to the UK have made to Britain's soft power, and their contribution to the UK's economy and human capital, not to mention the financial and cultural contribution they have made to our universities (see Chapter 9). The attractiveness of the UK to international students is enhanced by teaching generally being in English, and in recent years by the automatic access of

---

5  I. Tracey and A. Williamson, 'Independent Review of University Spin-out Companies: Final Report and Recommendations', Department for Science, Innovation and Technology and HM Treasury, 2023, <https://www.gov.uk/government/publications/independent-review-of-university-spin-out-companies>.

international students who graduate in the UK to a graduate-route visa (a post-study two-year work visa). This has the dual advantage of being an attractive opportunity for prospective international students and an economic benefit to the UK by way of brain gain, employee availability and tax receipts from the international graduates while in employment. The political uncertainty surrounding the graduate-route visa in absolute and qualitative terms (making it dependent on salary level for example) appears to have been resolved as a result of the positive findings of the MAC and QAA (see Chapter 9). It should be baked into the policies of all our political parties and not used in the vote-winning rhetoric of politicians trying to demonstrate an impact on immigration statistics.

## Governance

My final recommendation relates to university governance in England at a sectoral level. The OfS is now sufficiently embedded to be able to move to a risk-based model, whereby evidence of good practice by universities should be rewarded by a lower burden of oversight and less intrusion. For instance, why do five-year rolling financial forecasts need to be provided every year? If a university has a history of strong finances and a sensible five-year forecast, why not only require it every five years? A new way of policy decision-making should also be sought. Consultations are time-consuming and do not seem to affect the decisions being made, which appear entirely political. Finally, a more transparent and independent (non-political) way of appointing the board of the OfS would give both students and universities more confidence in its decision-making.

None of the recommendations in this chapter specifically ask for more real-term funding from government. The recommendation relating to sustainable funding certainly asks for more from the student (but only inflation-linked uplifts) and will require bold political direction to enact. Most of the other recommendations require collective action on the part of the university sector itself. I believe each recommendation would improve our universities and enhance their reputation internationally. Only two are genuinely existential and they are interrelated. A sustainable funding system must be found in the longer term, for teaching UK undergraduates and for research. In the immediate and longer term, a competitive visa-system must be found, which encourages international students who currently fill the funding gap and which, over the longer term, will consolidate our international competitiveness and add lustre to our universities.

Unlike other authors writing about universities, I do not think they need radical change forced upon them, either to survive or to improve; they do that for themselves. Our universities are fabulous organisations, they anchor our communities, enhance our human capital, stimulate our economy and shape our culture. I can do no better than finish by quoting John Masefield, then Poet Laureate, at the installation of the 6th Earl of Harewood as Chancellor of the University of Sheffield, on 25 June 1946.

*There are few earthly things more splendid than a university. In these days of broken frontiers and collapsing values, when every future looks somewhat grim and the dams are down and the floods are making misery, when every ancient foothold has become something of a quagmire, wherever a university stands, it stands and shines; wherever it exists, the free minds of men, urged on to full and fair enquiry, may still bring wisdom into human affairs.*

*There are few earthly things more beautiful than a university. It is a place where those who hate ignorance may strive to know, where those who perceive truth may strive to make others see; where seekers and learners alike, banded together in the search for knowledge, will honour thought in all its finer ways, will welcome thinkers in distress or in exile, will uphold ever the dignity of thought and learning, and will exact standards in these things.*

*They give to the young in their impressionable years, the bond of a lofty purpose shared, of a great corporate life whose links will not be loosed until they die.*

*They give young people that close companionship for which youth longs, and that chance of the endless discussion of the themes which are endless, without which youth would seem a waste of time.*

*There are few things more enduring than a university. Religions may split into sect or heresy; dynasties may perish or be supplanted, but for century after century the university will continue, and the stream of life will pass through it, and the thinker and the seeker will be bound together in the undying cause of bringing thought into the world. To be a member of these great societies must ever be a glad distinction.*

# Bibliography

Aaltonen, S., Latvala, A., Jelenkovic, A., Rose, R.J., Kujala, U.M., Kaprio, J. and Silventoinen, K., 'Physical Activity and Academic Performance: Genetic and Environmental Associations', *Medical Science Sports Exercise*, 52/2 (2020), pp. 381–90, <https://doi.org/10.1249/mss.0000000000002124>.

Advance HE, 'Professional Standards Framework for Teaching and Supporting Learning in Higher Education 2023', <www.advance-he.ac.uk>.

Aitken, M., 'The Rise of Women in the Profession', *In Practice*, 25/5 (2003), pp. 292–4.

Alatas, S.F., 'From Jami'ah to University Multiculturalism and Christian-Muslim Dialogue', *Current Sociology*, 54/1 (2006), pp. 112–32, <https://doi.org/10.1177/0011392106058837>.

Amis, K., 'Lone Voices', *Encounter*, July 1960, pp. 6–11.

Andrade, M.S. and Alden-Rivers, B., 'Developing a Framework for Sustainable Growth of Flexible Learning Opportunities', *Higher Education Pedagogies*, 4/1 (2019), pp. 1–16, <https://doi.org/10.1080/23752696.2018.1564879>.

Ashwin, P., 'What is the Teaching Excellence Framework in the United Kingdom, and Will it Work?', *International Higher Education*, 88 (2017), pp. 10–11, <https://doi.org/10.6017/ihe.2017.88.9683>.

Association of Public & Land-Grant Universities, 'How Does a College Degree Improve Graduates' Employment and Earnings Potential?', 2022, <https://www.aplu.org/our-work/4-policy-and-advocacy/publicuvalues/employment-earnings>.

Aznar, A.R., Forth, J., Mason, G., O'Mahony, M. and Bernini, M., 'UK Skills and Productivity in an International Context', BIS research paper 262, BIS/15/704, December 2015, <www.gov.uk/bis>.

Badran, A., Baydoun, E. and Hillman, J.R. (eds), *Higher Education in the Arab World: Research and Development* (Cham, 2022), <https://doi.org/10.1007/978-3-030-80122-9>.

Ball, P., 'The Lightning-fast Quest for COVID Vaccines – and What it Means for Other Diseases', *Nature*, 589 (2021), pp. 16–18, <https://doi.org/10.1038/d41586-020-03626-1>.

Barber, M., Bird, L., Flemming, J., Titterington-Giles, E., Edwards, E. and Leyland, C., 'Gravity Assist: Propelling Higher Education towards a Brighter Future', Report of the Digital Teaching and Learning Review, OfS, 1 March 2021, <https://www.officeforstudents.org.uk/digitalreview/>.

Barnett, C., *The Audit of War: The Illusion and Reality of Britain as a Great Nation* (London, 1986).

Barnett, R., 'Conditions of Flexibility: Securing a more Responsive Higher Education System', Advance HE, 2014, <https://www.advance-he.ac.uk/knowledge-hub/conditions-flexibility-securing-more-responsive-higher-education-system>.

Barrows, H.S., 'Problem-based Learning in Medicine and Beyond: A Brief Overview', *New Directions for Teaching and Learning*, 68 (1996), pp. 3–12, <https://doi.org/10.1002/tl.37219966804>.

Bekhradnia, B., 'Foreword: The Early Years', in Carasso (ed.), *UK Higher Education*.

Beloff, M., *The Plateglass Universities* (London, 1968).

Blackman, T., 'What Affects how much Students Learn?', HEPI policy note 5, January 2018, <https://www.hepi.ac.uk/wp-content/uploads/2018/01/HEPI-Policy-Note-5-What-affects-how-much-students-learn08_01_17.pdf>.

Blackman, T., 'What Affects Student Wellbeing?', HEPI policy note 21, February 2020, <https://www.hepi.ac.uk/wp-content/uploads/2020/02/HEPI-Policy-Note-21-What-affects-student-wellbeing-13_02_20.pdf>.

Bloom, N., Jones, C.I., Van Reenen, J. and Webb, M., 'Are Ideas Getting Harder to Find', National Bureau of Economic Research working paper 23782, September 2017, doi. 10.3386/w23782, <https://www.nber.org/papers/w23782>.

Bogle, D., '100 Years of the PhD in the UK', <www.vitae.ac.uk>.

Boliver, V., 'How Fair is Access to More Prestigious UK Universities?',

*The British Journal of Sociology*, 64/2 (2013), pp. 344–64, <https://onlinelibrary.wiley.com/doi/full/10.1111/1468-4446.12021>.

Bols, A., 'Why it is time for University Governors to do more on Academic Quality', HEPI policy note 36, July 2022, <https://www.hepi.ac.uk/wp-content/uploads/2022/07/Why-it-is-time-for-university-governors-to-do-more-on-academic-quality.pdf>.

Bolton, P., 'Education: Historical Statistics', House of Commons Library SN/SG/4252, 28 November 2012.

Bolton, P., 'Higher Education Student Numbers', House of Commons Library research briefing 7857, 2 January 2024, <https://commonslibrary.parliament.uk/research-briefings/cbp-7857/>

Booth, J., Miller, J., Halterbeck, M. and Conlon, G., 'The Impact of the Higher Education Sector on the UK Economy', Summary Report for UUK, August 2023.

Bouchrika, I., 'College Dropout Rates: 2023 Statistics by Race, Gender & Income, Universities & Colleges', 26 September 2022, <https://research.com/universities-colleges/college-dropout-rates>.

Braguinsky, S. and Rose, D.C., 'Competition, Cooperation, and the Neighbouring Farmer Effect', *Journal of Economic Behaviour and Organization*, 72/1 (2009), pp. 361–76.

The British Academy, 'Shape Skills at Work', November 2022, <https://www.thebritishacademy.ac.uk/documents/4414/BA1096_SHAPE_SkillsAtWork_V8_Digital_Pages.pdf>.

Britton, J., Dearden, L., Shephard, N. and Vignoles, A., 'How English Domiciled Graduate Earnings vary with Gender, Institution Attended, Subject and Socio-economic Background', IFS working paper W16/06, 13 April 2016, doi.10.1920/wp.ifs.2016.1606.

Britton, J., Dearden, L., Waltmann, B. and van der Erve, L., 'Most students get a big pay-off from going to university – but some would be better off financially if they hadn't done a degree', IFS, 29 February 2020, <https://ifs.org.uk/news/most-students-get-big-pay-going-university-some-would-be-better-financially-if-they-hadnt-done>.

Britton, J., van der Erve, L., Belfield, C., Vignoles, A., Dickson, M., Zhu, Y., Walker, I., Dearden, L., Sibieta, L. and Buscha, F., 'How much does Degree Choice Matter?', *Labour Economics*, 79 (2022), <https://doi.org/10.1016/j.labeco.2022.102268>.

Brooks, R. and Youngson, P.L., 'Undergraduate Work Placements: An Analysis of the Effects on Career Progression', *Studies in Higher Education*, 41/9 (2014), pp. 1563–78, <https://doi.org/10.1080/03075079.2014.988702>.

Broughton, N. and Ussher, K., *Venturing Forth: Increasing High-value Entrepreneurship* (London, 2014).

*Browne Report*, 'Securing a Sustainable Future for Higher Education: An Independent Review of Higher Education Funding and Student Finance', BIS/10/1208, 12 October 2010, <https://www.gov.uk/government/publications/the-browne-report-higher-education-funding-and-student-finance>.

Bruce, G., 'Rechargeable Lithium Batteries', *Philosophical Transactions of the Royal Society A* (1996), <https://doi.org/10.1098/rsta.1996.0066>.

Buckley, P. and Lee, P., 'The Impact of Extra-Curricular Activity on the Student Experience', *Active Learning in Higher Education,* 22 (2021), pp. 37–48.

Buckminster Fuller, R., *Critical Path* (London, 1983).

Budge, D., 'Millennium Mothers want University Education for their Children', Centre for Longitudinal Studies, Institute of Education, 2010, <https://cls.ucl.ac.uk/millennium-mothers-want-university-education-for-their-children/>

Byrne, E. and Clarke, C., *The University Challenge: Changing Universities in a Changing World* (London, 2020).

*Cadbury Report*, Report of the Committee on the Financial Aspects of Corporate Governance (London, 1992).

Callendar, G.S., 'The Artificial Production of Carbon Dioxide and its Influence on Temperature', *Quarterly Journal of the Royal Meteorological Society*, 64 (1938), <https://doi.org/10.1002/qj.49706427503>.

Cantwell, B., Luca, S.G. and Lee, J.J., 'Exploring the Orientations of International Students in Mexico: Differences by Region of Origin', *Higher Education*, 57/3 (2009), pp. 335–54, <https://doi.org/10.1007/s10734-008-9149-x>.

Carasso, H. (ed.), *UK Higher Education – Policy, Practice and Debate during HEPI's First 20 Years*, HEPI report 161 (Oxford, 2023).

Carasso, H. and Plume, A., 'To Measure is to Know: Two Decades of Change in UK Higher Education through the Lens of the Sector's own Statistics', in Carasso (ed.), *UK Higher Education.*

Carvalho, A., 'Wishful Thinking about R&D Policy Targets: What Governments Promise and What They Actually Deliver', *Science and Public Policy*, 45/3 (2018), pp. 373–91, <https://doi.org/10.1093/scipol/scx069>.

Cassan, E., '"A New Logic": Bacon's *Novum Organum*', *Perspectives on Science*, 29/3 (2021), pp. 255–74, <https://doi.org/10.1162/posc_a_00368>.

CBI Economics, 'To what Degree? Understanding what UK Businesses look for in Graduates', 2024, <cbi.org.uk/cbi-economics>.

Centre for Entrepreneurs, 'Putting the Uni in Unicorn: The Role of Universities in Supporting High-growth Graduate Startups', April 2017, <https://centreforentrepreneurs.org/wp-content/uploads/2017/08/CFE-University-Entrepreneurs-Report-WEB.pdf>.

Centre for Entrepreneurs, *Incubation Nation: The Acceleration of UK Startup Support* (London, 2022).

Chapin, D.M., Fuller, C.S. and Pearson, G.L., 'A New Silicon p-n Junction Photocell for Converting Solar Radiation into Electrical Power', *Journal of Applied Physics*, 25 (1954), pp. 676–7.

Chartered Association of Business Schools, 'Business Schools delivering Value to Local and Regional Economies', September 2016, <https://charteredabs.org/wp-content/uploads/2016/09/Chartered-ABS-Delivering-Value-Report-2.pdf>.

Chickering, A.W. and Ehrmann, S., 'Implementing the Seven Principles: Technology as Lever', *AAHE Bulletin*, 49 (1996), pp. 3–6, <https://sphweb.bumc.bu.edu/otlt/teachingLibrary/Technology/seven_principles.pdf>.

Chickering, A.W. and Gamson, Z.F., 'Seven Principles for Good Practice in Undergraduate Education', *AAHE Bulletin*, 3 (1987), pp. 3–7, <https://eric.ed.gov/?id=ED282491>.

'Child Development: In the Beginning was the Word – How Babbling to Babies can Boost their Brains', *The Economist*, 22 February 2014, <https://www.economist.com/science-and-technology/2014/02/20/in-the-beginning-was-the-word>.

Choukeir, J., Kenyon, T. and Meghji, Z., 'Entrepreneurs for Change', *RSA Journal*, 4 (2022), <https://www.thersa.org/comment/2022/11/entrepreneurs-for-change>.

Clark, G., Marsden, R., Whyatt, J.D., Thompson, L. and Walker, M., '"It's everything else you do…": Alumni Views on Extracurricular Activities and Employability', *Active Learning in Higher Education*, 16/2 (2015), pp. 133–47.

Coate, K., Barnet, R. and Williams, G., 'Relationships Between Teaching and Research in Higher Education in England', *Higher Education Quarterly*, 55/2 (2001), pp. 158–74, <https://onlinelibrary.wiley.com/doi/abs/10.1111/1468-2273.00180>.

Commission on Race and Ethnic Disparities, 'The Report', March 2021, <https://assets.publishing.service.gov.uk/government/uploads/system/uploads/attachment_data/file/974507/20210331_-_CRED_Report_-_FINAL_-_Web_Accessible.pdf>.

Competition and Markets Authority (CMA), 'UK Higher Education Providers – Advice on Consumer Protection Law', CMA 33, 12 March 2015, <https://assets.publishing.service.gov.uk/government/uploads/system/uploads/attachment_data/file/428549/HE_providers_-_advice_on_consumer_protection_law.pdf>.

Connor, H., Tyers, C., Modood, T. and Hillage, J., 'Why the Difference? A Closer Look at Higher Education Minority Ethnic Students and Graduates', DfES research report 552, June 2004.

Cook, S., Watson, D. and Vougas, D., 'Solving the Quantitative Skills Gap: A Flexible Learning Call to Arms!', *Higher Education Pedagogies*, 4/1 (2019), pp. 17–31, <https://doi.org/10.1080/23752696.2018.1564880>.

Corver, M., 'The Perennial Challenge of Funding Undergraduate Higher Education', in Carasso (ed.), *UK Higher Education*.

Corver, M., 'Predicted Grades and University Admissions', in R. Hewitt (ed.), *Where Next for University Admissions?*, HEPI report 156 (Oxford, 2021).

'Contextual admissions "as abhorrent as racism" – ex-DfE adviser', *Times Higher Education*, 3 October 2022, <https://www.timeshighereducation.com/news/contextual-admissions-abhorrent-racism-ex-dfe-adviser#:~:text=In%20an%20apparent%20reference%20to,as%20abhorrent%20as%20discrimination%20on>.

Cross-Border Education Research Team (C-BERT), 'Branch Campus Listing', 2015, <http://www.globalhighered.org/branchcampuses.phd>.

CUC, 'Guide for Members of Higher Education Governing Bodies in the UK', November 2004, <dera.ioe.ac.uk>.

CUC, 'The Higher Education Code of Governance', 2020, <https://www.universitychairs.ac.uk/wp-content/uploads/2020/09/CUC-HE-Code-of-Governance-publication-final.pdf>.

Dandridge, N., 'The Relationship between Teaching and Research in UK Universities – What is it and does it Matter?', HEPI report 162, July 2023.

*Dearing Report*, Reports of the National Committee of Inquiry into Higher Education (London: HMSO, 1997).

DeBaun, B. and Roc, M., 'Saving Futures, Saving Dollars: The Impact of Education on Crime Reduction and Earnings', Alliance for Excellent Education, 2013, <www.all4ed.org>.

Department for International Trade, 'Inward Investment Report', August 2021, <https://www.gov.uk/government/statistics/department-for-international-trade-inward-investment-results-2020-to-2021>.

DfES, *Widening Participation in Higher Education* (London: HMSO, 2003).

Ding, D., Kolbe-Alexander, T., Nguyen, B., Katzmarzyk, P.T., Pratt, M. and

Lawson, K.D., 'The Economic Burden of Physical Inactivity: A Systematic Review and Critical Appraisal', *British Journal of Sports Medicine*, 51/19 (2017), pp. 1392–409.

Directorate-General for Education, Youth, Sport and Culture (European Commission), *ECTS Users' Guide 2015*, <https://data.europa.eu/doi/10.2766/87192>.

Drawdown, 'Table of Solutions', 2023, <drawdown.org/solutions/table-of-solutions>.

Eaton, G., 'How the Tax System Squeezes Graduates', *The New Statesman*, 8 September 2021, <https://www.newstatesman.com/economy/2021/09/how-the-tax-system-squeezes-graduates>.

'The Economic Impact of the UK Film Industry', *Oxford Economics*, 2010, <www.oxfordeconomics.com>.

Education and Skills Committee, *The Future of Higher Education*, 23 June 2003, HC 425-I.

Education Committee, *The Impact of COVID-19 on Education and Children's Services*, HC 254 2020, <https://committees.parliament.uk/event/1755/fomral-meeting-oral-evidence-session/>.

Education Encyclopaedia, 'Higher Education Curriculum – Traditional and Contemporary Perspectives', <https://education.stateuniversity.com/pages/1895/Curriculum-Higher-Education-TRADITIONAL-CONTEMPORARY-PERSPECTIVES.html>.

Emmerich, C.H., Gamboa, L.M., Hofmann, M.C.J., Bonin-Andresen, M., Arbach, O., Schendel, P., Gerlach, B., Hempel, K., Bespalov, A., Dirnagl, U. and Parnham, M.J., 'Improving Target Assessment in Biomedical Research: The GOT-IT Recommendations', *Nature Reviews Drug Discovery*, 20/1 (2021), pp. 64–81, <https://doi.org/10.1038/s41573-020-0087-3>.

Erudera, 'World's Most Educated Countries and their Main Common Characteristics', 5 October 2022, <https://erudera.com/resources/worlds-most-educated-countries-their-main-common-characteristics/>.

EU, European Commission, Directorate-General for Education, Youth, Sport and Culture, 'Erasmus + Higher Education Impact Study', Final Report, 2019, <https://data.europa.eu/doi/10.2766/162060>.

*European Education Area*, official website of the European Union, <https://education.ec.europa.eu>.

Evans, N., 'Diotima and Demeter as Mystagogues in Plato's Symposium', *Hypatia*, 21/2 (2006), pp. 1–27, <https://doi.org/10.1111/j.1527-2001.2006.tb01091.x>.

Fazackerley, A., 'Research Linked to Teaching – Official', *Times Higher Education*, 19 Nov 2004.

Fennell, A., 'Average Graduate Salary UK', 2022, <https://standout-cv.com/average-graduate-salary-uk>.

Fisher, R., 'Grade Inflation: What can Universities do about It?', UUK, 3 August 2022, <https://www.universitiesuk.ac.uk/latest/insights-and-analysis/grade-inflation-what-can-universities-do>.

Flynn, J.R., 'The Mean IQ of Americans: Massive Gains 1932 to 1978', *Psychological Bulletin*, 95/1 (1984), pp. 29–51, <https://doi.org/10.1037/0033-2909.95.1.29>.

Flynn, J.R., 'Massive IQ Gains in 14 Nations: What IQ Tests really Measure', *Psychological Bulletin*, 101/2 (1987), pp. 171–91, <https://doi.org/10.1037/0033-2909.101.2.171>.

Ford, J.A. and Schroeder, R.D., 'Higher Education and Criminal Offending over the Course of a Lifetime', *Sociological Spectrum*, 31/1 (2010), pp. 32–58, <https://doi.org/10.1080/02732173.2011.525695>.

Fox, A., 'Class and Equality', *Socialist Commentary*, May 1956, p. 13.

Fryer, T., Westlake, S. and Jones, S., 'Reforming the UCAS Personal Statement: Making the Case for a Series of Short Questions', HEPI Debate Paper 31, November 2022.

'Funder's errors do not excuse London Met, audit finds', *THE*, 13 August 2009, <https://www.timeshighereducation.com/news/funders-errors-do-not-excuse-london-met-audit-finds/407756.article>.

Fung, D., *A Connected Curriculum for Higher Education* (London, 2017).

Garrison, D.R. and Kanuka, H., 'Blended Learning: Uncovering Its Transformative Potential in Higher Education', *The Internet and Higher Education*, 7/2 (2004), pp. 95–105, <https://www.researchgate.net/publication/222863721_Blended_Learning_Uncovering_Its_Transformative_Potential_in_Higher_Education>.

Gilbert, B., McDougall, P. and Audretsch, D., 'New Venture Growth: A Review and Extension', *Journal of Management*, 32/6 (2006), pp. 926–50, <https://doi.org/10.1177/0149206306293860>.

Gladwell, M., *Outliers: The Story of Success* (London, 2009).

Goldfinch, S., Dale, T. and DeRouen Jr., K., 'Science from the Periphery: Collaboration, Networks and "Periphery Effects" in the Citation of New Zealand Crown Research Institutes Articles, 1995–2000', *Scientometrics*, 57/3 (2003), pp. 321–37, <https://doi.org/10.1023/A:1025048516769>.

González-Zamar, M.-D., Abad-Segura, E., Luque de la Rosa, A. and López-Meneses, E., 'Digital Education and Artistic-visual Learning in Flexible

University Environments: Research Analysis', *Education Sciences*, 10/11 (2020), p. 294, <https://doi.org/10.3390/educsci10110294>.

Good Governance Institute, Review of Governance for Plymouth University, March 2015, <https://www.plymouth.ac.uk/students-and-family/governance/review>.

Gordon, N., 'Flexible Pedagogies: Technology-enhanced Learning', The Higher Education Academy, January 2014, <https://www.advance-he.ac.uk/knowledge-hub/flexible-pedagogies-technology-enhanced-learning>.

'Graduate Labour Market Statistics', 9 June 2022, <explore-education-statistics.service.gov.uk/find-statistics/graduate-labour-markets/2021>.

Green, A. and Mason, G., 'The Case for an All-Age Graduate Tax in England', London Centre for Learning and Life Chances in Knowledge Economies and Societies LLAKES Research Papers 61, 2017.

Haidt, J. and Lukianoff, G., *The Coddling of the American Mind: How Good Intentions and Bad Ideas are Setting up a Generation for Failure* (London, 2019).

*Haldane Report*, Report of the Machinery of Government Committee (London: HMSO, 1918).

Hamilton, E. and Cairns, H., 'Introduction', in E. Hamilton and H. Cairns (eds), *The Collected Dialogues of Plato: Including the Letters*, Bollingen Series LXXI (Princeton, 1961).

Hansen, K., Jones, E., Joshi, H. and Budge, D. (eds), *Millennium Cohort Study, Fourth Survey: A User's Guide to Initial Findings* (London, 2010), <www.cls.ioe.ac.uk/MCSFfindings>.

Harper, R., Bretag, T., Ellis, C., Newton, P., Rozenberg, P., Saddiqui, S. and van Haeringen, K., 'Contract Cheating: A Survey of Australian University Staff', *Studies in Higher Education*, 44/11 (2018), pp. 1857–73, <https://doi.org/10.1080/03075079.2018.1462789>.

Harte, N.B. and North, J.A., *The World of UCL, 1828–2004* (London, 2004).

Hattie, J. and Marsh, H., 'The Relationship between Research and Teaching: A Meta-Analysis', *Review of Educational Research*, 66/4 (1996), pp. 507–42.

Hayton, J., 'Leadership and Management Skills in SMEs: Measuring Association with Management Practices and Performance', BIS research paper 224, March 2015, <https://assets.publishing.service.gov.uk/government/uploads/system/uploads/attachment_data/file/418404/bis-15-204-leadership-and-management-skills-in-sme.pdf>.

Hazelkorn, E., 'The Geopolitics of Rankings: The Positioning of UK Higher Education and Research', in Carasso (ed.), *UK Higher Education*.

HEPI, 'Digging in? The Changing Tenure of UK Vice-chancellors', HEPI policy note 34, May 2022, <https://www.hepi.ac.uk/2022/05/26/digging-in-the-changing-tenure-of-uk-vice-chancellors/>.

HEPI, 'UK student recruitment numbers down, but is that the whole story?', May 2024, <https://www.hepi.ac.uk/2024/05/30/uk-student-recruitment-numbers-down-but-is-that-the-whole-story/>.

Hermann, K., 'Developing Entrepreneurial Graduates: Putting Entrepreneurship at the Centre of Higher Education', National Endowment for Science, Technology and the Arts (NESTA), 2008, <https://ncee.org.uk/wp-content/uploads/2018/01/developing_entrepreneurial_graduates.1.pdf>.

HESA, 'Higher Education Student Statistics: UK 2018/19 – Qualifications Achieved', 16 January 2020, <hesa.ac.uk>.

HESA, 'Higher Education Student Statistics: UK, 2020/21', <hesa.ac.uk/news/01-02-2022/sb261-higher-education-staff-statistics>.

HESA, 'Non-UK HE Students by the Provider and Country of Domicile', 2022.

HESA, 'Higher Education Student Statistics: UK, 2021/22 – Where Students come from and go to Study', 2023, <https://www.hesa.ac.uk/news/19-01-2023/sb265-higher-education-student-statistics/location>.

HESA, 'What Do HE Students Study?', 31 January 2023, <https://www.hesa.ac.uk/data-and-analysis/students/what-study>.

Hillman, N., 'UK slips behind the US, which takes the number one slot, for educating the world's leaders', *HEPI blog*, 14 August 2018, <https://www.hepi.ac.uk/2018/08/14/uk-slips-behind-us-takes-number-one-slot-educating-worlds-leaders/>.

Hillman, N., 'From T to R Revisited: Cross-subsidies from Teaching to Research after Augar and the 2.4% R&D Target', HEPI report 127, 9 March 2020, <https://www.hepi.ac.uk/wp-content/uploads/2020/03/From-T-to-R-revisited.pdf>.

Hjalmarsson, R. and Lochner, L., 'The Impact of Education on Crime: International Evidence', CESifo DICE Report, *ifo Institut – LeibnizInstitut für Wirtschaftsforschung an der Universität München*, 10/2 (2012), pp. 49–55.

Holland, D., Liadze, I., Rienzo, C. and Wilkinson, D., 'The Relationship between Graduates and Economic Growth across Countries', BIS research paper 110, August 2013, <www.gov.uk/bis>.

'How Education as a Human Right is Changing the World We Live in', *University of the People*, 8 December 2023, <https://www.uopeople.edu/blog/how-education-as-a-human-right-is-changing-the-world-we-live-in/>.

Independent Review of the Office for Students – Fit for the Future: Higher Education Regulation towards 2035, July 2024, <assets.publishing.service.gov.uk/media/66a261fda3c2a28abb50d758/Indpendent_review_of_the_office_for_students.pdf.pdf>.

Innovation, Universities, Science and Skills Committee, *Withdrawal of Funding for Equivalent or Lower Level Qualifications (ELQs)*, 17 March 2008, HC 187-I 2007–08.

Institute of Directors in Southern Africa, 'King IV: Report on Corporate Governance for South Africa 2016', <https://www.adams.africa/wp-content/uploads/2016/11/King-IV-Report.pdf>.

Institute of Fiscal Studies, 'The Impact of Undergraduate Degrees on Lifetime Earnings', 29 February 2020, <https://ifs.org.uk/publications/impact-undergraduate-degrees-lifetime-earnings>.

Intellectual Property Office, 'Graphene: The Worldwide Patent Landscape in 2015', UK Intellectual Property Office Informatics Team, March 2015, <www.ipo.gov.uk/informatics>.

Intergovernmental Panel on Climate Change, *Technical Summary* (Cambridge, 2021), <https://doi.org/10.1017/9781009157896.002>.

International Human Genome Sequencing Consortium, 'Initial Sequencing and Analysis of the Human Genome', *Nature*, 409 (2001), pp. 860–921, <https://doi.org/10.1038/35057062>.

Jackson, S. and Bohrer, J., 'Quality Assurance in Higher Education: Recent Developments in the United Kingdom', *Research in Comparative and International Education*, 5/1 (2010), pp. 77–87, <https://doi.org/10.2304/rcie.2010.5.1.77>.

Jacobson, M.J., 'Educational Complex Systems and Open, Flexible, and Distance Learning: A Complexity Theoretical Perspective', *Distance Education*, 40/3 (2019) pp. 419–24, <https://doi.org/10.1080/01587919.2019.1656152>.

Jeffery, A.J., Rogers, S.L., Jeffery, K.L.A. and Hobson, L., 'A Flexible, Open, and Interactive Digital Platform to Support Online and Blended Experiential Learning Environments: Thinglink and Thin Sections', *Geoscience Communication*, 4/1 (2021), pp. 95–110, <https://doi.org/10.5194/gc-4-95-2021>.

JISC, Effective Practice in a Digital Age, 2009, <https://www.Jisc.ac.uk/practice>.

JISC, 'The Future of Assessment: Five Principles, Five Targets for 2025', 2020, <https://repository.jisc.ac.uk/7733/1/the-future-of-assessment-report.pdf>.

JISC, 'Student Digital Experiences Insights Survey: Higher Education Findings', 2021, <Jisc.ac.uk/reports/

student-digital-experience-insights-survey-2021-22-higher-education-findings>.

Kari, J.T., Viinikainen, J., Böckerman, P., Tammelin, T.H., Pitkänen, N., Lehtimäki, T., Pahkala, K., Hirvensalo, M., Raitakari, O.T. and Pehkonen, J., 'Education Leads to a more Physically Active Lifestyle: Evidence based on Mendelian Randomization', *Scandinavian Journal of Medicine and Science in Sports*, 30/7 (2020), pp. 1194– 204, <https://doi.org/10.1111/sms.13653>.

Keeling, C.D., 'The Concentration and Isotopic Abundances of Carbon Dioxide in the Atmosphere', *Tellus*, 12/2 (1960), pp. 200–2023.

Kelsey, S., 'Explore the World's Top Universities', *US News & World Report*, 8 Oct 2013, <news.yahoo.com/explore-worlds-top-universities-142243604.html?>.

Kent, D.C., 'Challenges in a Disrupted World: Branch Campuses from the United States', *International Higher Education*, 104 (2020), pp. 14–15, <https://ejournals.bc.edu/index.php/ihe/article/view/14343>.

Kernohan, D., 'National Student Survey 2024', Wonkhe, <https://wonkhe.com/blogs/national-student-survey-2024/>.

Kerr, C., *The Gold and the Blue: A Personal Memoir of the University of California 1949–1967*, vol. i (Berkeley, CA, 2001).

King, M. and Woolley, E., 'Estimating the Effect of UK Direct Public Support for Innovation', BIS analysis paper 4, BIS/14/1168, November 2014, <www.gov.uk/bis>.

Kondakci, Y., 'Student Mobility Reviewed: Attraction and Satisfaction of International Students in Turkey', *Higher Education*, 62/5 (2011), pp. 573–92, <https://doi.org/10.1007/s10734-011-9406-2>.

Kruse, O., 'The Origins of Writing in the Disciplines', *Written Communications*, 23/3 (2006), pp. 331–52.

Lanford, M. and Tierney, W.G., 'The International Branch Campus: Cloistered Community or Agent of Social Change?', in C.S. Collins, M.N.N. Lee, J.N. Hawkins and D.E. Neubauer (eds), *The Palgrave Handbook of Asia Pacific Higher Education* (New York, 2016), <https://doi.org/10.1057/978-1-137-48739-1_11>.

Larson, R.W., Hansen, D.M. and Moneta, G., 'Differing Profiles of Developmental Experiences across Types of Organized Youth Activities', *Developmental Psychology*, 42/5 (2006), pp. 849–63.

Laurillard, D., 'Thinking about Blended Learning. A Paper for the Thinkers in Residence Programme', in G. Van der Perre and J.V. Campenhout (eds), *Higher Education for the Digital Era; A Thinking Exercise in Flanders* (Brussels, 2015), <https://discovery.ucl.ac.uk/id/eprint/1549749>.

Learning and Work Institute, 'Employer investment in training plummets 28% since 2005, putting the Government's ambition of a high skill, high wage economy at risk, report warns', April 2022, <https://learningandwork.org.uk/news-and-policy/employer-investment-in-training-plummets-28-since-2005-putting-the-governments-ambition-of-a-high-skill-high-wage-economy-at-risk-report-warns/>.

Leon, L.M., 'Flexible Learning in Higher Education', Advance HE, 2021, <https://www.advance-he.ac.uk/guidance/teaching-and-learning/flexible-learning>.

Lewis, C.T. and Short, C. (eds), *A Latin Dictionary: Founded on Andrews' Edition of Freund's Latin Dictionary* (Oxford, 1963).

Lewis, J., 'Free Speech in Universities; What are the Issues?', House of Commons Library, 19 March 2021, <https://commonslibrary.parliament.uk/free-speech-in-universities-what-are-the-issues/>.

Lewis, J. and Bolton, P., 'Student Mental Health in England: Statistics, Policy and Guidance', House of Commons Library, 30 May 2023, <https://commonslibrary.parliament.uk/research-briefings/cbp-8593/>.

Lin, L.C., Lee, G.W., Hung, H.C. and Shih, N.M., 'The Influence of People's Cultural Activities Participation and Sense of Gain on Life Satisfaction', *Leis Soc Res*, 17 (2018), pp. 75–84, <http://lawdata.com.tw/tw/detail.aspx?no=336194>.

Lo, C.-M., Han, J., Wong, E.S.W. and Tang, C.-C., 'Flexible Learning with Multicomponent Blended Learning Mode for Undergraduate Chemistry Courses in the Pandemic of COVID-19', *Interactive Technology and Smart Education*, 18/2 (2021), pp. 175–88, <https://doi.org/10.1108/ITSE-05-2020-0061>.

London Economics, 'The Outcomes Associated with the BTEC Route of Degree Level Acquisition: Report for Pearson', May 2013, <www.london.co.uk>.

London Economics, 'The Costs and Benefits of International Higher Education Students to the UK Economy', 2021, <www.london.co.uk>.

Loon, M., 'Flexible Learning: A Literature Review 2016–2021', 1 March 2021, <advance-he.ac.uk/news-and-views/flexible-learning-literature-review-2016-2021>.

Lundvall, B.A. and Johnson, B., 'The Learning Economy', *Journal of Industry Studies*, 1/2 (1994), pp. 23–42.

Macmillan, L. and Wyness, G., 'Should we stop using predicted A-level grades in university applications?', *Economics Observatory*, 3 September 2020, <https://www.economicsobservatory.com/should-we-stop-using-predicted-level-grades-university-applications>.

MacNeill, S. and Beetham, H., 'Approaches to Curriculum and Learning Design across UK Higher Education', JISC, November 2022, <https://repository.jisc.ac.uk/8967/1/approaches-to-curriculum-and-learning-design-across-uk-higher-education-report.pdf>.

Maitlis, P., 'The Revolution in England's Universities 1980–2000', May 1998, <https://warlight.tripod.com/ MAITLIS.html>

Makoff-Clark, A., 'Is Blind Recruitment the Secret to the Perfect Hire?', *People Management*, 24 January 2019.

Marginson, S., 'The UK in the Global Student Market: Second Place for How Much Longer?', Centre for Global Higher Education research finding, HEFCE, 2018, <www.researchcghe.org>.

Markopoulos, A., 'Education', in E. Jeffreys, J.F. Haldon and R. Cormack (eds), *The Oxford Handbook of Byzantine Studies* (Oxford, 2008), pp. 785–95.

McGarry, J., 'Understanding the Burden of Regulation', Moorhouse Consulting, 2023, <https://www.universitiesuk.ac.uk/sites/default/files/uploads/Reports/Moorhouse-regulatory-burden-report.pdf>.

McKellar, Q., 'Business Engagement is no longer an Optional Extra for Universities', in A. Badran, E. Baydoun and J.R. Hillman (eds), *Universities in Arab Countries: An Urgent Need for Change* (Cham, 2018), pp. 123–41, <https://doi.org/10.1007/978-3-319-73111-7_6>.

McKellar, Q., 'Friend or Foe? Governors and Governance in Higher Education', in A. Badran, E. Baydoun and J.R. Hillman (eds), *Higher Education in the Arab World, Government and Governance* (Cham, 2020), pp. 81–95, <https://doi.org/10.1007/978-3-030-58153-4_2>.

Meikle, J. and Malik, S., 'London Met Crisis will Damage UK's Brand, says Vice-Chancellor', *The Guardian*, 30 August 2012.

Meriouma, S., 'The Role of Education in Reducing Health Inequalities', Health Action Research Group, July 2021, <https://www.healthactioncampaign.org.uk/tackling-obesity/the-role-of-education/>.

Migration Advisory Committee (MAC), 'Rapid Review of the Graduate Route', May 2024, <https://assets.publishing.service.gov.uk/media/6641e1fbbd01f5ed32793992/MAC+Rapid+Review+of+Graduate+Route.pdf>.

Millward, C., 'What happened to the Masterplan? The Relationship between Government and Higher Education', in Carasso (ed.), *UK Higher Education*.

Mohamed, H., *People Like Us: What it Takes to Make it in Modern Britain* (London, 2020).

Moore, N. and Breeze, V., 'China tops US and UK as Destination for Anglophone African Students', *The Conversation*, 27 June 2017, <https://theconversation.com/china-tops-us-and-uk-as-

destination-for-anglophone-african-students-78967#:~:text=According%20to%20the%20UNESCO%20Institute>.

Morgan, J., 'South Korean Universities Lead Way on Industry Collaboration', *Times Higher Education*, 9 March 2017.

Moubayed, S., 'The Founding of Damascus University 1903–1936: An Essay in Praise of the Pioneers', *Journal of Arabic and Islamic Studies*, 18 (2018), pp. 179–200.

'MPs and their Degrees: Here's Where and What our UK Politicians Studied', *Studee*, 2019, <https://studee.com/media/mps-and-their-degrees-media/>.

Mueller-Vollmer, K. and Messling, M., 'Wilhelm von Humboldt', in E.N. Zalta (ed.), *The Stanford Encyclopaedia of Philosophy* (summer 2022 edn).

Müller, C. and Mildenberger, T., 'Facilitating Flexible Learning by Replacing Classroom Time With an Online Learning Environment: A Systematic Review of Blended Learning in Higher Education', *Educational Research Review*, 34 (2021), p. 100394, <https://doi.org/10.1016/j.edurev.2021.100394>.

Murray, R. (ed.), *The Scholarship of Teaching and Learning in Higher Education* (Maidenhead, 2008).

'Must Do Better: The Office for Students and the Looming Crisis facing Higher Education', Industry and Regulators Committee, 2nd Report of Session 2022–23, HL Paper 246, 13 September 2023.

NASA, 'Global Climate Change: Vital Signs of the Planet', NASA's Jet Propulsion Laboratory, California Institute of Technology, 2022, <climate.nasa.gov/evidence/>.

National Academic Recognition Information Centre, <www.naric.org.uk>.

National Center for Education Statistics, 'Undergraduate Enrollment', Condition of Education, US Department of Education, Institute of Education Services, 2023, <https://nces.ed.gov/programs/coe/indicator/cha>.

National Centre for Universities and Business, 'State of the Relationship 2024', <info@ncub.co.uk>.

Naylor, R. and Smith, J., 'Schooling Effects on Subsequent University Performance: Evidence for the UK University Population', Department of Economics, University of Warwick Economic Research Paper 657, 2002.

Neves J. and Brown, A., 'Student Academic Experience Survey 2022', Advance HE and HEPI, <https://www.hepi.ac.uk/wp-content/uploads/2022/06/2022-Student-Academic-Experience-Survey.pdf>.

Neves, J., Freeman, J., Stephenson, R. and Sotiropoulou, P., 'Student Academic Experience Survey 2024', Advance HE and HEPI, <https://www.hepi.ac.uk/wp-content/uploads/2024/06/SAES-2024.pdf>.

Neves, J. and Hillman, N., 'Student Academic Experience Survey 2019', Advance HE and HEPI, <https://www.hepi.ac.uk/2019/06/13/student-academic-experience-survey-2019/>.

Newman, J.H., *The Idea of a University*, ed. F. Turner (1852; New Haven, CT, 1996).

Nikravan, L., 'More than 1 in 4 Employers are Hiring Employees with Master's Degrees for Positions that had been primarily held by those with Four-Year Degrees in the Past', *PR Newswire*, 17 March 2016, <prnnewswire.com/news-release/more-than-1-in-4-employers-are-hiring-employees-with-masters-degrees>.

Nisbet, I. and Shaw, S., *Is Assessment Fair?* (London, 2020) <https://dx.doi.org/10.4135/9781529739480>.

*Nolan Report*, First Report of the Committee on Standards in Public Life, cm 2850-I, May 1995, London: HMSO.

Nunes, A., 'Automation Doesn't Just Create or Destroy Jobs — It Transforms Them', *Harvard Business Review*, 2 November 2021.

Nurse, P., 'Independent Review of the UK's Research, Development and Innovation Organisational Landscape', March 2023, <https://www.gov.uk/government/publications/research-development-and-innovation-organisational-landscape-an-independent-review>.

OECD, 'Education at a Glance 2009: OECD Indicators', <https://www.oecd.org/edu/eag 2009>.

OECD, *Frascati Manual 2015: Guidelines for Collecting and Reporting Data on Research and Experimental Development*, The Measurement of Scientific, Technological and Innovation Activities (Paris, 2015), <https://doi.org/10.1787/9789264239012-en>.

OECD, 'Good Laboratory Practice (GLP)', 2022, <https://www.oecd.org/chemicalsafety/testing/good-laboratory-practiceglp.htm>.

OECD, Graduation and Entry Rates, <https://stats.oecd.org/Index.aspx?DataSetCode=EAG_GRAD_ENTR_RATES>.

OfS, 'Public Interest Governance Principles', 2017, accessed January 2024, <https://www.officeforstudents.org.uk/advice-and-guidance/regulation/registration-with-the-ofs-a-guide/public-interest-governance-principles/>.

OfS, 'Regulator Bans Controversial "Conditional Unconditional" Offers during Pandemic', 3 July 2020, <https://www.officeforstudents.org.uk/news-blog-and-events/press-and-media/regulator-bans-controversial-conditional-unconditional-offers-during-pandemic/>.

OfS, Transparent Approach to Costing (TRAC), published data 2020–21, <https://officeforstudents.org.uk/data-and-analysis/trac-data/published-data-2020-21/>.

OfS, 'Young Participation by Area: About POLAR and Adult HE', 30 September 2022, <https://www.officeforstudents.org.uk/data-and-analysis/young-participation-by-area/about-polar-and-adult-he/>.

OfS, 'Financial Sustainability of Higher Education Providers in England: 2023 Update', OfS 2023.20, updated 23 June 2023, <https://www.officeforstudents.org.uk/media/0b7d9daa-d6c7-477e-a0b2-b90985d0f935/financial-sustainability-report-2023-updated-june-2023.pdf>.

OfS, 'Transnational Education: Protecting the Interests of Students Taught Abroad', 2023, <https://www.officeforstudents.org.uk/publications/transnational-education-protecting-the-interests-of-students-taught-abroad/>.

OfS, 'Financial Sustainability of Higher Education Providers in England 2024', OfS 2024.21, 16 May 2024, <www.nationalarchives.gove.uk/doc/open-government-licence/version/3/>.

OfS, 'Financial Sustainability of Higher Education Providers in England: November 2024 Update', <https://officeforstudents.org.uk/publications/financial-sustainability-of-higher-education-providers-in-england-november-2024-update/>.

ONS, Employment by Occupation, 2021, <https://www.ons.gov.uk/employmentandlabourmarket/peopleinwork/employmentandemployeetypes/datasets/employmentbyindustryemp13>.

ONS, 'Ethnic Group Differences in Health, Employment, Education and Housing shown in England and Wales', Census 2021, 15 March 2023.

ONS, 'How has Life Expectancy Changed Over Time?', Census 2021.

Orr, S., Highton, M., Lieven, N., Thomas, D.S.P. and Lawson, M., 'Blended Learning Review Report of the OfS-appointed Blended Learning Review Panel', OfS, October 2022.

Ortiz-Ospina, E., Beltekian, D. and Roser, M., 'Trade and Globalisation', *ourworldindata.org*, 2018, <https://ourworldindata.org/trade-and-globalization>.

Ostby, G., Urdal, H. and Dupuy, K., 'Does Education Lead to Pacification? A Systematic Review of Statistical Studies on Education and Political Violence', *Review of Educational Research*, 89/1 (2019), pp. 46–92, <https://doi.org/10.3102/0034654318800236>.

Owston, R., York, D. and Murtha, S., 'Student Perceptions and Achievement in a University Blended Learning Strategic Initiative', *The Internet and Higher Education*, 18 (2013), pp. 38–46, <https://doi.org/10.1016/j.iheduc.2012.12.003>.

Page, A., Petteruti, A., Walsh, N. and Ziedenberg, J., 'Education and Public Safety', The Justice Policy Institute Report, 30 August 2007, <www.justicepolicy.org>.

Panjwani, A., 'Research and Development Spending', House of Commons Library, 11 Sept 2023, <https://commonslibrary.parliament.uk/research-briefings/sn04223/>.

PatSeer, 'Worldwide Innovation Filing Trends 1995–2015', <http://www.slideshare.net/gridlogics/patseer-worldwide-filing-trend-report>.

Peers, E.A., 'Redbrick University Revisited: Autobiography of Bruce Truscot', in A.L. MacKenzie and A.R. Allan (eds), *E. Allison Peers Lectures* (Liverpool, 1996).

Popov, D., 'Large Economic Contribution of Universities in England', *Frontier Economics*, 29 September 2021, <https://www.frontier-economics.com/uk/en/news-and-articles/news/news-article-i8785-large-economic-contribution-of-universities-in-england/>.

Portes, R., 'I think the people of this country have had enough of experts', think at London Business School, 2017, <london.edu/think/who-needs-experts>.

Purcell, K. and Elias, P., *Seven Years On: Graduate Careers in a Changing Labour Market* (Manchester, 2004).

PWC, 'Will Robots really Steal our Jobs?', 2018, <https://www.pwc.co.uk/economic-services/assets/international-impact-of-automation-feb-2018.pdf>.

Rafiq, A.-K., *Tarikh al-Jami 'ah al-Suriyyah: al-bidayah wa' l-numuww, 1901–1946* (Damascus, 2004).

Raghupathi, V. and Raghupathi, W., 'The Influence of Education on Health: An Empirical Assessment of OECD Countries for the Period 1995–2015', *Archives of Public Health*, 78 (2020), <https://doi.org/10.1186/s13690-020-00402-5>.

Reeves, A., 'Neither Class nor Status: Arts Participation and the Social Strata', *Sociology*, 49/4 (2015), pp. 624–42, <https://doi.org/10.1177/0038038514547897>.

Rhead, S., Black, B. and Pinot de Moires, A., 'Marking Consistency Metrics', Ofqual/18/6449/2, November 2018, <www.gov.uk/ofqual>.

Ritchie, H. and Roser, M., 'Age Structure Our World in Data', 2019, <https://ourworldindata.org/age-structure>.

*Robbins Report*, Report of the Committee on Higher Education (London: HMSO, 1963).

Rollot, O., 'C'est quoi une Grande École?', *Le Monde*, 11 Feb 2011, <https://www.lemonde.fr/education/article/2011/02/11/c-est-quoi-une-grande-ecole_1477588_1473685.html>.

Roser, M., Hasell, J., Herre, B. and Macdonald, B., 'War and Peace', *ourworldindata.org*, 2016, <https://ourworldindata.org/war-and-peace>.

Ruiu, G. and Ruiu, M., 'The Complex Relationship between Education and Happiness: The Case of Highly Educated Individuals in Italy', *Journal of Happiness Studies*, 20/8 (2019), pp. 2631–53, <https://doi:org/10.1007/s10902-018-0062-4>.

The San Francisco Declaration on Research Assessment (DORA), 2012, <https://sfdora.org/read/>.

Sandford, A., 'Coronavirus: Half of Humanity now on Lockdown as 90 Countries Call for Confinement', *euronews*, 2 April 2020, <https://www.euronews.com/2020/04/02/coronavirus-in-europe-spain-s-death-toll-hits-10-000-after-record-950-new-deaths-in-24-hou>.

Santacreu, A.M. and Zhu, H., 'Domestic Innovation and International Technology Diffusion as Sources of Comparative Advantage', *Federal Reserve Bank of St. Louis' Review*, Fourth Quarter (2018), pp. 317–36, <https://doi.org/10.20955/r.100.317-36>.

Santacreu, A.M. and Zhu, H., 'Which Countries and Industries Contributed the Most to the Decline in Trade Barriers Around the World?', *Economic Synopses*, 26 (2018), <https://doi.org/10.20955/es.2018.26>.

Scannell, J.W., Blanckley, A., Boldon, H. and Warrington, B., 'Diagnosing the Decline in Pharmaceutical R&D Efficiency', *Nature Reviews Drug Discovery*, 11/3 (2012), pp. 191–200.

Schilling, D.R., 'Knowledge Doubling Every 12 Months, Soon to be Every 12 Hours', *Industry Tap into News*, 19 April 2013, <https://www.industrytap.com/knowledge-doubling-every-12-months-soon-to-be-every-12-hours/3950>.

Schmitz, L., 'Academus', in W. Smith (ed.), *Dictionary of Greek and Roman Biography and Mythology*, vol. i (London, 1867).

Schwartz, S., 'Fair Admissions to Higher Education: Recommendations for Good Practice', Admissions to Higher Education Review AHER3, DfES, 2004, <www.admissions-review.org.uk>.

Seow, P.S. and Pan, G., 'A Literature Review of the Impact of Extracurricular Activities Participation on Students' Academic Performance', *Journal of Education for Business*, 89 (2014), pp. 361–6.

Shattock, M., 'University Governance Reformed: The Transformation of a "Self-governed" to a "Regulated" University System', in Carasso (ed.), *UK Higher Education*.

Shattock, M., *The UGC and the Management of British Universities* (Buckingham, 1994).

Shuo, Z., 'China's Higher Education System is World's Largest, officials say', *China Daily*, 3 December 2020, <https://www.chinadaily.com.cn/a/202012/03/WS5fc86ab2a31024ad0ba9999e.html>.

Sianesi, B. and Van Reenen, J., 'The Returns to Education: Macroeconomics', *Journal of Economic Surveys*, 17/2 (2003), pp. 115–226, <https://onlinelibrary.wiley.com/doi/abs/10.1111/1467-6419.00192>.

Smith, Z., *White Teeth* (London, 2000).

Snow, C.P., *The Two Cultures and the Scientific Revolution*, The Rede Lecture (Cambridge, 1959).

Sooryamoorthy, R., 'Do Types of Collaboration Change Citation? Collaboration and Citation Patterns of South African Science Publications', *Scientometrics*, 81/1 (2009), pp. 177–93, <https://doi.org/10.1007/s11192-009-2126-z>.

Sperlinger, T., McLellan, J. and Pettigrew, R., *Who are Universities For? Re-making Higher Education* (Bristol, 2018).

Statista, 'Online Education – Worldwide, Statista Market Forecast', 2023, <https://www.statista.com/outlook/dmo/eservices/online-education/worlwide#key-players>.

Stephenson, R. (ed.), 'How Should Undergraduate Degrees be Funded? A Collection of Essays', HEPI Report 173, April 2024, <www.hepi.ac.uk>.

Stewart, C., 'Middle Class Pupils missing University Place will see Reform', *The Herald*, 13 January 2023, https://www.heraldscotland.com/opinion/23247308.middle-class-pupils-missing-university-place-will-see-reform/>.

Strand, S., 'Ethnic, Socio-economic and Sex Inequalities in Educational Achievement at age 16', Report for the Commission on Race and Ethnic Disparities, 3 February 2021, <https://www.gov.uk/government/publications/the-report-of-the-commission-on-race-and-ethnic-disparities-supporting-research/ethnic-socio-economic-and-sex-inequalities-in-educational-achievement-at-age-16-by-professor-steve-strand>.

Strathclyde Business School, 2019, <https://www.strath.ac.uk/business/>.

'Student Loan Forecasts for England Financial Year 2021–22', 14 July 2022, <https://explore-education-statistics.service.gov.uk/find-statistics/student-loan-forecasts-for-england/2021-22>.

'Study Projects Dramatic Growth for Global Higher Education through 2040', *ICEF Monito*, 3 October 2018, <monitor.icef.com/2018/10/study-projects-dramatic-growth-global-higher-education-2040>.

Swisher, R.R. and Dennison, C.R., 'Educational Pathways and Change in Crime Between Adolescence and Early Adulthood', *Journal of Research in Crime and Delinquency*, 53/6 (2016), pp. 840–71, https://doi.org/10.1177/0022427816645380>.

'Swiss spend almost CHF 23 billion on research', SWI Annual Report, 2021, <swissinfo.ch>.

ThinkImpact, 'College Dropout Rates', 2021, <https://www.thinkimpact.com/college-dropout-rates/>.

Tight, M., 'Examining the Research/Teaching Nexus', *European Journal of Higher Education*, 6/4 (2016), pp. 293–311, <https://doi.org/10.1080/21568235.2016.1224674>.

*Times Education Commission: Bringing out the Best*, 2022, <https://www.thetimes.co.uk/society/education/education-commission>.

'Tips for Applying to the University of California System', *IvyWise*, <https://www.ivywise.com/ivywise-knowledgebase/resources/article/tips-for-applying-to-the-university-of-california-system/>.

Tollefson, J., 'China Declared World's Largest Producer of Scientific Articles', *Nature*, 553/390 (2018), <https://doi.org/10.1038/d41586-018-00927-4>.

Tracey, I. and Williamson, A., 'Independent Review of University Spin-out Companies: Final Report and Recommendations', Department for Science, Innovation and Technology and HM Treasury, 2023, <https://www.gov.uk/government/publications/independent-review-of-university-spin-out-companies>.

Trostel, P., 'It's Not Just the Money, The Benefits of College Education to Individuals and to Society', Lumina issue papers, Lumina Foundation, 14 October 2015, <https://www.luminafoundation.org/resource/its-not-just-the-money/>.

Tyler, R.W., *Basic Principles of Curriculum and Instruction* (Chicago, 1949).

UCAS, 'Entry into Higher Education', 16 February 2021, <https://www.ethnicity-facts-figures.service.gov.uk/education-skills-and-training/higher-education/entry-rates-into-higher-education/latest>.

UCAS, Undergraduate End of Cycle Data Resources, 2022, <https://www.ucas.com/data-and-analysis/undergraduate-statistics-and-reports/ucas-undergraduate-end-cycle-data-resources-2022>.

UCAS, 'Future of Undergraduate Admissions', MD-8018, January 2023, <https://www.ucas.com/file/672901/download?token=VccObZXZ>.

'UCAS to Reform University Personal Statements', *BBC News*, 18 July 2024, <https://www.bbc.co.uk/news/articles/cger11kjk1jo>.

UIS, 'Global Education Digest 2010: Comparing Education Statistics Across the World', <http//www.uis.unesco.org/>.

UIS, 'Pupil–Teacher Ratio, Tertiary', The World Bank, February 2020, <https://data.worldbank.org/indicator/SE.TER.ENRL.TC.ZS>.

UIS, Stat Bulk Download Service, 2022, <apiportal.UIS.UNESCO.org/bolds>.

The UK National Agency for International Qualifications and Skills, <enic.org.uk>.

UK Research and Innovation, 'Costs you can apply for, Principles of full economic costings (fEC)', 17 August 2021, <https://www.ukri.org/councils/epsrc/guidance-for-applicants/costs-you-can-apply-for/>.

UK Science Parks Association, accessed December 2022, <http://www.ukspa.org.uk>.

UK Soft Power Group, 'The Future of UK Soft Power: Building a Strategic Framework', 2023, <https://www.ed.ac.uk/sites/default/files/atoms/files/the_future_of_uk_soft_power_-_building_a_strategic_framework.pdf>.

Ulrichsen, T.C., 'Assessing the Economic Impacts of the Higher Education Innovation Fund: A Mixed Method Quantitative Assessment', HEFCE, Bristol, UK, 2015.

Ulster University Business Institute, 2019, <https://www.ulster.ac.uk/business/business-institute/services>.

UNESCO, 'Inbound Internationally Mobile Students by Country of Origin', September 2021, <data.uis.unesco.org>.

United Nations Conference on Trade and Development, 'Global trade hits record high of $28.5 trillion in 2021, but likely to be subdued in 2022', <https://unctad.org/news/global-trade-hits-record-high-285-trillion-2021-likely-be-subdued-2022>.

United Nations Population Division (Median Age), 2017, <https://ourworldindata.org/age-structure>

Universities UK/GuildHE, 'Fair Admissions Code of Practice', 2022, <https://www.universitiesuk.ac.uk/what-we-do/policy-and-research/publications/fair-admissions-code-practice>.

Urban, T., 'Why Generation Y Yuppies are Unhappy', *Wait But Why*, 9 September 2013, <https://waitbutwhy.com/2013/09/why-generation-y-yuppies-are-unhappy.html>.

US Bureau of Labor Statistics, 2021, <www.bls.gov/nls>.

UUK, *Achieving our Vision: Universities UK 2004 Spending Review Submission for England and Northern Ireland* (London, 2004).

UUK, *The Funding Environment for Universities 2015: The Economic Role of UK Universities* (London, 2015).

UUK, *Fair Admissions Review June 2019 – November 2020* (London, 2020).

UUK, *Busting Graduate Job Myths* (London, 2022).

UUK, *Our Universities: Generating Growth and Opportunity* (London, 2022).

UUK, *Sustainable University Funding: Why it's Important and What is Needed* (London 2023).

UUK, 'New Data shows Universities Open their Doors to Local Communities',

2024, <https://www.universitiesuk.ac.uk/latest/insights-and-analysis/new-data-shows-universities-open-their>.

UUK, 'New Report Reveals Key Role Universities Play in Boosting Growth and Productivity Across the UK', 6 September 2024, <https://www.universitiesuk.ac.uk/latest/news/new-report-reveals-key-role-universities#:~:text=The%20London%20Economics%20report%20also,will%20be%20involved%20in%20crime.>.

UUK/GuildHE, *Fair Admissions Code of Practice* (London, 2022).

UUKi, 'The Scale of UK Higher Education Transnational Education 2018/19', October 2020, <https://www.universitiesuk.ac.uk/sites/default/files/field/downloads/2021-08/the-scale-of-UK-HE-TNE-2018-19.pdf>.

Van Damme, D., 'Trends and Models in International Quality Assurance and Accreditation in Higher Education in Relation to Trade in Education Services OECD/US Forum on Trade in Educational Services', 23–24 May 2002, <https://www.oecd.org/education/skills-beyond-school/2088479.pdf>.

Van Der Wende, M.C., 'The Bologna Declaration: Enhancing Transparency and Competitiveness of European Higher Education', *Higher Education in Europe*, 25/3 (2010), pp. 305–10, <https://doi.org/10.1080/713669277>.

Vattori, O., 'Curriculum Design', Learning and Teaching Paper 8, Thematic Peer Group Report, European University Association, 2020, <www.eua.eu.info>.

Veletsianos, G., 'Best Evidence on Supporting Students to Learn Remotely', 2020, <https://educationendowmentfoundation.org.uk/guidance-for-teachers/covid-19-resources/best-evidence-on-supporting-students-to-learn-remotely>.

Verger, J., 'Patterns', in H. De Ridder-Symoens (ed.), *A History of the University in Europe, vol. I Universities in the Middle Ages* (Cambridge, 1991).

Vo, H.M., Zhu, C. and Diep, N.A., 'The Effect of Blended Learning on Student Performance at Course-level in Higher Education: A Meta-analysis', *Studies in Educational Evaluation*, 53 (2017), pp. 17–28, <https://doi.org/10.1016/j.stueduc.2017.01.002>.

Volkmann, C., Wilson, K.E., Mariotti, S., Rabuzzi, D., Vyakarnam, S. and Sepulveda, A., 'Educating the Next Wave of Entrepreneurs: Unlocking Entrepreneurial Capabilities to Meet the Global Challenges of the 21st Century', A Report of the Global Education Initiative for the World Economic Forum, Switzerland, April 2009, <https://papers.ssrn.com/sol3/papers.cfm?abstract_id=1396704>.

Wadhwa, V., Aggarwal, R., Holly, K. and Salkever, A., 'The Anatomy of an Entrepreneur: Making of a Successful Entrepreneur', Kauffman Foundation Small Research Projects research paper 2, 17 November 2009, <http://dx.doi.org/10.2139/ssrn.1507384>.

Walker, I. and Zhu, Y., 'The Impact of University Degrees on the Lifecycle of Earnings: Some Further Analysis', BIS research paper 112, August 2013, pp. 44–6.

Walker, I. and Zhu, Y., 'University Selectivity and the Relative Returns to Higher Education: Evidence from the UK', *Labour Economics,* 53 (2018), pp. 230–49, <https://doi.org/10.1016/j.labeco.2018.05.005>.

Waterbury, J., 'Governance of Arab Universities: Why does it Matter?', in E. Baydoun and J.R. Hillman (eds), *Universities in Arab Countries: An Urgent Need for Change* (Cham, 2018), pp. 55–70, <https://doi.org/10.1007/978-3-319-73111-7_2>.

Watson, D., 'Quality, Standards and Institutional Reciprocity', in J. Brennan, P. de. Vries and R. Williams (eds), *Standards and Quality in Higher Education* (London, 1997).

Whalley, B., France, D., Park, J., Mauchline, A. and Welsh, K., 'Towards Flexible Personalized Learning and the Future Educational System in the Fourth Industrial Revolution in the wake of Covid-19', *Higher Education Pedagogies,* 6/1 (2021), pp. 79–99, <https://doi.org/10.1080/23752696.2021.1883458>.

Whitchurch, C., 'The Changing Profile and Work Experiences of Higher Education Staff in the 21st Century', in Carasso (ed.), *UK Higher Education.*

Willetts, D., *A University Education* (Oxford, 2017).

WIPO, *Global Innovation Index 2019: Creating Healthy Lives – The Future of Medical Innovation,* 12th edn, eds S. Dutta, B. Lanvin and S. Wunsch-Vincent (Ithaca, NY, 2019).

WIPO, *Global Innovation Index 2022, What is the Future of Innovation Driven Growth?,* 15th edn, eds S. Dutta, B. Lanvin, L. Rivera Leon and S. Wunsch-Vincent (Geneva, 2022), <https://doi.org/10.34667/tind.46596>.

Witty, A., 'Encouraging a British Invention Revolution: Sir Andrew Witty's Review of Universities and Growth', BIS/13/1241, 2013, <www.gov.uk/bis>.

Wolf, A., *Does Education Matter? Myths About Education and Economic Growth* (London, 2002).

Wood, M., *The Story of China* (London, 2020).

The World Bank, 'Higher Education', 22 October 2021, <worldbank.org/en/topic/tertiaryeducation>.

World Economic Forum, 'These 3 Charts Show the Global Growth in Online Learning', 27 January 2022, <https://www.weforum.org/agenda/2022/01/online-learning-courses-reskill-skills-gap/>.

World Health Organisation, 'The Global Health Observatory, GHE: Life Expectancy and Healthy Life Expectancy', 2022, <https://www.who.int>.

'World Industry Outlook: Healthcare and Pharmaceuticals', *Economist Intelligence Unit*, June 2017.

YouGov, 'Government Approval', 2022, <https://yougov.co.uk/topics/politics/trackers/government-approval>.

Young, C., 'The Pecking Disorder: Social Justice Warriors Gone Wild', *Observer*, 11 June 2015, <https://observer.com/2015/06/the-pecking-disorder-social-justice-warriors-gone-wild/>.

Zhang, Z. and Chen, W.A., 'A Systematic Review of the Relationship Between Physical Activity and Happiness', *Journal of Happiness Studies*, 20 (2019), pp. 1305–22, <https://doi.org/10.1007/s10902-018-9976-0>.

Zhong, H., 'An Over Time Analysis on the Mechanisms behind the Education–Health Gradients in China', *China Economic Review*, 34 (2015), pp. 135–49, <https://doi.org/10.1016/j.chieco.2015.04.003>.

# Index

2017 Higher Education and Research Act 24–5

Academic
    ability 3, 20, 49–50, 59, 62, 75, 107, 217, 228
    board 213–14
    exchanges *see* Exchange programmes
    freedom 11, 121, 127, 224, 243
    quality 205, 213–18
    registrar 210

Academus 6

Academy 6, 7, 94 *see also* Higher Education Academy

ACCA *see* Association of Chartered Certified Accountants

Accelerators (for business start-ups) 155 *see also* Entrepreneurship

Access to higher education 27–63
    fair access 27, 30–3, 40, 50, 60 *see also* Admissions
        for disadvantaged students 28, 36, 40, 45, 47–9, 58, 63 *see also* Disadvantage
        of the privileged 5, 20, 37, 43, 58–9

Accommodation (at university) 91

Accountability 205–6, 208, 211, 213, 220–1, 224 *see also* Nolan principles
    public 164

Accounting 190, 224 *see also* Resource Accounting and Budgeting charge
    firms *see* Arthur Andersen

Accreditation
    of degree programmes 179
    multi-accreditation 218
    of Prior Experiential Learning (APEL) 61
    processes 23
    by professional bodies 79, 162, 183, 233

Active learning 7, 67, 71

Adaptive 2 *see also* Artificial intelligence
    comparative judgement 85
    teaching 71
    technology 71, 79

Adequacy 32, 50

Admissions (to university)
    fairness of 32–3, 37–48, 50–3, 57 *see also* Universities UK Fair Admissions Code of Practice

impartiality 33, 43–46, 50
Oxbridge 30, 44, 58–9
portfolios 35, 53, 56, 58, 60
system 27, 30, 53, 59–60, 63
tests 34
   Bio Medical Admissions Test (BMAT) 34
   Scholastic Aptitude Tests (SATs) 34
   Universities and Colleges Admissions Service (UCAS) 28, 36, 38, 42, 56, 61, 241–2
validity (of the admissions process) 33–5, 38–9, 51, 54, 55
Advance HE 78, 83
   Fellowships 89
   Professional Standards Framework 89
Advanced Research and Invention Agency (ARIA) 159–60
Africa 9, 180, 185
   sub-Saharan 110
Agriculture 13, 15, 122, 137
   agricultural productivity 135
   agricultural technology 137
AI *see* Artificial Intelligence
Alan Turing Institute 135
A-levels 22, 28–30, 34, 39, 45–7, 50, 52, 55, 60, 202, 240–1
   actual results 27, 40–1
Alumni 10, 12, 43, 94, 154–5, 173, 237–8
Amis, Kingsley 62
   'more [students] means worse [students]' 62–3
Anglo-Persian Oil company (later Anglo-Iranian, British Petroleum, BP) 207
Anonymisation 44–5
Antiquity 5–9, 119, 285
Anxiety 59, 98–100
Apprenticeships 61, 225, 231–3
   degree apprenticeships 69, 156–7, 242, 248–9

   integrated degree apprenticeships 157, 231
   end-point assessments 157, 231
   in Germany 156
   higher level (level 4 and above) 157
   levy 2, 195, 248–9
   standards 157
Aptitude 34–5, 54
ARIA *see* Advanced Research and Invention Agency
Aristotle *see* Philosophy
Arthur Andersen LLP 207
Articulation agreements *see* Collaboration
Artificial Intelligence (AI) 17, 64, 71, 74, 124, 133, 135, 240, 242
Arts, the 11, 129–30
   liberal arts 13, 34, 65
Assessment (while studying at university) 29, 34, 49, 73, 84–7, 179, 214–17 *see also* Cheating, Plagiarism, Student feedback
   automation of 71, 85–6
   formative 77, 86
   principles of good assessment 85–7
Association of Chartered Certified Accountants (ACCA) 170
Asynchronous delivery (of education) 70, 75
Attainment gap *see* Black, Asian and Minority Ethnic
Attendance paradox 73
Attributes 35, 54, 68 *see also* Graduate attributes, Interviews
Audio *see* technology
Audio-visual *see* connectivity
Audit 208
   committees 214, 220
Australia 138, 175–6
   differential fees banding 203, 247
Automation 226–7 *see also* Assessment
Autonomy (of universities) 7, 11, 14,

21-2, 54, 205, 211, 214, 219, 221, 224, 244
   in Scotland 31, 58
Aviation 132, 169
Awarding gap *see* Black, Asian and Minority Ethnic students

Babylon 5
   *edubas* (scribal schools) 5
Baccalaureate 30
   International Baccalaureate (IB) 34
Bacon, Francis 12, 119
   sceptical methodology 12
Bangladesh 14-15 *see also* Universities
   Bangladeshi students 99
Banks 206 *see also* Lehman Brothers bank
   Bank of England
   Bank of Italy 114
   Royal Bank of Scotland 207
   World Bank 103, 110, 112
Barnett, Correlli 150
Barnett, Ronald 83-4
Barriers
   to education 35, 37, 58
   trade barriers 102, 170
Battery technology *see* Lithium
Behaviours 56, 70, 78, 94-7, 103, 111-12, 148, 170 *see also* Graduate attributes and behaviours
   enterprising 152, 233
   work-related 156, 228-30
Beliefs (of students) 94-7, 170
*Bimaristan see* Medicine
Bio Medical Admissions Test (BMAT) *see* Admissions tests
Biology 6, 202
Black, Asian and Minority Ethnic (BAME) students 44-6, 99
   Commission on Race and Ethnic Disparities 45
   attainment gap 96
Blair, Tony 197
Blended learning 70-4, 75, 77-83 *see also* Technology-enhanced learning
   *Blended Learning in Practice* 78
   Curriculum Design Toolkit 77
   digital 76
   face-to-face 70-7, 79-83
Block release 235
BMAT *see* Admissions tests
Bologna accord/protocol 66, 174, 218
Boston, Maine, USA 167
   Boston Symphony Orchestra 45
Brexit 177
British East India Company 206
British Government/s
   coalition (Conservative/Liberal) 2010-15 200
   Conservative
      1979-97 21, 197
      2015-24 2, 23, 91, 95, 157, 178, 217, 222, 227
   departments
      Department for Business, Innovation and Skills (BIS, formerly Department for Innovation, Universities and Skills) 25
      Department for Education (DfE) 25, 63, 142
      Department for the Economy in Northern Ireland 24, 210
      Department for Science, Innovation and Technology (DSIT, formerly Department for Business Energy and Industrial Strategy, BEIS) 25
      The Meteorological Office (Met Office)
         climate and weather science 136
      Ministry of Defence 136
   Labour

1997–2010 197
2024 (current at time of writing) 2, 95,144, 179, 193, 222, 241
Secretaries of State for Education 63
British values 170, 211, 232
Browne Review 200
BTECs *see* Business and Technology Education Council qualifications
Business 34, 137, 144, 156, 195, 196, 239, 248
   administration (university subject) 13
   business-facing (universities) 120 *see also* Entrepreneurship; Knowledge Transfer
   community 156, 204
   engagement 120, 149–51, 158–67, 249–50
   and management (university subject) 154
   schools 153, 154
   universities as businesses 116–17, 205, 213
Business and Technology Education Council qualifications (BTECs) 28, 34, 49–50

California 115 *see also* Universities
   ban on affirmative action 44
   guaranteed university places (index-eligibility) 49
Campus 14, 16–17, 72–3, 75, 89, 186–7
   experience 72–3, 75, 90–1, 232
Capital
   construction 245
   costs 22, 197
   cultural 170
   grants 22, 77, 173, 197
   human 25, 92, 101, 107–10, 144, 147, 151–2, 169, 172, 195, 250, 252
   social 36
   venture 161

Carbon dioxide *see* Climate change
Careers advice 42–3, 83, 91, 229, 241
Catalyst funding scheme 165
Catapult centres 120, 137
CATs *see* Colleges of advanced technology
Centres for Excellence in Teaching and Learning (CETL) 77 *see also* Blended Learning
CERN *see* Conseil Européen pour la Recherche Nucléaire
CETL *see* Centres for Excellence in Teaching and Learning
Charities
   donations to (by graduates) 116
   fundraising for 238
   Rag weeks 238
   research funding from 244
ChatGPT 133
Cheating 84, 86–7, 133 *see also* Plagiarism
Chief Executives 209
China 8–9, 17, 36, 79, 112, 141, 163–4, 177, 184–5, 222
   Chinese education 8–9
      Han empire 8
      imperial colleges 8
      Song dynasty 8
         Kaifeng 8
      Sui dynasty 8
         Jinshi (degree) 8
   Chinese Mandarin 176
   Cultural Revolution 9
Christakis, Erika 96
Citation (of published research) 139–40
   field-weighted citation indices 140
   metrics 139
Civilisation (of society) 129, 150
Civilisations 5, 132
Classes (at university)
   classrooms 77, 79, 81, 175, 202, 247

class size 22, 203, 245
Clearing 56–7
Climate change 103, 130–1
　carbon dioxide 130–1
　deniers 131
　Keeling Curve 131
　mitigation 101
Cluster effect 167, 171, 181–2
CMA *see* Competition and Markets Authority
CNAA *see* Council for National Academic Awards
Collaboration 150
　collaborative provision or articulation agreements 180
　collaborative research 133, 136, 158–9, 165, 173
　international 170–3, 185, 222
Colleges of advanced technology (CATs) 20
Commission for Tertiary Education and Research 24, 210
Committee of University Chairs (CUC) 197, 213
　Code of Governance 213, 220
Commodification (of education) 169
Communication 16, 30, 62, 69, 78, 118, 132–3, 155, 169, 172
　skills 8, 68, 93, 229
Communities 3, 29, 115, 179, 239 *see also* Business community
　academic communities 5, 7, 10–11, 90, 95, 143, 213, 219
　community activities 116, 238
　in halls of residence 91
　local 224, 239
　research communities 121, 126
Commuting (students) 75, 83, 99
Competency (in one's degree subject) 54, 68, 107, 151, 243
　competence 29, 35, 65, 84, 88, 107–8, 119, 174–5, 227–9, 242

Competition 77 *see also* Selection, Research Excellence Framework, Research funding
　between universities for students 23, 31, 205
　for university places 27
　alternatives to competition 32
Competition and Markets Authority (CMA) 42
Completion (of university courses) 24, 48, 51, 84, 156, 180, 214, 216–18
　failure to complete 27
　　cost of living crisis 82–3
　　Covid-19 pandemic 82
　potential to complete (as a reason for selection) 33, 37
Computers 16, 69–70, 86, 133, 155, 227
　computerisation 169
　laptops 77
Confucius 8
Connectivity 76
　audio-visual 77
　global 79
Conseil Européen pour la Recherche Nucléaire (CERN) 138, 171
Consultancy work (by academics) 151, 154, 161–2
Consultants (external) 212, 223
Contact hours (of students with academics) 72, 82, 215
Contextualisation (of applicants to university)
　previous educational advantage or disadvantage 45–8, 50, 57–9
Continuation (of students from year 1 to 2 of their courses) 24
　rates 88, 214, 216–17
Continuing professional development (CPD) 162, 234, 238
Copyright *see* Intellectual property
Coronavirus *see* Covid-19 pandemic
Corporate providers (of higher education) 15

online 184
Corporations 206
  multinational 207
Cost of living crisis 82
Council for National Academic Awards (CNAA) 21
Counselling *see* Mental health
Coursera *see* MOOCs
Courts (in Scottish universities) 219
Covid-19 pandemic 75, 79, 80, 82, 87, 100, 227
  disinfection 81, 123
  lockdowns 81, 91, 182
  post-Covid 'bounce' 72
  vaccine 123–4
CPD *see* Continuing professional development
Creative arts *see* Arts, The
Credentials 84, 184, 218
  micro-credentials 87
Credits 234, 247
  European Credit Transfer and Accumulation System (ECTS) 66
Crime 61, 116
  rates 48, 115
    violent crime rates 115
Critical thinking 30, 34, 54, 68, 127, 225, 228, 242–3
Cross-border 102
  institutions 169
  recognition 218
  relationships 101, 174
Cross-subsidy *see* Subsidy
Culture 8, 11, 30, 118, 129–30, 168–70, 174, 213, 243, 252 *see also* Research culture
  cultural 175, 237
    activities 113
    attributes 8
    barriers 58
    capital 170

change 78
contribution (of international students) 250
facilities 239
impact 163
inclusion 69
integration 174
participation 113
progress 8
proximity 176
sensitivity 96
Cultural Revolution *see* China
educational culture 78
ethical culture 206–8
multicultural
  friendships 91
  on campus 75
Curricula 29, 65–9, 179, 228
  co-curricular societies 233
  content 233
    adjustments for international students 173–5
  Curriculum Design Toolkit *see* Blended learning
  design 64–5, 66, 68–9, 71, 215
  evaluation of 83
  evolution of
    learner-focused curricula 67
    methodological-based 67
  flexibility of 235
  inclusive 69, 96, 243
  problem-based 67
  review of 29, 87
  spiral 67
Curtice, John 94
Customers (students as) 24, 172, 220, 238

DARPA *see* Defense Advanced Research Projects Agency
Data

analytics 71, 242, 244
science 135
Davies, Howard 221
Davies, Sir Graeme 143
Dearing
   Committee (National Committee of Inquiry into Higher Education) 197
   Report 214, 219
Debt (of students) *see* Loans (for students)
Defense Advanced Research Projects Agency (DARPA) 159–60
Deficits (in university finances) 145, 190–3
Degree-awarding powers 15, 21, 23, 214
Degrees 2, 7, 8, 16–17, 49, 74, 175, 234
*see also* Degree apprenticeships, Joint honours
   bachelor's 21–2, 24, 29–30, 66, 106–7, 111–12
      four-year bachelor's 22, 30, 34, 241
   degree outcomes 92
   doctoral degree 66–7, 178
      Doctor of Philosophy (PhD) 12, 119, 126, 127, 144, 178, 221, 236
   double degrees 180
   'good' degree (2:1 or First) 33, 47, 51, 58, 230
   'low-value' degrees 91
   master's 66–7, 235
      taught 236
Demographics 94, 168, 175, 185
   ageing demographic 237
Dentistry 202–3
Descartes, René 12
   rationalism 12
Deservedness 47, 50
Destination of Leavers from Higher Education (DLHE) 216

Devolution (within the UK)
   Acts of Parliament 22
   devolved nations 22, 24–5, 177, 202, 204, 210, 220
Diamond Light Source *see* Particle accelerator
Digital
   competence 227
   poverty 76
   skills 30, 74
   teaching and learning 17, 70, 72–3, 77, 79–82
   technologies 76, 85, 227
Disadvantage (in university candidates) *see also* Index of Multiple Deprivation, Scottish Index of Multiple Deprivation 28, 36, 40–1, 47, 50, 53, 201
   compensating for 44–5, 55, 57–8, 63, 241
Dissemination (of knowledge) 11, 119, 133, 150, 168–9, 181
Dissertations 12, 152
Distance learning 14–15, 59, 74, 186
   delivery 16–17, 70, 203
   international 172–3, 179, 182–5
   Open University 59, 185, 187
   pioneered by University of London 16, 70, 169
   supported distance learning (SDL) 185
Diversity (of higher education institutions) 5, 26, 35, 44, 60–1, 138, 143
DLHE *see* Destination of Leavers from Higher Education
DNA 124
Dogma 11, 127
Donations 44, 188
   due diligence with regard to 221
DORA *see* San Francisco Declaration on Research Assessment
Double marking 39
Dropout rates 217

Drugs (pharmaceutical) 214 *see also* Pharmaceuticals, Medical research
　drug-regulating authorities 139
　efficacy and safety of new drugs 124
Dual support system 159

Earnings 27, 108, 113 *see also* Graduate earnings
　earn while you learn 232
　Earnings Before Interest, Tax, Depreciation and Amortisation (EBITDA) 190
　lifetime 32, 61, 106, 110, 195–6, 246
EBITDA *see* Earnings
Economic benefits of higher education *see* Higher education
Economy 1, 25, 61, 106, 108–9, 116–17, 130, 150–1, 153, 249–50 *see also* Gross Domestic Product, Knowledge economy, Taxation
　global 226
　Gross Value Added (GVA) 130
ECTS *see* Credits: European Credit Transfer and Accumulation System
Education hubs 18
edx *see* MOOCs
Electric cars 29, 132
Electronic delivery (of education) 76, 203 *see also* Digital teaching and learning
Electronic voting 77
Electronics 158
Elite universities 9, 107, 111
ELQs *see* Equivalent or lower-level qualifications
Employability 30, 50–1, 71, 92–3, 127, 149, 156, 184, 217, 225, 228–9, 242
Employers 28–30, 32, 42, 60, 63, 69, 84, 93, 107, 156–7, 217, 226–7, 229–31, 235
Employment 55, 83, 85, 103, 147, 226 *see also* Work
　graduate employment 67, 106, 150, 156, 236, 248, 251
　rates 27, 105
　outcomes (for university graduates) 50, 88, 216–17
Endowments 145, 222, 237
Engineering 13, 19, 34, 67, 202–3, 214
　engineers 33, 110, 115, 151, 195
English language 169, 176, 250
　English-speaking countries 175
　proficiency in 51
　tests of 51
Enlightenment 1, 27, 29, 240
Enron 207
Enterprise 149, 151–3, 154, 155, 233, 239, 250
Entrepreneurship 149, 154–161
　business spin-outs/start-ups 131, 160–1, 167, 249–50
　centres for 120, 153–5, 160
　entrepreneurial education 120, 152, 154, 233
　entrepreneurial graduates 149, 153
Entry qualifications 28, 105
Environmental 174
　catastrophe 148
　hazards 122
　impact 125
　regulations 124
Equality 40, 47, 50, 97
　intergenerational 246
　of standards (between institutions) 215
Equity (of access to university) 27–63
Equity (in start-ups) 150, 153, 156, 161, 249
Equivalent or lower-level qualifications (ELQs) 24, 235
Erasmus programme *see* European Union
Erudera 103
Essay mills 86

Ethics 8, 52, 68, 221 *see also* Governance
  ethical culture 206–8
Ethnicity 46, 60, 170 *see also* Black, Asian and Minority Ethnic (BAME) students
EU *see* European Union
Europe 5, 7, 11, 12, 13, 65, 174
  European Higher Education Area 66
  European Quality Assurance Register for Higher Education 218
  Northern 11, 158
  Southern 10
European Union (EU) 43
  Erasmus programme 174
  Horizon Europe 171
  tuition fees 52
European University Association 68
Evidence 3, 81, 106, 107–8, 110, 125–7, 130–1, 178, 233–4, 251
Exchange programmes 169–70, 172, 173–4
Expansionism (university) 41
Expectation/s 55, 76
  of employers 229
  of teachers 41, 71
  of university applicants 54
    'expectation frustration' 114
    'expectation inflation' 235–6
    legitimate 33, 41–2, 63
    unrealised 56, 97
Expenditure 23, 187–8, 193 *see also* Health expenditure
Experiential
  activity 152
  learning 153, 156 *see also* Accreditation of Prior Experiential Learning (APEL)
Experimental 54, 80
  development 120
  investigation 119
Expertise 85, 126–7, 213, 220, 228, 242

experts 73, 126, 171
External 78
  examining 87–8, 214–15
  funding 145
  governors 219
  horizon 168
  seminars 77
  speaker 95
  stakeholders 69
Extracurricular activities 36, 90, 92–4

Face-to-face learning 72, 81 *see also* Blended learning
Feedback *see* student feedback
Financial security 211
Financial sustainability 89, 187–93, 197, 212–13, 220, 223, 245, 247, 251–2 *see also* Deficits, Office for Students (OfS)
Flexible
  classrooms 235
  learning 64, 73, 74–81, 89, 223, 235, 239, 242
    successful outcomes of 82–4
  modularisation 75
  working 226–7
    locations 75, 227
Flynn, James 62
  Flynn effect 62, 228
Forecasts *see* Office for Students
Fox, Alan *see* meritocratic society
Franchise activity 172, 179 *see also* International branch campuses
  assessment accreditation 179
  curriculum 179
  'fly-in' faculty 179
  overseas campuses 185
  teaching support 179
Francis Crick Institute 135
Frascati definitions of research 119
Fraunhofer Institutes *see* Germany
Freedom of speech 94–6, 222, 243

FTSE 100 155
Funding (of universities) 2, 5, 24, 186–204, 245–9, 251–2 *see also* Research funding
  funding-body grants 20–1, 188–91
  gap 252
  models 22, 48, 158, 193–7, 202, 234
  state funding 13, 234
Fundraising (by universities) 238
Further and Higher Education Act 1992 21

Gaddafi, Saif al-Islam 221
Gaddafi Foundation 221
Gaokao (Chinese National Higher Education Entrance Examinations) 9
'*Gaudeamus igitur*' 4
GCSEs 45, 111
GDP *see* Gross Domestic Product
General Medical Council 107
Genetically modified (GM) crops 125
Germany 11, 119, 136 *see also* Universities
  apprenticeships 156
  Dresden *see* Innovation hubs
  German model of institutes 136
    Fraunhofer Institutes 120, 136
    Helmholtz Institutes 136
    Leibniz Institutes 136
    Max Planck Institutes 136
Gig economy *see* Work
Global
  economy 226
  enrolment to higher education 17
  interconnectivity *see* Connectivity
  league tables 13
  median age *see* Median age
  online education 183–5
  recession 102, 207
  warming 103, 118, 121, 125, 130–2 *see also* Climate change

Globalisation 169, 175, 181
GLP or GCP *see* Good laboratory (or clinical) practice
Good laboratory (or clinical) practice (GLP or GCP) 139
Gove, Michael 126
Governance 8, 24, 197, 205–24, 251
  board effectiveness reviews 223–4
  corporate 205–7
  governing bodies 206, 208, 213, 219–20, 223, 239
    governors 205, 209–10, 214, 220, 224
      responsibilities 205, 213, 219, 220
    senior independent governor 209
    staff and student governors 219–20
    at Oxford and Cambridge 12, 219
  models 211, 218–21, 224
  monitoring of institutional performance 220
  operational control 208
GPA *see* Grades
Grades (in examinations) 37, 42, 129
  actual and/or predicted 27, 32, 39–41, 42, 55–7, 241
  entry grades 58
  as a proxy for university quality 42
  grade boundaries 39, 85
  grade inflation 211, 215
  grade outcomes 214
  grade point average (GPA) 49, 93, 217
Graduate
  attributes and behaviours 28, 68–9, 93, 114, 152, 157, 228
    better health 31, 61, 101, 111–13
    embrace of climate-change-mitigation behaviours 101, 103

INDEX                                291

promotion of sustainability 101
greater happiness 101, 103–4, 113–14, 186
greater productivity 101, 107–11, 150–2
greater respect for the law 101
inventiveness 109
peacefulness 101
employability 30, 50, 93, 127, 156, 217, 225, 228–9
employment rates 27
endowment 198
jobs and/or job market 24, 34, 62, 107, 151, 236
'oven-ready' graduates 29, 42, 227–8, 242
progression 24, 88, 216–17
prosperity 101, 103, 115, 153, 172
    earnings 24, 104–7, 195, 203, 247
        Graduate Outcomes Survey 216
    premia 31, 104–106, 173
    trajectory 105
tax 61, 108, 110, 196, 246–7
Grandes Écoles, France 12, 127
Graphene 164
Greek (language) 7 see also Philosophy
Greer, Germaine 95
Gross Domestic Product (GDP) 116, 122, 124, 130, 143–4, 158
    per capita (as measure of prosperity) 103–4
Growth (of universities) 5, 11, 15–17, 20–3, 85, 101, 192, 197, 200, 218, 220–1
GuildHE 37–8
Gutenberg, Johannes 11, 132

Haldane
    committee 20, 121
    principle 121, 243
Happiness 100, 101, 103–4, 113–14, 186 see also Graduate attributes
Haptics 71
HEA see Higher Education Academy
Health 48, 101, 111–13, 125, 242 see also Life expectancy, Mental health
    exercise and sport 61, 93
    expenditure 112
    health:education gradient 112
    impact of research on health 118, 121–4, 147
    insurance 114
HEFCE see Higher Education Funding Council for England
HEFCW see Higher Education Funding Council for Wales
HEIF see Higher Education Innovation Funding
Helmholtz Institutes see Germany
Henry Royce Institute 135
HERA see Higher Education and Research Act
HESA see Higher Education Statistics Agency
Higher education
    economic benefits of 104–11
    evolution of 5–8, 12–18, 64, 67, 76, 87, 218, 240
    institutions 1, 11, 46, 72, 146, 191, 217, 238, 241
Higher Education Academy (HEA) 78
Higher Education and Research Act (HERA) 24–5
Higher Education Freedom of Speech Bill 222
Higher Education Funding Council for England (HEFCE) 24, 77, 121, 197, 208, 211
Higher Education Funding Council for Wales (HEFCW) see Commission for Tertiary Education and Research
Higher Education Innovation Funding (HEIF) 25, 151, 155, 159, 165
Higher Education Statistics Agency

(HESA) 187, 216
  finance records 191
Highers *see* Scotland
Hirsch-Index (H-Index) 139
Home nations (of the UK) 188
  differences in university regulations 24, 210
  differences in growth of student numbers 23
  funding levels and sources 189
Horizon Europe *see* European Union
Human genome 124
Human rights 221-2
Humanities 28-30, 64, 155, 203
  employability outcomes 217
  research 129, 136
Hybrid delivery (of education) 72-5, 87

IBCs *see* International branch campuses
IMD *see* Index of Multiple Deprivation
Impact Factors (from Clarivate Analytics) 139
Impact of research (in the REF) 140, 149, 163, 165-6
  case studies 140, 244
In-person teaching 14-15, 72, 79, 172, 183
Incubators (for start-up businesses) 153, 155-6 *see also* Entrepreneurship
Independent schools 36-7, 47
Index of Multiple Deprivation (IMD) 49 *see also* Scottish Index of Multiple Deprivation
Index-eligibility *see* California
India 7, 14, 15, 86, 177, 185 *see also* Universities
  Indian National Testing Agency 86
Industry 73, 121, 125-6, 131, 144, 163, 195, 209, 244, 248
  industrial
    partner/s 136-7, 158-9, 161-2, 164, 166

  research *see* Contract research
  revolution 225
  strategies 129
industry-sponsored research 145, 151
  UK creative industries 130
    UK film industry 130
  university engagement with industry 116, 160, 165-6, 249
Infant mortality 112
Information technology (IT) 34, 186
Infrastructure 121, 122, 161, 186-7, 192, 204, 233
  communication infrastructure 155
  costs 22, 137-8, 147, 173
  programmes 171
  projects 125
  operational infrastructure 137
  research infrastructure 147
Innovation 2, 14, 64, 102-3, 122, 137, 149, 152, 160, 165 *see also* United Kingdom Research and Innovation (UKRI)
  centres 120, 160
  funding *see* Higher Education Innovation Funding
  hubs 166
    Dresden (Germany) 166
    Malmö (Sweden) 166
    Oregon (USA) 166
Insurance 90 *see also* Health insurance, National Insurance
  indemnity insurance 162
Intellectual property (IP) 160, 162-4
  commercialisation of 161, 163
  infringement of 222
Intelligence 62-3, 107 *see also* Artificial Intelligence
Intelligence Quotient (IQ) 62-3, 116, 228
Interconnectivity *see* connectivity
Interest (on loans) 108, 200-3, 246

International
  recruitment 172–4, 192
  students 3, 9, 23, 51–3, 61, 147, 172–3, 175–9, 187, 192–3, 208, 250–2
  trade 102–3
International branch campuses (IBCs) 181–2, 185
  Curtin University Malaysia 181
  Georgia Tech-Europe 18
  Heriot-Watt Dubai 181
  Nottingham Ningbo 181
  RMIT Vietnam 181
International Holocaust Remembrance Alliance 211
Internationalisation 69, 168–9, 173, 181, 250
  curriculum 173
Internships 230, 242
Interviews (for university places) 35, 45, 53–6, 58, 60 *see also* Admissions
  affirmative action 35
  as barriers to applicants 35
  bias 35
  at Oxbridge 44
  standardised or common 35, 53–4, 241–2
Investment
  by employers in students 230, 232
  equity investment 161, 222
  in facilities 192
  by government (in universities) 115, 167
  income 188
  in international branch campuses 181
  in research and development 121–2, 130, 137, 153, 158, 171, 244
  return on investment 124, 137, 147, 193–5, 249
  in staff development 87
IP *see* Intellectual property

IQ *see* Intelligence Quotient
Iran 207
Islam 7
  Baghdad libraries 7
  Judeo–Islamic teaching 7
Israel 104, 122

Jodrell Bank Observatory 138
Joint Honours 29
Joint Information Systems Committee (JISC) 84–5

KE *see* Knowledge Exchange
Keeling, Charles David 131
  Keeling Curve *see* Climate change
King, Mervyn 206
Kings College, Aberdeen 11
Knowledge 5, 11–12, 25, 28–9, 31, 34, 42, 64–8, 80, 86, 89, 107, 112, 115, 126–8, 132–3, 138, 148, 150, 152, 154, 156, 161–3, 168–71, 181, 213, 227–8, 233, 242, 248, 252
  economy 235
  growth of 29, 118–20, 149, 225–6, 234–5, 239
  total of human knowledge 225
Knowledge Exchange (KE) 156, 166
  income 166
  Partnerships (KEPs) 151
Knowledge Transfer (KT)
  Partnerships (KTPs) 151, 159

Laboratories 75–6, 80, 90, 128, 155, 160, 202, 235, 247
Labour market 107, 218
Large Hadron Collider *see* Conseil Européen pour la Recherche Nucléaire
Latin 4, 7, 10, 168
Laureate Education *see* Universities
Law (university subject) 7, 9–10, 11, 64, 74, 107, 111, 149, 151, 152, 202–3

Leadership 93, 152, 206
  skills 154, 209
League tables 84, 141, 142, 188, 215, 223
  International 13, 173
Learning
  designs 87
  environments 12, 62, 174 *see also* Virtual Learning Environments
  experience 65, 69, 87, 185, 230, 233
  methods 175
  outcomes 68, 82, 126
  process 84, 230
  time 82–3
Learning resource centres 74, 90, 237
Leave to remain 208
Lectures 64, 73, 89
  public 2, 239
  recorded 72–3, 76
Lehman Brothers bank 207
Leibniz Institutes *see* Germany
Levies 162, 196, 203, 248 *see also* Apprenticeship levy
Liberal
  arts *see* Arts, the
  education 150
  Party, the (UK) 200
  values 222
Libraries
  ancient 7, 8 *see also* Islam
  as collections of study material 80
  as places of study 72–4, 90, 132, 137, 237
Licences 161
Life expectancy
  impact of education 112–13
  impact of research 122–3
Lifelong learning 86, 234–5, 239 *see also* Flexible learning
  accounts 162
  entitlements 238

Literacy 34, 64, 108
Lithium
  battery 132
  Bell Laboratories, New Jersey 131
Loans (for students) 23, 105, 156, 220, 234–5, 245, 248
  loan repayments 108–9, 111, 217, 245–6, 247
  loan schemes 44, 186, 195, 197, 200–1, 232, 247–8
    in Scotland 49, 186, 202
  maintenance loans 49, 82, 201, 249
  total student loan debt 109 *see also* Resource Accounting and Budgeting Charge
Logic 6, 10, 64–5, 119
Lyceum (ancient school) 6, 65

Maintenance
  grants 82
  loans *see* Loans (for students)
Management 173, 213, 221 *see also* Business and management (university subject)
  apprentices 196
  estate management 137
  managerial malfeasance 208
  managerial structures 221
  managers 209–10
  time management 93
Mariscal College, Aberdeen 11
Massive Open Online Courses (MOOCs) 16, 17, 74
  Coursera 16, 182
  revenues from 16, 74
  Udacity 16
Mature students 59, 61, 83
Max Planck Institutes *see* Germany
May, Theresa 176
Median age (of a country's population) 237
  global median age 236

Medical *see also* General Medical Council
  research 122–3, 135
  Medical Research Council 135
    Laboratory of Molecular Biology (LMB) 136
Medicine (university subject) 11, 19, 64–5, 67–8, 107, 111, 149, 151, 174, 196, 202–3, 214, 247
  assessment of Medicine students during admission process 32–4, 42, 53 *see also* Admission tests
  *bimaristan* (ancient medical schools) 7
  dissection 76
Medieval
  period 64, 169
  scholars 168
  universities 94, 219, 5
Mega-versities 15
Members of parliament 92, 126
Mental health
  counselling and support 75, 83, 91, 97, 203
  mental ill-health 97–9
    anxiety 59, 98–9
    causes
      economic uncertainty 97
      influence of social media 98
    depression 31
    suicide 98
      in men 98
      in women 98
  self-esteem 133
  sport (benefits of) 93
Merit 44, 47, 50–1, 53, 54, 243
  artistic 35
Meritocracy 8
  meritocratic society 50
Meteorological Office (Met Office) *see* British Government departments
Mexico 13, 176

Middle East 176, 180
Mobility (of university staff and students) 170, 175–9, 185
Mohamed, Hashi 229
Monographs 140
MOOCs *see* Massive Open Online Courses
Morrill Land-Grant Acts 13–14
Multiple choice questions 85, 86
Mumps 123

NARIC *see* National Academic Recognition and Information Centre
National
  National Academic Recognition and Information Centre (NARIC) 43, 51
  Insurance 108
  service 56
  National Student Survey (NSS) 91, 211, 214, 216
  National Vocational Qualifications (NVQs) 157
Natural justice 32, 44, 50
Nestor (in *The Iliad*) 227
Net liquidity (of UK education providers) 190
Net Present Value 105
Net zero 125, 132, 192
Netherlands 32, 159, 182
Newman, Cardinal John Henry 66, 150
  reason and reflection 150
Nicolaus Copernicus 10
Niger 237
Nobel Prize 12, 14, 136
Nolan principles 206
Non-economic benefits (of higher education) 17, 104, 111–14, 115–16
Non-EU students 177, 191, 198
No-platforming 95, 243
North America 12, 65, 143
Northern Europe *see* Europe

Northern Ireland 22–4, 177, 188–9, 198–9, 202, 220
Norway 56, 159
Not-for-profit (organisations) 13
NSS *see* National Student Survey
Numeracy 34, 54, 64, 108
NVQs *see* National Vocational Qualifications

OECD *see* Organisation for Economic Co-operation and Development
'Off the job' study 231–2, 249
Offers (of a place at university) 31, 40, 42, 48, 58
   'conditional unconditional' 41, 59–60
   post-qualification 55–7, 59, 63
   unconditional 59–60
Office for Standards in Education (Ofsted) 232–3
Office for Students (OfS) 24–5, 42, 60, 72–3, 210–13, 218, 232, 242 *see also* Teaching Excellence Framework
   demands made by OfS of universities 212–13
      annual accounts 220
      annual sustainability assessments 220
      five-year forecasts 220, 251
      House of Lords report 212
      Transparent Approach to Costing (TRAC) 220
   consultations (of the university sector) 211
      on the National Student Survey 211
      on the Teaching Excellence Framework 211
   financial sustainability update 190, 192
OfS *see* Office for Students
Ofsted *see* Office for Standards in Education

Oldest university 7, 9
Olympics 93
   athletes 92
   Paris (2024) 92
   Rio (2016) 92
Online (education) 16–17, 74, 184 *see also* Massive Open Online Courses
   delivery (of education) 16, 70, 75, 79–81, 87, 179, 187, 235
   learning platforms 76, 78, 182–3
   lectures 73
Organisation for Economic Co-operation and Development (OECD) 110, 112
   member countries 122, 143–4, 194
Owens College, Manchester, part of Victoria University 19
Oxbridge 58, 219, 229 *see also* Admissions, Interviews
   governance models 219

Pacification 102
Pandidakterion 7
Papal bulls 10, 11
Paris Accord (of 2016) 125
Participation
   in assessment panels (for quality assurance) 218
   in clubs and societies 93, 233
   in cultural activities 113
   in higher education 17–18, 99, 194, 201
Particle accelerator
   CERN (Conseil Européen pour la Recherche Nucléaire) 138, 171
   Diamond Light Source at the Rutherford Appleton laboratories, Harwell, Oxfordshire 138
Part-time
   academics 227
   courses 234
   students 24, 60, 74
   work 52, 75, 82, 83, 227, 232, 239,

249
Patents 161, 163–4, 222, 249
Pedagogy 76, 77, 80–1, 83, 88, 126, 234, 242
  principles of 70–1
Peer Group report (of the European University Association) 68
Personal
  essays 36
  statements 36–8, 241
    disadvantage gap 36
    short-response questions 37–8, 241
  tutors 7, 8
Personalisation 64, 71, 86
Pharmaceuticals
  products 124, 161
    Humira 124
    Keytruda 124
Philanthropy 158, 181, 188
Phillipson, Bridget 2, 179
Philosophy 6, 11, 119, 126–7, 129, 204 see also Bacon, Francis, Descartes, René, Doctor of Philosophy
  educational 22, 66
  Greek
    mythology 6
    philosophers 6, 94
      Aristotle 6, 12, 65, 150
      Plato 6
      Pythagoras 6
      Socrates 6
  political 6
Physical activity 112–13 see also Sports
Placements see Work
Plagiarism 84, 86, 215
Podcasting 74, 76, 77
POLAR classification 99, 201
Polarisation (of the humanities and sciences) 29–30
Politics 10, 31, 90, 94–7, 121, 125–6, 175,
176, 186, 188, 193, 195, 221, 245, 251
  political doctrine 204, 243
  in the nations of the UK 22
  politicians 1, 6, 11, 81–2, 92, 94–5, 115, 156, 170, 206, 233, 236, 242, 251
Polytechnics 20–1
Population
  growth 17–18, 112
  steady state 18
POSCO 158
Postgraduates 24, 33, 114, 127, 192–3
  postgraduate (research) 177
  postgraduate (taught) 177
Post-qualification admissions 43, 55–7, 59, 63, 241 see also Pre-qualification admissions
Post-study work 176
  visas see Visa system, UK
Potential (in applicants to university) 28, 47, 59
  to complete the course 37
  to succeed 35
Practicals 65, 75–6, 79–80, 128, 202
Pre-92 universities
  lack of diversity 44
Predicted grades 40, 55, 57, 241
Pre-qualification admissions 60 see also Post-qualification admissions
Primary education 88, 110
Print
  printed material 8, 16, 169
  printing press 11, 132, 168
  wood-block printing 8
Private sector 134, 137, 144, 206
  of higher education 134
    for-profit 13, 184
    non-profit 13, 184
Problem-based learning 67–8, 69
Problem-solving 68, 93, 127, 225, 228, 242–3

Productivity 17, 108, 109–10, 118, 121–2, 124, 139, 150–1, 152, 154, 233
  agricultural 135
  data 107
  German 136, 156
  improved productivity 61, 102–3, 108, 248
  labour productivity 109
  poor/er productivity 111, 156, 248
Professional, statutory and regulatory bodies (PSRBs) 76, 80, 84, 107, 162, 170, 225, 233–4, 242
  accreditation *see* Accreditation by professional bodies
Programme revalidation 87
Progression
  of academics in their careers 88–9, 128
  of recent graduates into employment 24, 88, 216–17
  of students through their university course 83, 88, 178, 215, 217
Prosperity 17, 101, 103, 116, 122, 150, 172, 185, 240, 242 *see also* Graduate prosperity, Gross Domestic Product
PSRBs *see* Professional, statutory and regulatory bodies
PSREs *see* Public Sector Research Establishments
Public good 121
  view of university education 195
Public Sector Research Establishments (PSREs) 135–6
Public universities (in the USA) 13, 158
Publications 9, 139–41, 158–9, 163–4, 171

QAA *see* Quality Assurance Agency
Qatar 181, 222 *see also* Universities
  Qatar Foundation 181
QR *see* Quality-related
Quality (of education provided by universities) 42, 76, 78, 84, 178, 197, 211, 212, 214, 216–18, 227, 245
  of delivery (of education) 17, 22, 88, 215–16
  Designated Quality Body 25, 213, 232
  enhancement 87
  quality assurance 25, 87, 139, 180, 213–18, 224, 232, 234
    international schemes 218
    Quality Assurance Agency (QAA) 25, 53, 88, 178–9, 197, 215, 218, 220, 232, 251
  quality-related (QR)
    funding 141, 142, 145, 243

RAB charge *see* Resource Accounting and Budgeting charge
Radio telescopes 138
RBS *see* Royal Bank of Scotland
Recession 106, 109
  global recession 102
  of 2008 207
Recreational learning 237
Recruitment (of students) 23, 41, 43, 44, 53, 55, 192, 230 *see also* International recruitment
  anonymised 45
REF *see* Research Excellence Framework
Regent House (Cambridge University) 12, 219
Regulators 24, 91, 180, 205, 212, 215, 219, 232 *see also* Office for Students, Professional, statutory and regulatory bodies
Regulatory
  compliance 212
  environment 24, 211, 224
  framework 157
  system 24
Relative Specialisation Index (RSI) 164
Religion 1, 19, 64, 129, 170, 253

religious
    groups 13
    instruction 5
    law 10
    leaders 11
    organisations 116
Remuneration 137, 163
    committee 220
Renaissance
    in China 8
    in Europe 11
Republic of Ireland 178 *see also* Universities
Reputation (of universities) 25, 84, 92, 106–7, 118, 129, 141, 145, 147, 173, 208, 210, 218, 220–1, 238, 243, 252
Research *see also* Collaborative research, Frascati definitions of research, Humanities research, Medical research, Research communities
    applied 119–20, 135–6
    basic 119, 136
    contract (or industrial) 161–2, 164–6
    councils 25, 140, 164 *see also* Medical Research Council
    and development (R&D) 2, 102, 122, 137, 144, 165
    developmental 119
    directed 121, 135, 243
        competitive or response-mode 25, 134, 136–7, 140–2, 145, 164, 243
    full economic cost of 134, 244
        cost recovery 145–6
    impact of research 118, 124, 140, 149, 163, 165–6, 244, 249
    measurement of 138–41
    pharmaceutical 123, 138
    research concentration 142–3
    research culture 136
    research funding 25, 121, 134, 137, 140–8, 188, 243–4
    research institutes 14, 134–6, 166
        Moredun, Edinburgh 1
    research-intensive universities 1, 37, 120, 129, 135, 141–3, 203
    research outputs/publications *see* Publications
    research quality 120, 125, 138–42, 165–6
Research Assessment Exercise (RAE) *see* Research Excellence Framework
Research Excellence Framework (REF) 120, 140–2, 145, 159, 163, 165–6, 223, 244
    Research Assessment Exercise (RAE) 140
    units of assessment 140
Reskilling 87, 88, 225, 227, 234–5 *see also* Upskilling
Resource Accounting and Budgeting charge (RAB) 108–9, 200
Restorative justice 50, 63
Retail Price Index (RPI) 108, 193–4, 198, 200–1, 246
Retirement plans (pensions) 106, 192, 223
Revolutions *see also* China, Industrial revolution, Technology
    American economic 119
    digital/technological 16, 76, 157, 240
    French 12
    Lebanese 181
    scientific 12
RMIT Vietnam *see* International branch campuses
Robbins
    Lord Robbins 20
    Principle 3, 58
    Report 20
Rome, ancient 7, 10
    Roman law 10
Rosalind Franklin Institute at Harwell

Science and Innovation Campus, Oxfordshire 135
Royal Bank of Scotland (RBS) 207
  2008 bail-out 207
Royal Charters 11, 19, 169, 214
Royal Melbourne Institute of Technology 181
Royal Society, the 12, 119,
RPI *see* Retail Price Index
Russell Group of universities 37, 53, 120, 192–3, 216
Russia 159, 221
Rutherford Appleton laboratories, Harwell, Oxfordshire *see* Particle accelerator
Rwanda 122

Salary bill 157, 231, 248
Samsung 158
San Francisco 167 *see also* Universities
  San Francisco Declaration on Research Assessment (DORA) 139, 244
Sandwich courses 231, 242
Sarbanes-Oxley Act 206–7
SARS–CoV-2 *see* Covid-19 pandemic
Satisfaction 4, 143, 186 *see also* Student satisfaction
  with life 99–100, 113
SATs *see* Admissions (to university)
Saudi Arabia 222
Scholarships 44, 173
School-leaving qualifications 22, 34
Schwartz review (of admissions) 46, 57
Science parks 160, 166–7
Scotland 22, 29–31, 48–9, 55, 57–8, 91, 177–8, 186, 188–9, 198–9, 201–2, 248
  cap on Scottish student numbers *see* Student numbers
  Scottish
    'ancients' 11, 19
    Highers 34, 202, 241

    government 23
    universities 22, 23, 219
Scottish Funding Council 24, 210
Scottish Index of Multiple Deprivation (SIMD) 48, 58
SDL *see* Supported distance learning 185, 179
Secretary/Registrar (of a university) 209
Secular education 5, 19
Selection (of students for university places) 27, 33, 34–5, 63
  affirmative action 44
  methods 34–5
  random 39
  semi-random 32–3
Self-determination 127
Seminars 73, 77, 90
Semmelweis, Ignaz 123
  disinfection in childbirth 123
Shephard, Gillian 197
'Signalling' 106
SIMD *see* Scottish Index of Multiple Deprivation
Simulations 75, 76
Singapore 182
Skills *see also* Communication skills, Digital skills, Leadership skills, Reskilling, Transversal skills, Upskilling
  gap 156
  soft skills 93
Small and medium-sized enterprises (SMEs) 158, 166
SMEs *see* Small and medium-sized enterprises
SNIP *see* Source Normalised Impact per Paper
Snow, John 123
  spread of cholera 123
Social
  barriers 35, 37, 58

INDEX 301

capital 36
care 111
contact 73
context 47, 50
enhancement 170
fabric 28, 115, 130
framework 75
injustice 97
learning spaces 72, 74, 90
media 85, 98, 133, 238
networks 94
sciences 103, 136, 155
socio-economic background 46, 48
Societies (university clubs) *see* Participation
Soft power 102, 147, 170–1, 250
Source Normalised Impact per Paper (SNIP) 139
South Africa 138, 206 *see also* Universities
South Korea 104, 122, 164 *see also* Universities
Space race 159
Specialisation 22, 66, 202
    in sciences or in the humanities 28–30
Spin-outs *see* Entrepreneurship
Sports
    activities at university 75, 92–3, 232
    excellence 92–3, 173
    facilities 90, 137, 237, 239
Sputnik 160
Square Kilometre Array, the 138
Staff
    development *see* Continuing professional development
    staff-student ratios 21–2, 197, 202, 233, 245
    workload allocation 87
Standardised tests *see* Admissions tests
Standards 14, 53, 107, 206–7, 211, 214–15, 224, 233, 252 *see also* Office for Standards in Education, Quality Assurance Agency
    in apprenticeships 157, 231
    ethical 52
    international 25, 27, 140, 171, 217
    living 147
    minimum standards of English *see* English language
State schools 36–7, 45–6, 47–49
Steel 158
Stewardship 205
Student
    feedback
        from teachers to students 71, 74, 83, 84, 85, 99
        from students 82
    numbers 9, 17, 147, 182, 187, 188, 192, 200
        caps 23, 57, 197, 200, 246
        in Scotland 23, 48
        cohort sizes 81, 235
    satisfaction 88
    unions 95
    wellbeing 98–9
Student Academic Experience Survey 82, 98–9
Student-centred learning 67, 69
Student-staff ratios *see* Staff-student ratios
Study abroad 168
StudyNet 78
Subject competency 54, 65, 68, 107, 151, 229, 243
Subject review 215
Subsidiary companies (of universities) 223
Subsidy 44, 90, 111, 135, 195
    cross-subsidy 134, 145, 147, 188, 202, 244–5, 247
    state-subsidised (university system) 186, 202

Summative examinations 27, 34, 50, 86
Sunak, Rishi 55, 241
Supported distance learning (SDL) *see* Distance learning
Surpluses (financial) 147, 190–1, 223
Sweden *see* Innovation
Switzerland 122, 138
Synchronous delivery of education 72, 75–6 *see also* Asynchronous delivery of education
    synchronous interaction 70
Syrian Protestant College *see* Universities

Tariffs (for entry to university)
    higher 129
    lower 58
    minimum 58
    standard 43
    supplementary 58
    uplift 58
Taxation 111, 130, 158, 172–3, 195–6, 223, 246–7 *see also* Graduate tax
    hypothecated 196
    relief 137, 250
Teachers (primary or secondary school) 33, 43, 88, 106, 115, 196
    accuracy of grades predicted by teachers 40–1
Teaching (at university)
    methods 6, 79, 83, 87, 126
    quality 40, 84, 215–16 *see also* Teaching Excellence Framework
Teaching and research (divide between) 128–9
Teaching Excellence Framework (TEF) 25, 28, 88, 141, 203, 211, 215–16, 223
Teamwork 93, 229
Technology 35, 102–3, 109–10, 120, 162, 168, 171, 185, 226, 242 *see also* Colleges of advanced technology, Computers, Information technology
    biotechnology 137

technological r/evolution 16, 69, 76, 157, 240
technology-enhanced learning 64, 70–87, 89
TEF *see* Teaching Excellence Framework
Telecommunication 169
Television 16, 69, 74, 93, 133, 238
Tenure
    of chairs of governing bodies 223
    of vice-chancellors 210
Terrorism 95–6, 102
Tertiary education 18, 21, 248
    benefits of 17, 103–4, 110, 112
Theodosius II 7
Trade 169, 206
    international 101–3, 170, 174, 181
    trade barriers 102, 170
    trading regulations 168
    unions 219
Trademarks 13
Trailblazers (employer groups) 157
Transnational education 102, 168, 179–80, 185 *see also* Franchise activity
Transparency 37, 41–2, 55, 63, 220, 251
Transparent Approach to Costing (TRAC) *see* Office for Students
Transport 132, 239
    services for students 90
    transportation 169
Transversal skills 68
Treasury, the 20, 195, 197
Trigger warnings 96, 243
Tuition fees 31, 49, 51, 61, 105, 108, 147, 158, 177–8, 182, 186–9, 193, 196–202, 203, 208, 211, 215–16, 221, 231, 245, 247–8 *see also* Loans
    burdens 195, 231, 249
    cap 172, 177
    ceiling 200
    at independent schools 47

for international students 147,
172–3, 187, 192–3, 208, 244
in Scotland 177–8, 188–9, 201–2
in Wales 177–8, 188–9, 202
unregulated 172, 177, 187–92
Turin programme 174
Turkey 14, 15, 176 *see also* Universities
Turnitin 86
Tutorials 76, 187
Tutors 7, 8, 36, 83, 185
Tyler, Ralph 65, 68

UCAS *see* Universities and Colleges Admissions Service
Udacity *see* Massive Open Online Courses
UGC *see* University Grants Committee
Ukraine, invasion of 221
Unemployment 104, 106, 226
Unit of resource 21, 197, 245
United Kingdom Border Agency 208
United Kingdom National Information Centre (for the recognition and evaluation of international qualifications and skills, also known as UK ENIC) 43
United Kingdom Research and Innovation (UKRI) 25, 121, 145, 158–9
United States of America (US) 16–17, 22, 29–30, 34, 36, 41, 43, 49, 92, 182–4, 188, 196, 206–7 *see also* Universities
    affirmative action in 44
    curriculum 65–6
    diversity policies in 44
    range of university types in 13
    state and federal funding for public universities in 13
    Supreme Court 44, 46
Universities (and other HEIs) *see also* International branch campuses
    in the Americas
        California 14, 49

Cornell 13
Harvard 13, 161, 188, 237
Johns Hopkins 127
Kerr, Clark (President 1958–67) 14
Laureate Education 15
Massachusetts Institute of Technology 13, 15, 16
McMaster University *see* Problem-based learning
Michigan 238
Michoacán 13
Princeton 13, 237
Santo Domingo 13
Stanford 15, 16, 92, 161
Texas 237
Texas A&M 181
William and Mary 13
Yale 12, 13, 15, 96, 119, 127
in Bangladesh
    National University of Bangladesh 15
in France
    Hautes Etudes Commerciales de Paris 181
    Paris 119
in Germany
    Humboldt University of Berlin 12, 127
in India
    Chaudhary 14
    Indira Gandhi National Open University 14, 183
    Mumbai 14
    Savitribai 14
in Italy
    Bologna 9–10
    Ferrara 10
    Naples 10
    Padua 10
in Lebanon

American University in
    Beirut (formerly the Syrian
    Protestant College) 181
in Malaysia
    EduCity 182
in Morocco
    Al-Qarawiyyin (Al-Karaouine) 7
'Plateglass' 20
post-92 2, 44, 120, 187, 216
in Qatar
    Education City 181
        Hamad Bin Khalifa
            University 181
        Hautes Etudes
            Commerciales de Paris 181
        Texas A&M 181
        University College London 181
'Redbrick' 44
in Republic of Ireland
    University College Dublin 66
in South Korea
    Pohang 158
        Graduate Institute of
            Ferrous Technology 158
    Sungkyunkwan 158
in Spain
    Salamanca 10
in Turkey
    Anadolu 15
    Imperial University of
        Constantinople 7
in the United Kingdom
    Aberdeen 11
    Aston 20, 230
    Bath 20, 230
    Bristol 19, 58
    Brunel 20
    Cambridge 10, 11–12, 19, 44, 59,
        93, 161, 167, 187–8, 219, 239
        Cambridge University Press 188
    Cardiff 95
    Coventry (CU) 223
    CU London 223
    CU Scarborough 223
    Cranfield 239
    Edinburgh 11, 19
    Glasgow 11, 54
    Harper Adams 15
    Hertfordshire 2, 3, 77, 221
    Lincoln 167
    London 143, 170
        City St George's (merger of
            City and St George's) 15
        distance-learning
            programmes 16, 59, 70,
            169, 185
        Imperial College 135
        Kings College 135
        London Metropolitan 208
        London School of
            Economics and Political
            Science (LSE) 221
        Royal Veterinary College 1,
            15, 54, 238
        University College London
            (UCL) 19, 135, 181, 187
        Westminster (formerly the
            London Polytechnic) 21
    Loughborough 20, 92
    Manchester 135, 164
    Northumbria 120
    Nottingham 181, 222
    Nottingham Trent 187
    Open 16, 59, 70, 74, 185, 187
    Oxford 10, 11–12, 19, 44, 59,
        93, 107, 142, 161, 219
        Oxford PV 131
    Oxford Brookes 170
    Plymouth 209–10
    Royal Agricultural 15
    Teesside 167

St Andrews 11
Sheffield 252
Surrey 167
vs polytechnics ('binary divide') 21
Universities and Colleges Admissions Service (UCAS) *see* Admissions
Universities UK (UUK) 53, 212
    Fair Admissions Code of Practice 37–8, 60
    Fair Admissions Review 45, 56, 60
    Presidents
        Thomas, Eric 227
University Grants Committee (UGC) 20
University status 19, 20, 21, 23
Upskilling 87, 88, 109, 157, 162, 225, 227, 234–5, 238
UUK *see* Universities UK

Vaccination 29, 112, 124
    against Covid-19 *see* Covid-19
    against smallpox 123
    of animals 135
Value for money 23, 81, 193, 224
Veterinary medicine 34, 35, 54, 67, 174, 202–3, 231, 238
Virtual
    classroom 77
    interview 35
    spaces 90
    technology 133
Virtual Learning Environments (VLEs) 76, 78, 80
Visa system, UK
    Graduate-route visa 3, 52, 176, 178–9, 192, 251–2

VLEs *see* Virtual Learning Environments
Vocational subjects 20, 30, 34, 65, 69, 149, 151, 223, 233 *see also* National Vocational Qualifications
Volunteer work 91, 116, 239
Von Humboldt, Wilhelm 12, 119, 126–7 *see also* Universities in Germany

Wealth 31, 44, 153, 197, 204, 238
Wi-Fi 74, 76
Willetts, David 30, 61–2, 243, 104, 110, 120–1
    *A University Education* (book) 104
Wireless network 77
Wolf, Alison 107, 157
Work 61, 85, 114, 125, 132, 152, 157, 225–8 *see also* Employment, Flexible working, Part-time work, Teamwork
    automation 226–7
    evolution of 234, 238–9
    experience 30, 36–7, 61, 75, 231
    freelance employment 226
    gig economy 226–7
    placements 75, 91–2, 154, 229–31
    working life 105
    workplace 29, 36, 71, 75, 242
Workforce (UK) 109, 121, 157, 186, 195–6
World innovation index 122
World Trade Organisation 181
Wren, Christopher 119

Youth Training Schemes 157